SOCIAL WORK: THE CASE OF A SEMI-PROFESSION

SOCIAL WORK:
The Case of a Semi-Profession

NINA TOREN

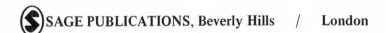

SAGE PUBLICATIONS, Beverly Hills / London

For information address:

SAGE PUBLICATIONS, INC.
275 South Beverly Drive
Beverly Hills, California 90212

SAGE PUBLICATIONS LTD
St George's House / 44 Hatton Garden
London E C 1

Printed in the United States of America

International Standard Book Number 0-8039-0087-2

Library of Congress Catalog Card No. 74-127996

First Printing

ACKNOWLEDGMENTS

I wish to convey my deep gratitude to Professor Terence Hopkins and Professor Amitai Etzioni for their constructive and generous counsel and guidance from which I have greatly benefited.

I am also indebted to the Department of Health, Education and Welfare for financial support of this study [Grant (WA) CRD 280-6-175], which was originally submitted in partial fulfillment of the requirements for the degree of Doctor of Philosophy in the Faculty of Political Science, Columbia University.

CONTENTS

Acknowledgments   5

About the Author   11

Introduction   13

The Problem   13
A Basic Dilemma of Social Work and its Implications   19
Outline of the Study   27

Part I. THE PROCESS OF PROFESSIONALIZATION AND BUREAUCRATIC CONTROL IN SOCIAL WORK

1. SOCIAL WORK AS A SEMI-PROFESSION   37

Typologies of Professions   38
The Position of Social Work on a Continuum of
    Professionalism   39
The Propensity Toward Deprofessionalization   43

2. SEMI-PROFESSIONS AND BUREAUCRACY   49

Contradiction and Compatibility between Bureaucracy
    and Professions   50
Heteronomy and Semi-Professionalism   52
The Helping Professions and Bureaucratic Control   57

3. SUPERVISION IN SOCIAL WORK   65

The Purposes of Supervision   67

Inherent Conflicts in the Established Pattern of Supervision 69
Visibility and Supervision 71
Critiques of Supervision 72
The Unique Features of Supervision in Social Work 75
Attitudes Toward Supervision 77
Concluding Remarks 80

Part II. THE RELATIONSHIP BETWEEN SOCIAL WORKER AND CLIENT

4. THE CASEWORK RELATIONSHIP *89*

Some Problems of Therapy and Socialization in
    Dyadic Settings 90
The Purposes of Casework 93
Casework as a Mechanism of Social Control 95
Types of Power and Their Application in Social Work 99
Possible Obstacles to the Exercise of Normative Power 105
Different Types of Power and Their Consequences 108
Some Research Problems and Findings 113

*5. THE EFFECTS OF THE NATURE OF THE PROFESSION
AND THE ORGANIZATIONAL SETTING ON THE
WORKER-CLIENT RELATIONSHIP* *129*

Prestige and Control 129
The Knowledge-Base 135
The Code of Ethics 137
Professional Autonomy 141
The Nature of the Clientele 147
Concluding Remarks 152

**Part III. INFLUENCE AND CHANGE THROUGH
SOCIAL GROUP WORK**

6. SOME ISSUES IN SOCIAL GROUP WORK *161*

From Movement to Profession 161
The Controversy about the Primary Purpose of Social
    Group Work 164
Different Techniques Employed in Group Work 169
Some Implications for Social Group Work from Sociological
    Theory and Research 171
Learning Theory and Laboratory Training 176

Bibliography   9

7. *THE EXERCISE OF NORMATIVE AND SOCIAL POWER*
   IN GROUP WORK   *189*
   The Group Setting and its Effects on Clients and Professionals   190
   The Process of Influence in Small Groups   196
   Cohesion and Credibility in Group Work and Casework   197
   The Contagion of Change   202
   The Proximity of the Group to Real Life   205
   Natural and Artificial Groups   208
   A Comparison between the Consequences of Casework and
        Group Work   212
   Concluding Remarks   215

Summary and Conclusion   225

Epilogue   229

Bibliography   233

Author Index   253

Subject Index   257

NINA TOREN is Lecturer of Sociology in the Department of American Studies, Hebrew University, Jerusalem, and Coordinator of the Department of Behavioral Sciences in the University of the Negev, Beer-Sheba, Israel.

Dr. Toren is a co-author (with S. N. Eisenstadt and D. Weintraub) of the study "Analysis of Processes of Role Change: A Proposed Conceptual Framework" (published by the Kaplan School of Economics and Social Sciences, the Hebrew University, Jerusalem, 1963; and has contributed a chapter to *The Semi-Professions and their Organization: Teachers, Nurses, Social Workers,* edited by A. Etzioni (Free Press, N.Y., 1969).

Dr. Toren received her Ph.D. from Columbia University in 1969, and her M.A. and B.A. degrees from the Hebrew University in Jerusalem. She was the recipient of Fellowships at both Columbia and the Hebrew University. She was born in Vienna, Austria, and emigrated to Israel with her family in 1939. At present she lives in Jerusalem with her husband and two children. Currently, her main interests are in the fields of theory, formal organizations, and the professions.

INTRODUCTION

The Problem

Lately, social work, and in particular social casework, the paramount method of the profession, have been extensively criticized on different grounds and from different directions. The current criticisms include two fundamental charges: first, that casework does not reach those persons who are most in need of social services, and second, that even when applied, casework is not an effective method for promoting the "better functioning of the individual in his environment."[1] Available research evidence has not demonstrated that social work intervention produces considerable positive change in the general "adaptive level" or "capacity to cope" of clients;[2] that it effects a decline in delinquency rates;[3] or that it promotes marital adjustment.[4]

Social work is defined here as a "semi-profession," and the ineffectiveness in obtaining proclaimed goals will be related to the various elements responsible for its semi-professional nature. It should be noted, however, that the main objectives of the treatment process as generally perceived by social workers, and as expressed in the professional literature and in social work schools' curricula, i.e. inducing clients to conform more closely to the conventional norms of society, are not necessarily identical with concepts of social work's role held by other groups, notably the clients themselves. Recent events have indicated that a considerable number of welfare clients are not in the mood to be "psychoanalyzed," and that their perception

13

of their "needs" is different from the professional definition. In addition, the doubts of many social workers concerning the problem of "imposing middle-class standards on the poor" are, at present, greater than ever before.[5]

In the following analysis of the structure and practice of social work we shall address ourselves to the formally established aims of social work, and we shall examine the means by which they can be achieved more effectively. This, however, does not imply that the attainment of these objectives will be regarded as better service by all parties involved, and that the views expressed in this study represent all the diverse perspectives of the goals to which social work should aspire.

The relative ineffectiveness of social workers in the spheres of psychological and sociological "rehabilitation" of their clients will be traced to three principal sets of factors:

(a) The undeveloped theoretical knowledge-base of social work practice, relative to that of full-fledged professions.
(b) The relative low professional autonomy and authority of social workers within the organizations in which social work is carried out.
(c) The dyadic structure of the practitioner-client relationship and its insulation from the client's social milieu.

The first two factors are the main elements of semi-professionalism; the third is a structural property of the professional-client relationship which, in conjunction with the two former variables, enhances the impact of semi-professionalism on social work performance and achievements. The elucidation of the significance of semi-professional attributes and their effects on social work practice are the main themes of this study.

We shall be primarily concerned with examining the implications of modifying the organizational setting, the social worker's role-definition within it, and the structure of the worker-client relationship. The knowledge-base of social work, and other features associated with it, will be taken as given, because it is not expected that these can, or will be changed to any great extent in the near future. Nevertheless, the repercussions of the present state of social work's theory will be constantly referred to in the analysis of the structural characteristics of the situation.

The practice of social work in public agencies on the one hand, and in private agencies on the other, provides a unique opportunity to observe, separately, the impact of some of the variables mentioned earlier. Most workers in public welfare agencies are nonprofessionals, the task of administering financial aid and those of casework are combined in one and the same role, and bureaucratic controls and supervision are strong. By comparison, the social worker's role in private agencies is detached from the tasks of eligibility determination and income maintenance, and is relatively more automous. Thus, attention may be focused on the effects of the casework relationship. As will be shown, even under these circumstances, the one-to-one relationship of casework has not, so far, demonstrated its effectiveness as a change-inducing technique.

Our contention is that by introducing a different structure of professional-client relationship in social work, namely, the group setting, and by systematically differentiating financial aid from professional counseling, the weaknesses of the present system can be partly overcome:

(a) The interaction between workers and clients will be less removed from "real life" and more anchored to the clients' social milieux.
(b) The role conflict emanating from the combination of inherently incompatible tasks in the same role and relationship can be avoided.
(c) The relatively low professional authority of the worker may be supplemented by such group processes as cohesion, contagion, and group sanctioning.

At present, social workers are seriously questioning the value of traditional social work methods, and although theirs has always been a practicing profession, many feel that social workers should become more actively involved in social issues, devoting their knowledge and skills to the solution of pressing social problems. It would, however, be inaccurate to give the impression that the profession as a whole is undergoing a total revolution in outlook and practice. Most public social work agencies are so busy administering public welfare acts, that there is not much time and effort left for anything else. Of course, there are also those who believe that casework cannot, and should not, be replaced by political and legislative action, in much the same way as the treatment of a man sick with malaria should not be postponed because the doctor is on his way to track down the anopheles mosquito.[6] Referring to the development of the recent community mental health movement, Cooper writes,

"It would be ironic, indeed, if the new thrust for social betterment—propelled by an essentially humanistic tradition—denied place and space for individualism. For whom are these new broadscale approaches to helping if not for people? And people do not live out their lives in masses. Are we returning to a love of mankind and finding ourselves incapable of helping one man in a mass?"[7]

By contrast, some of the more radical solutions that have been proposed lately emphasize the need to change social institutions, namely, the social system, *instead* of changing the individuals who do not live up to prevailing social norms and who have no place within the established structural arrangements. This idea evolved as a reaction to the disappointment with traditional social work, including economic relief and the provision of social services, which is described as

"a form of amelioration which is handled essentially by designated agents of the social system. (And) . . . while social planning may be devised as an economic or political strategy, it is often administered by persons who work, not only to administer a law but also to change the distressed individual, i.e., to change not the system but the self."[8]

Several suggestions for modifying the established organizational structure of social work, and the role of the individual practitioner, have been forwarded. Piliavin, for example, proposes to shift the institutional base of practice from the social agency to the private practitioner, so that social workers will become once more the advocates of those in need of help.[9] Miller demands that the profession "get out of the business of dealing with involuntary clients, with people who do not want us," and strongly opposes the imposition of unsolicited advice upon clients. He regards counseling under these conditions as humiliating, demeaning, and robbing the client of his dignity. He concludes with a plea to social workers: "Let us join with these clients in a search for and reaffirmation of their dignity. Let us become their allies and champion their cause. Let us become mercenaries in their service—let us, in a word, become their advocates."[10]

A different type of approach, which also grew out of the dissatisfaction with traditional ways of dealing with the problem of poverty, is expressed by the idea of "maximum feasible participation" of communities and individuals in the decisions concerning the measures to be taken to improve their economic and social conditions. However, the community action programs, provided for by the antipoverty legislation, have not proven very successful so far.[11]. One problem, though not the only one, in implementing these programs is posed by the great difficulty in involving local residents of slum areas in community programs. In part, the failure to do so is due to certain general attributes of the urban poor as described by Piven:

> "Low income people are overwhelmed by concrete daily needs. Their lives are often crisis ridden, deflecting from any concern with community issues. They often have no belief in their ability to affect the world in which they live, and so they are not easily induced to try to affect it. Frequently they lack the necessary resources of knowledge and information to enable them to scrutinize social policies. Leadership capabilities are also scarcer among the poor. . . . Finally, the institutions whose services might offer incentives for low-income interest and activity are often effectively insulated from the low-income community by their structure, practices, and cultural style."[12]

Piven's recommendations to overcome the lack of interest and incapability of low-income local residents to participate in community programs are mainly on the organizational level. She suggests that residents should be put on the local board, should be employed as staff in the project, and should be formed into active constituent groups. However, if the problem is, in part, rooted in lack of knowledge, motivation, and social skills (e.g. leadership) of the target population, as Piven herself points out, then structural and organizational changes will have to be accompanied by a process of socialization and learning. In other words, the provision of economic and political resources to a certain group of people will not be effective (for example, bring about resident involvement), unless the individual has the knowledge, motivation, and competence to use them constructively, and derive satisfaction from participation in community activities. Group work can contribute a great deal in training low-income people toward democratic action and leadership roles. For this purpose the group setting is most appropriate for obvious reasons; in the group a person gains experience in group-living and learns about intragroup relationships, collective decision-making, cooperation, conflict, and so forth.

Our analysis will be focused on the problems of the operation of a semi-profession, and will not address itself to a detailed consideration of controversial political issues. The few comments on the subject have been presented above because recent social and political developments are being reflected in ideological debates as well as in new projects undertaken by social workers. In addition, the theoretical arguments in favor of group work as a medium of behavioral change, and the suggestion to dissociate income-maintenance from treatment, gain further support in view of these broader social developments.

Problems of poverty and discrimination in a society cannot be solved by any one professional group. The need for institutional, structural change by way of reallocating economic, political, and educational resources, and in particular the modification of the principles and procedures of relief-dispensation are, therefore, taken for granted here.[13] Furthermore, it is realized that certain types of problems, such as those of the aged and the disabled, have to be coped with by the provision of services on an individual basis. Working with groups of welfare clients is, therefore, not suggested as a substitute for societal, institutional change, or as a substitute for all individual treatment techniques. However, it is proposed that specific types of group work command a crucial position as a bridging mechanism between these two approaches. The reform approach, by itself, is as one sided as the orientation that concentrates upon the adjustment of the individual to existing social and economic conditions. A redistribution of benefits always entails individual readjustment, both on part of those who are to gain, and of those who are to "lose" by the new order.[14] On the other hand, attempts to produce normative change will not have lasting effects if individuals lack the instrumental and relational assets needed to implement and sustain newly acquired attitudes and patterns of behavior.

Thus, in discussing the barriers to the exertion of influence on welfare clients by social workers, and by attempting to suggest more effective ways of doing so, we assume that clients and their families are provided for by an "adequate" income, and that they do not suffer from physical or mental handicaps that a priori preclude their participation in interpersonal relationships, in group experience, and in the process of learning.

A Basic Dilemma of Social Work and its Implications

The purpose of the following discussion is to explore further the controversy between the social reform approach and the individual adjustment approach. As has been pointed out, we shall not address ourselves directly to the ideological and political issues related to this problem. Rather, the strain between reform and rehabilitation is treated here as an inherent feature of social work, pervading the professional and organizational levels and the sphere of worker-client interaction, which are the major subject matter of this study.

Two basic orientations toward the achievement of social welfare can be found in social work literature, to quote Meyer:

"In its history, social work has long had a double focus: on social reform, on the one hand; and on facilitating adjustment of individuals to existing situations, on the other. These two themes reappear in various forms: as environmental manipulation or promotion of psychological functioning; as concern with people through mass programs; or as casework with persons 'one by one.' Social workers have been conscious of these two approaches to

> social welfare and have often sought to reconcile them. Mary
> Richmond, symbol of the case by case approach, is reported to have
> said to Florence Kelley, symbol of reform in the grand style: We
> work on the same program. I work on the retail end of it, but you
> work on the wholesale."[15]

As we shall see later, this duality turns into a dilemma when a
"zero-sum" attitude is taken, as it often is, regarding the two
general approaches, that is, if one is adhered to or exercised at
the expense of the other.

Social reform and the one-by-one approach are both rooted
in the same ultimate values and goals—the promotion of human
welfare. The first was dominant in social work until World War
I, and attempts to promote welfare mainly by changing
man's economic and social environment. The other—the individual-focused approach—which developed in the second decade
of this century, tries to achieve "improved social functioning"
by changing the individual's inner-world—his perceptions, attitudes, commitments, and behavior—and consequently to enhance
his adjustment to the environment. This orientation, emphasizing the individual case and neglecting issues of broad social
reform, was related to a change in the basic perceptions of
social work: "From viewing the case as a product of impersonal
forces in the social and economic environment, social work
came to the image of the case as a product of unconscious
impulse, needing restoration to an unchanged environment by
self-mastery."[16]

The shift was by no means complete. Following World War
II, a trend of "revision" became visible; voices of warning were
raised against the "flight from reform" caused by the drive
toward professionalism.[17] The debate on the relative weight
to be given to each orientation is still going on, as has been
recently expressed at the 94th annual forum of the National
Conference of Social Welfare held in Dallas on May 27, 1967.
Charles Y. Schottland, Dean of Graduate Studies in Welfare at
Brandeis University and former Commissioner of Social
Security, said, "We need to place less emphasis on psychotherapy—that is, person-to-person casework methods—and
begin putting more stress on broad social policy. . . . In short,
we must make an impact on the physical planners, the people

who run things, as well as the individual unwed mother and the individual delinquent."[18] Few, if any, of the leaders or the rank-and-file social workers would suggest giving up the accomplishments of better knowledge, training, and competence. However, the tendency is to achieve some kind of synthesis by broadening the perception of narrow professionalism, and by incorporating it within the former concern with social reform.

The basic ideological duality of society and individual, reform and therapy, situation and motivation, casework and welfare, or whatever other terms we use, is also discernible on the structural level. The development of a profession is usually accompanied by a more precise definition of its sphere of competence and responsibility, e.g. the identification of social work as dealing with "casework" instead of "the welfare of mankind." Within this limited area, a process of further specialization and differentiation takes place.[19] In social work, the differentiation between public and private agencies increased, especially during and after the Great Depression, with the former assuming the burden of financial assistance, and the latter concentrating on the treatment of psychological, intra- and interpersonal problems. Specialization along these lines also cuts across the public and private sectors, exemplified by such programs as family counseling, child welfare, vocational rehabilitation, probation, public health, and so forth; each of these programs has its own purposes, techniques, sponsors, and clientele.

The implications of interagency specializations are that some subfields are more "professional" than others. For example, longer training and higher qualifications—a more theoretical and scientific basis of knowledge—are required in family counseling or corrections than in public assistance agencies. This also means that workers in public welfare agencies enjoy lower prestige, receive lower salaries, and have less autonomy than those in specialized agencies. In turn, this affects recruitment by directing the better-trained social workers toward the more professional agencies by social and self-selection. In *Social Workers in 1950,* a report by the Bureau of Labor Statistics of the U.S. Department of Labor, published by the American

Association of Social Workers, the following information is provided: Of the estimated total of 74,240 persons in the United States in social work positions in 1950, only 16% had completed the full two-year graduate curriculum. According to the same source, in 1960, 75% of the estimated 116,000 social welfare positions in the United States were occupied by persons without graduate degrees. Public assistance workers who made up 41% of the total number of social workers (in 1950) were mostly without professional training. Only 4% of them had two or more years in graduate social work schools, whereas other programs had higher percentages of trained personnel (two or more years of graduate studies)—for example, work with physically handicapped: 8%; group work: 13%; child welfare work, institutional: 23%; family services: 42%; and psychiatric social work in clinics: 83% (the highest percentage of professional workers in any one program).

The dilemma of "reform" and "welfare" versus "casework" on the ideological and structural levels has its repercussions on the role level, that is, on the orientation and performance of the individual social worker. The growing emphasis on the personality-focused therapeutic approach was accompanied by a transition "from preoccupation with reform to preoccupation with technical professionalism." Wilensky and Lebeaux remark,

> "a professional absorbed in the technical side of his work, aiming at full use of his skills and training, preoccupied with that competent, efficient performance of which his professional colleagues would approve—this person does not have the time, energy, or inclination necessary for social reform, for dedicated attention to the broader public purpose."[20]

The tendency of the social worker to identify his tasks as "casework" instead of "public welfare" is part of the process of professionalization.[21] It is an attempt to base the role on scientific knowledge and methods acquired by distinctive training, and thus to protect it from encroachment by anyone without proper training. By comparison, it is much more difficult to monopolize social welfare or to give it a scientific base. It is realized that "We lacked then [in the pre-World War I period when social work was committed to social reform] and lack today any adequate scientific base that would make possible professionalization of a social action approach."[22] On the lowest, most concrete level, welfare can be conceived of as relief dispensation which is basically an administrative function that does not require special knowledge or training. On a higher level of operation, social reform concerns political and legislative action for which "social workers as now trained are less equipped as reformers by school curricula than lawyers, labor leaders, politicians, public administrators, and others who know the political-social map and how to find their way around it."[23]

The conflict between the organization and the profession, in terms of the dilemma described above, is most apparent and most strongly felt in the role of the trained social worker in public welfare agencies. This role entails an inherent conflict between the task of eligibility investigation and financial dispensation and between intensive, therapeutic casework. The conflict has been reconciled, theoretically, by pointing out the interdependence of the two tasks—eligibility decisions almost always involve the establishment of some personal relationship and casework; on the other hand, Charlotte Towle has described the value in casework of "the giving of money."[24] Empirically, this role-conflict could be solved by separating financial assistance from professional casework and performing each in special units and different roles. But the Social Security Act amendments of 1962 established a new policy according to which welfare agencies were not only to dispense financial aid to the needy as before, but in addition, they were to provide social services designed to restore the indigent to self-support, strengthen the family-life of recipients, and prevent dependency. Although the law's intention is to integrate financial aid and psychological help in one and the same role, it has not provided the necessary resources for implementation. The new policy implies, for example, that agencies would have to recruit more professionally trained social workers. But if amendments in recruitment and allocation of trained personnel have occurred since the 1962 legislation, they have not been far-reaching enough to satisfy many professionally conscious social workers. It is claimed that of the few workers with graduate social work education in public welfare agencies, a large percentage is assigned to supervisory and administrative positions, resulting in feelings of inadequacy and dissatisfaction. The authors of an article on this problem write,

> "Public assistance may need trained administrators and supervisors, but what happens to the trained *caseworker*? He may emerge from school convinced that his talents lie in the world of the casework relationship. He may also feel that full integration of his knowledge and skills demands concentrated work with clients for an extended time. When he returns instead to supervision, resultant frustration is often responsible for his decision to obtain casework experience elsewhere."[25]

"Elsewhere" signifies other agencies with different purposes, utilizing professional skills and dealing with a different type of clientele. Thus, talent, training, and competence are drained off to the more professional agencies, and public welfare is left staffed mostly by nonprofessional, bureaucratic-like personnel.

The great difficulty in carrying out casework due to organizational pressures was one of the pertinent issues in the "work-in" declared in 1967 by the Social Service Employees' Union in New York City. One caseworker with the City Welfare Department told a reporter:

> "You know, the basic frustration of the caseworker is that you can only help your client's material needs. What they really ought to have is help in getting rehabilitated, in taking a big step along the way toward becoming better citizens. But you have 60 cases to take care of and a mountain of paper work. The department sets up no program of effective rehabilitation. And it seems to have an attitude like a vindictive parent. It's tough to do the kind of job you'd like to do."[26]

Thus, it is not surprising that professional social workers try to "get rid" of their administrative tasks. It has been recently suggested that the traditional eligibility investigation by social workers should be replaced by a "declaration of eligibility" by clients themselves. This is designed to free the social worker from paper work and red tape so that he may devote his time and energy to more intensive rehabilitative casework.

Proposals of this nature are also based on professional-ethical arguments. The strain in the social worker's role is due not only to lack of appropriate organizational resources (e.g. time), or of having to perform different tasks with relation to different role-partners, namely, managing one's "role-set."[27] The incompatibility of the practitioner's various tasks frequently appears in the same role-relationship, that is, with one client. In his encounter with the client, the social worker commands several types of "power," or means, which he can use to elicit compliance on the client's part. He has "utilitarian power" in the form of financial assistance that he can either give or withhold from the client; he has "normative power" by way of personal influence and "activation of commitments"; he has "coercive power," i.e. physical means of control, through his ability to initiate court proceedings.[28]

In using these different types of power, the social worker is faced with professional and moral problems. From these points of view it is clear that he should not use his economic or coercive power to persuade the client to behave or not to behave in a certain manner. For example, the client must not be made to feel that he has to change his behavior or interpersonal relationships in order to be eligible for financial assistance. The immanent problems of the situation were presented by McEntrie and Haworth:

> "Many of the problems of dependency are completely interwoven with financial need. . . . To draw the conclusion, however, that the same worker who determines the client's financial need should also offer therapeutic service means that assistance applicants are to be treated differently from other people who receive money from public sources. It also implies the possibility that an applicant's financial need may be judged according to his acceptance of or response to services offered—if not formally, at least in various subtle ways inherent in the relationship between caseworker and client. Furthermore . . . to combine the two in the same job is wasteful of scarce professional time."[29]

A fair decision about eligibility and reception of financial assistance is the client's right; to try to help him by means of other services may be the worker's right, but it is not clear whether the acceptance of these services is the client's "duty" or is subject to his own free choice. In regard to this problem, the semi-professional status of social work is apparent. In the well-established professions, particularly in medicine and law, the professional will decide, according to his own judgment, what his client's "real needs" are and how they will best be served. Not so in social work in which the goals and techniques of the professional are much more given to control and criticism by outside groups, including the wider public.

The use of coercive power by the social worker raises similar problems. The threat or the actual use of force will surely evoke the client's hostility, and in any case, its intended effects will not be long-lasting.[30] Aside from this, the ability of the social worker to "trigger off" court action is somewhat dubious since he is not at liberty to decide in which cases to use this authority; his records and testimony are liable to be subpoenaed by the court's decision. In this matter, the social worker's position is different from that of full-fledged professionals who have successfully obtained the right of privileged communication—the classic example in this respect being the clergy.[31] Nevertheless, the actual encounter and interaction between social worker and client is relatively invisible, that is, hidden from the public eye and from any other observer. It so happens that the practitioner will, under certain circumstances, employ utilitarian or coercive power to motivate the client to comply with his demands,[32] and "far too many applicants believe that acceptance of services for which they feel no impelling need is the price they must pay in order to get financial aid."[33]

We have delineated what seems to us to be a central dilemma in the profession of social work, and have traced its manifestations on different levels. First, on the level of ideology and *Weltanschauung,* there is the controversy between the ideas of "social reform" and "individual rehabilitation." Second, on the organizational level, there is the phenomenon of differentiation and specialization of agencies according to the two functions of "welfare" and "therapy" or "intervention for change." Third, on the level of the social worker's role, there is the role conflict between the more routine task of eligibility determination and administering financial assistance, and bringing about changes in people's norms and behavior. And finally, the dilemma is discernible in the basic unit of interaction between the social worker and his client in the form of alternation and manipulation of instrumental and normative sanctions.

As noted earlier, the discussion in subsequent chapters will be restricted to the implications of this essential duality for the process of professionalization of social work, for its operation within a bureaucratically organized framework, and for the degree of effectiveness of the worker-client relationship regarding the enhancement of the client's personal gratification and the improvement of his interpersonal competence.

Outline of the Study

The first part of the study is devoted to the analysis of social work as a semi-profession. In Chapter 1, the main dimensions that characterize the professions in general are defined, and the position of social work is located on a continuum of professionalism. Chapter 2 deals with the relations between bureaucratic organizations and the professions, paying special attention to the features of this relationship in the case of the helping, human-relations professions. The discussion in Chapter 3 is focused on the problem of professional autonomy and the prevailing pattern of supervision in social work.

The second part of the study approaches the examination of the worker-client relationship on the assumption that the caseworker is engaged in performing a social control function vis-a-vis his client. In Chapter 4 the structure and purposes of the casework-relationship, as defined in social work literature, are presented, noting in particular various orientations of social workers toward the inherent element of power in their role. Different types of power exercised by workers in their interaction with clients are discussed, and several obstacles to the acceptance of control by clients are pointed out. Possible consequences of the application of different types of power and their significance for the major goals of social work are discussed. Chapter 5 relates the attributes of semi-professionalism to the actual ability of the worker to produce change in the attitudes and behavior of clients.

The third part analyzes the processes of influence and personal change in small, face-to-face groups. Chapter 6 describes some of the diverse approaches and techniques currently applied in social group work. Theories and empirical studies of small groups, the process of learning, laboratory training, and group psychotherapy are drawn upon, and their possible contributions for the conduct of social group work are examined.

The last chapter contrasts the group setting with the casework situation, and examines the significance of group structure and dynamics for the interacting parties. The mechanisms of influence exertion and acceptance within groups are compared with those in casework. The attractiveness and salience of the group for its members are regarded as the two major factors that enhance the individual's susceptibility to change within a peer-group framework. The findings of several evaluative studies are employed to support the proposition that groups are more effective for inducing personal change than the professional-client configuration. Different types of groups are distinguished according to their proximity or distance from real-life situations and relationships, and the implications of this factor for change induction are analyzed.

The epilogue discusses prospects for the change of social work itself, its fundamental approach, and established practices, as related to its semi-professional nature and position.

Notes

1. Research evidence from evaluative studies of social work practice, supporting this notion, is still quite scarce. For a review of available evaluation studies in family services see Scott Briar, "Family Services," in Henry S. Maas, ed., *Five Fields of Social Service: Reviews of Research* (New York: National Association of Social Workers, 1966), pp. 16-21. For more general analyses questioning the effectiveness of traditional casework techniques see Scott Briar, "The Casework Predicament," Social Work 13 (January 1968): 5-11, and "The Current Crisis in Casework," Social Work Practice, 1967 (New York: Columbia University Press, 1967); Earl C. Brennen, "The Casework Relationship: Excerpts from a Heretic's Notebook," New Perspectives: The Berkeley Journal of Social Welfare 1 (Spring 1967): 75-82; and Richard A. Cloward and Irwin Epstein, "Private Social Welfare's Disengagement from the Poor: The Case of Family Adjustment Agencies," in Mayer N. Zald, ed., *Social Welfare Institutions* (New York: John Wiley and Sons, 1965), pp. 623-644.

2. See for example, McVicker J. Hunt and Leonard S. Kogan, *Measuring Results in Social Casework: A Manual on Judging Movement* (New York: Family Service Association of America, 1950); Leonard S. Kogan, McVicker J. Hunt, and Phyllis Bartelme, *A Follow-Up Study of the Results of Social Casework* (New York: Family Service Association of America, 1953); and Malcolm G. Preston, Emily Mudd, and Hazel B. Froscher, "Factors Affecting Movement in Casework," Social Casework 34 (March 1953): 103-111.

3. Edwin Powers and Helen L. Witmer, *An Experiment in the Prevention of Delinquency: The Cambridge-Somerville Youth Study* (New York: Columbia University Press, 1951); Helen L. Witmer and Edith Tufts, The Effectiveness of Delinquency Prevention Programs (Washington, D.C.: Children's Bureau, Publication 350, 1954); and Henry J. Meyer, Edgar F. Borgatta, and Wyatt C. Jones, *Girls at Vocational High: An Experiment in Social Work Intervention* (Russell Sage Foundation, 1965).

4. For example, see Robert G. Ballard and Emily H. Mudd, "Some Theoretical and Practical Problems in Evaluating Effectiveness of Counseling," Social Casework 38 (October 1957): 533-538; and Robert G. Ballard and Emily H. Mudd, "Some Sources of Difference Between Client and Agency Evaluation of Effectiveness of Counseling," Social Casework 39 (January 1958): 30-35.

5. See, for example, Frank Riessman, Jerome Cohen, and Arthur Pearl, eds., *Mental Health of the Poor: New Treatment Approaches for*

Low Income People (New York: Free Press, 1964); Henry Miller, "Value Dilemmas in Social Casework," Social Work 13 (January 1968): 27-33; and Paul Terrell, "The Social Worker as Radical: Roles of Advocacy," New Perspectives: The Berkeley Journal of Social Welfare 1 (Spring 1967): 83-88.

6. See Helen Harris Perlman, "Casework is Dead," Social Casework 48 (January 1967): 22-25.

7. Shirley Cooper, "The Swing to Community Mental Health," Social Casework 49 (May 1968): 279.

8. David J. Kallen, Dorothy Miller, and Arlene Daniels, "Sociology, Social Work, and Social Problems," The American Sociologist 3 (August 1968): 236. The authors classify the possible ways by which a society can handle a recognized social problem into four types: (1) amelioration of the negative outcomes without affecting the underlying causes, (2) prevention by modifying a single social institution, (3) revolutionary restructuring of the society, and (4) symptom exacerbation with no clear plan for solution of the problem.

9. Irving Piliavin, "Restructuring Social Services," Social Work 13 (January 1968): 34-41.

10. Miller, "Value Dilemmas in Social Casework," p. 33. See also Paul Terrell, "The Social Worker"; Robert H. McRae, "Social Work and Social Action," Social Service Review 40 (March 1966): 1-7; and Harry Specht, "Casework Practice and Social Policy Formulation," Social Work 13 (January 1968): 42-52.

11. The implementation of the Community Action Program by the Government has been strongly criticized by Daniel P. Moynihan in *Maximum Feasible Misunderstanding* (New York: Free Press, 1970).

12. Frances Piven, "Participation of Residents in Neighborhood Community Action Programs," Social Work 11 (January 1966): 75. See also Melvin B. Mogulof, "A Developmental Approach to the Community Action Program Idea," Social Work 12 (April 1967): 12-20 and Charles Grosser, "Community Development Programs Serving the Urban Poor," Social Work 10 (July 1965): 15-21. See also "Having the Power We Have the Duty," Report to the Secretary of Health, Education and Welfare, by the Advisory Council on Public Welfare (Washington, D.C.: U.S. Department of Health, Education and Welfare, June 29, 1966).

13. Several proposals for radical changes in public assistance programs have been suggested; see, for example, The National Symposium on Guaranteed Income (Washington, D.C.: Chamber of Commerce of the U.S., December 9, 1966); George Harris (Look Senior Editor), "Do We Owe People a Living," Look 32 (April 30, 1968); Richard A. Cloward and Frances F. Piven, "A Strategy to End Poverty," The Nation 202 (May 2,

1966): 510-517; Milton Friedman, *Capitalism and Freedom* (Chicago: University of Chicago Press, 1962); Robert Theobald, *Free Men and Free Markets* (New York: Clarkson and Tatten, 1953); and, Edward E. Schwartz, "A Way to End the Means Test," Social Work 9 (July 1964): 3-12.

14. By this we mean, for example, people who will not be directly affected having to pay more taxes to finance urban renewal and other antipoverty projects, or having to give up privileged social positions and high prestige.

15. Henry J. Meyer, "Professionalization and Social Work," in Alfred Kahn, ed., *Issues in American Social Work* (New York: Columbia University Press, 1959), pp. 319-340.

16. Harold Wilensky and Charles N. Lebeaux, *Industrial Society and Social Welfare* (New York: Free Press, 1965), p. 325.

17. See the discussion of this problem in Part I of this study.

18. New York Times, May 28, 1967.

19. A classic example in this respect is the development of medicine during the past two centuries. The process of "segmentation" in the medical profession is described in Rue Bucher and Anselm Strauss, "Professions in Process," American Journal of Sociology 66 (January 1961): 325-334; see also Abraham Zlozower, *Career Opportunities and the Growth of Scientific Discovery in 19th Century Germany* (Jerusalem: The Hebrew University, 1966).

20. Wilensky and Lebeaux, *Industrial Society and Social Welfare*, p. 330.

21. See D. G. French, *Statistics on Social Work Education* (New York: Council on Social Work Education, 1957), p. 16; more time is devoted to the subject of "human growth and development" in the curriculum of social work schools than to the history of social reforms and the structure of welfare services, and most students choose casework as their specialization.

22. Alfred Kadushin, "The Knowledge Base of Social Work," in Alfred J. Kahn, ed., *Issues in American Social Work,* p. 56.

23. Wilensky and Lebeaux, *Industrial Society and Social Welfare,* pp. 329-330.

24. Charlotte Towle, *Common Human Needs* (New York: National Association of Social Workers, 1965).

25. Jane K. Thompson and Donald P. Riley, "Use of Professionals in Public Welfare: A Dilemma and a Proposal," Social Work 11 (January 1966): 23-24. Italics added.

26. D. Stetson, "Welfare Workers, They Say They Can't Do Their Job," New York Times (June 25, 1967).

27. This term was conceived by Robert K. Merton in "The Role Set: Problems in Sociological Theory," British Journal of Sociology 8 (1957): 106-120.

28. This three-fold typology of power was formulated by Amitai Etzioni, *A Comparative Analysis of Complex Organizations* (New York: Free Press, 1961), pp. 3-22, and *Modern Organizations* (New Jersey: Prentice-Hall, 1964), pp. 58-67. Parsons introduced a similar typology of the ways by which compliance can be achieved: (a) "inducement" (situational—positive), the typical means employed in this case is "money"; (b) "deterrence" (situational—negative), by means of power; (c) "persuasion" (intentional—positive), by means of "influence"; and (d) activation of commitments" (intentional—negative), by means of "general commitments"; see Talcott Parsons, "On the Concept of Influence," Public Opinion Quarterly 27 (Spring 1963): 37-62. The problems entailed in the application of different types of power will be discussed in detail in Part II, Chapter 4.

29. Davis McEntrie and Joanne Haworth, "The Two Functions of Public Welfare: Income Maintenance and Social Services," Social Work 12 (January 1967): 22-30.

30. The consequences of control by coercion are an important issue in studies of custodial institutions such as prisons, correctional agencies, and mental hospitals. See, for example, Charles R. Tittle and Drollene P. Tittle, "Structural Handicaps to Therapeutic Participation: A Case Study," Social Problems 13 (Summer 1965): 75-82.

31. Our discussion does not imply that there are no professional and moral problems involved in the use of "normative power." Much has been said and written about imposing middle-class values on lower-class clients by teachers, social workers, and others. This, and related problems of "persuasion" will be discussed later.

32. The resources which the social worker has at his disposal in the situation are numerous and include, besides decision on eligibility for welfare payments, institutionalization of children, hospitalization, referral to other service organizations, and the like.

33. Mary E. Burns, "What's Wrong with Public Welfare?" Social Service Review 30 (June 1962): 116.

In this part we shall first present some typologies of the professions advanced by sociologists, and the dimensions along which these classifications are made. Then we shall apply these criteria to social work, assessing its present position on a continuum of professionalism, and establish our classification of social work as a semi-profession. As mentioned earlier, the present state of social work as a profession is the main factor that accounts for the disappointing consequences of social work practice. The diverse aspects of this problem will be discussed in following chapters.

It should be noted again, that increased professionalization is functional if we limit ourselves to the attainment of the traditional goals of social work, namely, helping people cope more effectively within the existing societal framework. Profes-

Part I

THE PROCESS OF PROFESSIONALIZATION
AND BUREAUCRATIC CONTROL IN
SOCIAL WORK

sionalization may, however, shift the emphasis of practice from the ordinary, routine problems of clients, such as relations with landlords or access to health services and education, to more professional tasks, e.g. therapeutic casework. By the same token, it seems plausible that this development will result in a transition of social work's clientele from a low-class to a more middle-class population. As we shall see later, our specific suggestions concerning the reconstruction of the social worker's role, and the worker-client relationship, largely avoid the possibility of a development in this direction.

Chapter 1

SOCIAL WORK AS A SEMI-PROFESSION

The nature of the professions and the process of professionalization have been dealt with extensively in recent sociological writings.[1] The various descriptions differ as to the number of attributes by which professions are defined and in regard to the relative importance given to each. However, most writers agree that the core characteristics which distinguish the professions from other occupations are that professions are based on a body of theoretical knowledge, that their members command special skills and competence in the application of this knowledge, and that their professional conduct is guided by a code of ethics, the focus of which is service to the client.

In view of the proliferation of professions in modern society, it is difficult and also misleading to talk about the professions as a whole. Rather, the extent of professionalization of an occupation should be measured by applying the general criteria used to define the professions. In this connection, two points should be noted. First, it is possible to distinguish among different types or degrees of each element, for example, the type of knowledge on which the profession is based, or the degree of public recognition enjoyed by its members. Second, different attributes of professionalization may have developed to varying degrees, so that a profession may rank higher in respect to one characteristic and lower in respect to another.

Thus, for example, although the service ideal is strongly emphasized in social work, its knowledge base is still in the process of crystallization, upgrading, and integration. These two distinctions have to be taken into account if we intend to rank an occupation on a continuum of professionalization.

Typologies of Professions

Measuring the degree of professionalization, particularly in respect to the type of knowledge upon which a profession is based, Carr-Saunders has differentiated four major types of professions in modern society.[3]

(a) The established professions of law, medicine, and the Church share two basic attributes; their practice is based upon the theoretical study of a department of learning, and the members of these professions feel bound to follow a certain mode of behavior.

(b) The new professions are those which are based on their own fundamental studies such as engineering, chemistry, accounting, and the natural and social sciences.

(c) The semi-professions replace theoretical study by the acquisition of technical skill. Technical practice and knowledge is the basis of such semi-professions as nursing, pharmacy, optometry, and social work.

(d) The would-be professions require neither theoretical study nor the acquisition of exact techniques but rather a familiarity with modern practices in business, administration practices, and current conventions. Examples of this type are hospital managers, sales managers, works managers, and so on.

In addition to the criteria of commitment to an ethical code (this aspect is mentioned explicitly only in reference to the old-established professions), and the type of knowledge base, a structural variable is introduced, namely, the degree to which members of different professional groups are independent or salaried workers. According to Carr-Saunders, the members of the older professions were originally independent practitioners; a certain proportion of members of the new professions have always been employed; and nearly all members of the semi-professions and would-be professions are salaried. The author apparently regards the transition from the independent practitioner to the salaried professional worker as a major factor undermining the professional code of ethics.

The characteristics of a semi-profession can be described more clearly by comparing it with an ideal-type, such as the model of professions provided by Greenwood,[4] which consists of five components: (1) a basis of systematic theory, (2) authority recognized by the clientele of the professional group, (3) broader community sanction and approval of this authority, (4) a code of ethics regulating relationships of professionals with clients and colleagues, (5) a professional culture sustained by formal professional associations.

The term semi-profession indicates that the profession in question is located somewhere along the middle of the continuum of professionalism, that is, between the full-fledged professions and those occupations which are professions in name only but do not, in fact, possess any of the attributes characterizing the professions.

The Position of Social Work on a Continuum of Professionalism

An occupation will be classified as a semi-profession if it lacks one or more of the professional qualities pointed out above, or if—which is empirically more frequent—one or more of these qualities are not fully developed. Thus, a semi-profession may lack a systematic theoretical knowledge base, and hence entail a shorter period of training for its members; it may not command a monopoly of control over its members, the criteria for their recruitment, training, licensing, or performance; its code of ethics may be vague or inconsistent; and the professional association may be divided, inefficient, or powerless.

Attempting to answer the question of whether social work is a profession, or to determine the extent of its professional character, different observers come to different conclusions, depending upon their general viewpoint and on the different degrees of importance they ascribe to various professional traits.

Many writers on this subject open their discussion of the problem by citing Flexner who, in 1915, argued that social work could not qualify as a full-fledged profession because it was not founded on a body of scientific knowledge.[5] Most of them also agree that since that time social work has gone a long way on the road toward professionalization.[6] Greenwood, for example, after presenting his model of the professions, comes to the conclusion that

> "Social work is already a profession; it has too many points of congruence with the model to be classified otherwise. Social work is, however, seeking to rise within the professional hierarchy, so that it, too, might enjoy maximum prestige, authority and monopoly which presently belong to a few top professions."[7]

As he sees it, social work possesses the main attributes characterizing a profession, but they are, as yet, less highly developed and integrated than in the established professions. Therefore, social work still ranks relatively low on the continuum of professionalism.

Carr-Saunders, whose typology of the professions was described earlier, classifies social work as a semi-profession, since he ascribes primary importance to the autonomy of the professional practitioner. He writes,

> "Social workers and school teachers, for example, have a dual responsibility to the employer as well as the client. But the employer lays down the limits to the service which can be rendered and to some extent determines its kind and quality. As a result, a social worker who is, say, a probation officer is far from free to treat a person committed to his charge in a manner indicated by his professional training and experience."[8]

While Greenwood is referring to the relatively lower degree of development of the main professional components in social work, Carr-Saunders emphasizes the lack of professional autonomy due to organizational pressures.

It is our contention that, as far as typologies go, social work should at present be classified as a semi-profession, although for somewhat different reasons than those provided by the authors quoted above. The phenomenon of uneven professionalization has already been mentioned; although the attributes of a profession are interdependent and hence tend to cluster around a certain point on the professional continuum, they may sometimes be less well integrated due to differences in the rates or directions of their development. This problem has been noted by some students of the process of professionalization;[9] considering social work, Boehm writes, "in social work, technical features, skills and techniques are relatively identified; its value system is well articulated, but its theory is less well developed than are its other features."[10] This means that the knowledge base of social work is still, to a large extent, drawn from experience, i.e. generalizations inferred from many specific cases, and that a great deal of intuition is required in the application of this knowledge. At the same time, the methods and particularly the service orientation of social work have attained a high level of development and crystallization.

Of course, the upward mobility of social workers toward a more "established" professional status is, in part, inhibited by a shortage of "authority recognized by the clientele of the professional group," and "broader community sanction and approval of this authority."[11] Social work also does not have, as yet, a strong inclusive professional association in which membership is a necessary prerequisite for the right to practice. However, these features are, to a considerable degree, the consequences of the fact that social workers have been unable until now to prove "exclusive competence" based on special training and knowledge in the treatment of their clients. Only a relatively small number of those practicing social work (16%) have had a full two-year graduate training and only one-third of the employed social workers are members of the National Association of Social Workers. Moreover, casework, i.e. therapeutic interviewing, which is the most "scientific" technique of the profession, is not the monopoly of social work but is used by other professional practitioners as well.

The discrepancy between the present development of theoretical knowledge and the value system of social work is one of the main factors contributing to its semi-professional status. Nowadays, it is difficult to claim full-fledged professional standing on

the basis of a commitment to help people in need and a concern
for humanitarian and social reform. As stated by Dollard,

> "The difficulty which has plagued social work in its development as
> a profession is that the social worker's dedication is to a degree
> shared by all good men and women. . . . Hence we all resist and
> resent the notion that the task of the social worker requires a
> peculiar combination of temperament, intelligence and exper-
> ience."[12]

To be granted the rights and rewards of an established
profession—autonomous control, high prestige, and high income—social work will have to demonstrate that its members
command esoteric knowledge and skills which enable them to
accomplish their task much more efficiently and with better
results than "any other enthusiastic amateur," as is clearly the
case, for example, in the medical professions.

The general conclusion which can be drawn from our
discussion at this point is that to claim and to be awarded an
"established" position (particularly in the sense of professional
autonomy), the profession must demonstrate a certain congruence between the two core elements—systematic knowledge
and professional norms. If a profession ranks high only on one
of these dimensions and low on the other, it will not be
accredited full professional status either by the public or by
social scientists. A profession may be based on a great amount
of systematic knowledge but lack a collectivity-oriented code of
ethics, as in the case of engineering specialists and other kinds
of technicians. Or, it may be committed to a service ideal but
lack a theoretical knowledge base, as in the case of social work,
nursing, and librarianship.

It should be mentioned here that the above analysis does not
account for the differentiated subdivisions of social work, for
example, public welfare, family counseling, child welfare, and
psychiatric casework. Some of these units command a more
systematic body of knowledge than others, and some are
organized in different structures from others. Therefore, our
analysis is a generalization of the concrete complexity of the
profession and should be considered as such.

The Propensity Toward Deprofessionalization

Another problem which deserves to be noted is that any classification of a profession is, by definition, more or less temporary. Professions, even the "established" ones, develop and change. Many developments and modifications have taken place in social work since the days of the charity organization; new changes are taking place at present so that the categorization of social work as a semi-profession is limited to the present time period.

It is usually taken for granted that members of a semi-profession and their leaders seek to achieve full professionalism so as to gain its accompanying rewards. However, while reviewing social work literature, a tendency toward "deprofessionalization" can be detected, namely, a resistance to full professionalization.[13] The source of this counter-trend is the concept that social work should retain some of its original and unique qualities. The writers who give expression to this tendency base their argument on two major issues: first, that "overprofessionalization" in social work will cause the loss of its basic humanitarian values, and second, that the profession will be drawn away from its commitment to social reform. This idea was eloquently expressed by Nathan Cohen: "Social work without service would be lame, but without values would be blind."[14]

Obviously, the ideals of social reform and the welfare of individuals are interrelated; however, some emphasize one or the other as being in danger of neglect as a result of professionalization.[15] Carr-Saunders, for example, deplores the decline of the true professional spirit in modern times; referring to social workers at the beginning of the century, he says,

"They were in effect general practitioners. In their place we now find specialist social workers of many kinds, such as probation officers, hospital social workers, psychiatric social workers, and others. . . . As a consequence of the trend toward specialization, the professional man no longer takes a comprehensive interest in his client. He feels that he has no general responsibility for those who come under his care, and the personal relationship between practitioner and client is weakened."[16]

Others, too, are convinced that social work should not and cannot desert its personal and humanitarian involvement: "It can never reach the point of scientific objectivity usually characterized by such terms as 'impersonal' and 'descriptive.' It will always have an element of the subjective, the personal, and the emotional."[17] The universalistic-specific orientation characterizing the professional's attitude is seen here from its negative side as infringing upon personal interest and total responsibility, which are fundamental to the helping professions.

The second issue—the effect of professionalization on the goals and values of social reform—is probably the more visible, and the more stressed in debates among social workers concerning the future of the profession. Some view the process of professionalization in social work as a two-edged sword; on the one hand, more knowledge and better training will eventually enhance the status of social work as a profession, but on the other hand, this process is regarded with apprehension because of the growing emphasis on methods and techniques at the expense of participation in wider social action and policy-making. Bisno observes that, "In assuming the rightness and naturalness of this trend (striving for more prestige by way of professionalization) we have tended to ignore the question of the price to be paid for the higher status and whether it is 'worth' it. Does it imply a weakening of the *social* in social work?"[18] He argues that if the trend of emphasizing methods and techniques continues, three consequences will follow:

"First, a continuing de-emphasis on controversial social action which has broad social implications; second, a related lessening of attempts to influence social policy and the acceptance of the role of technician-implementer; and third, change in the ideology of social work that will lessen the gap between its system of ideas and that of the dominant groups in society."[19]

In other words, a displacement of goals is likely to occur in which means (techniques and methods) will take the place of goals (social reform).[20]

Thus, we see that the opposing trends in social work, which

have been described earlier as a basic dilemma, constitute another factor inhibiting the process of professionalization of social work.

Notes

1. See, for example, Alexander M. Carr-Saunders and P. A. Wilson, *The Professions* (Oxford: Clarendon Press, 1933), Part III; Everett C. Hughes, *Men and their Work* (New York: Free Press, 1958), Chs. X and XI; Harold L. Wilensky, "The Professionalization of Everyone?" American Journal of Sociology 70 (September 1960): 33-50; William J. Goode, "Encroachment, Charlatanism, and the Emerging Professions: Psychology, Sociology and Medicine," American Sociological Review 25 (December 1960): 902-914; Ernest Greenwood, "Attributes of a Profession," Social Work 2 (July 1957): 45-55; Howard S. Becker, "The Nature of a Profession," in Nelson B. Henry, ed., *The Sixty-first Yearbook of the National Society for the Study of Education* (Chicago: University of Chicago Press, 1962), Part II; for studies on specific aspects of professionalization and of different professions, see Kenneth S. Lynn and the Editors of Daedalus, eds., *The Professions in America* (Boston: Beacon Press, 1967); Howard M. Vollmer and Donald L. Mills, eds., *Professionalization* (Englewood Cliffs, N.J.: Prentice-Hall, 1966); William J. Goode, Mary Jean Huntington, and Robert K. Merton, The Professions in Modern Society (Columbia University, unpublished manuscript).

2. See, for example, Wilensky, "The Professionalization of Everyone?"; Alfred Kadushin, "The Knowledge Base of Social Work"; and Alfred J. Kahn, "The Nature of Social Work Knowledge," in Cora Kasius, ed., *New Directions in Social Work* (New York: Harper, 1954), pp. 194-214.

3. Alexander M. Carr-Saunders, "Metropolitan Conditions and Traditional Professional Relationships," in Robert M. Fisher, ed., *The Metropolis in Modern Life* (Doubleday & Company, 1965), pp. 279-287.

4. Greenwood, "Attributes of a Profession," p. 45.

5. Abraham Flexner, "Is Social Work a Profession?" *Proceedings of the National Conference of Charities and Corrections* (Chicago, 1915), pp. 576-590.

6. For discussions dealing with social work's position as a profession, see for example Werner W. Boehm, "The Nature of Social Work," Social Work 3 (April 1958): 10-18, and "Relationship of Social Work to Other Professions," in Harry L. Lurie, ed., *Encyclopedia of Social Work* (New York: National Association of Social Workers, 1965), pp. 640-648; John C. Kidneigh, "Social Work as a Profession," in Russell H. Kurtz, ed., *Social Work Yearbook* (New York: National Association of Social Workers,

1960), pp. 563-572; Nathan E. Cohen, "Social Work as a Profession," *Social Work Yearbook* (1957), pp. 553-562.

7. Greenwood, "Attributes of a Profession," p. 54.

8. Carr-Saunders, "Metropolitan Conditions," p. 283.

9. See, for example, Goode, "Encroachment, Charlatanism, and the Emerging Professions."

10. Boehm, "Relationship of Social Work," p. 644.

11. See the list of components of Greenwood's model above.

12. Charles Dollard, Proceedings of the First Annual Trustees Reception of the New York School of Social Work, Bulletin of New York School of Social Work, Columbia University (September 1952): 4.

13. "Deprofessionalization" is used here in a similar manner to Eisenstadt's "debureaucratization"; both terms signify a process that leads in the opposite direction of the "ideal type" of professionalization and bureaucratization, respectively. See, S. N. Eisenstadt, "Bureaucracy, Bureaucratization, and Debureaucratization," Administrative Science Quarterly 4 (1959): 302-320; and Elihu Katz and S. N. Eisenstadt, "Some Sociological Observations on the Response of Israeli Organizations to New Immigrants," Administrative Science Quarterly 5 (1960): 113-133.

14. Cohen, "Social Work as a Profession," p. 559.

15. This is related to the basic duality in the values and goals of social work analyzed in the introduction.

16. Carr-Saunders, "Metropolitan Conditions," p. 283.

17. Cohen, "Social Work as a Profession," p. 559. An analysis of the special character of the social worker-client relationship can be found, for example, in Mary J. McCormick, "Professional Responsibility and the Professional Image, "Social Casework 47 (December 1966): 635-641.

18. Herbert Bisno, "How Social Will Social Work Be?" Social Work 1 (April 1956): 17. Italics added.

19. Ibid., p. 18.

20. This problem is noted in many discussions about the nature of the profession; see Greenwood, "Attributes of a Profession"; Alvin L. Schorr, "The Retreat to the Technician," Social Work 4 (January 1969): 29-33; and Harry L. Lurie, "The Responsibilities of a Socially Oriented Profession," in Cora Kasius, ed., *New Directions in Social Work,* pp. 31-33.

Chapter 2

SEMI-PROFESSIONS AND BUREAUCRACY

The preceding discussion has pointed out the factors underlying our classification of social work as a semi-profession. This characteristic of social work, the role-definition of social workers in agencies, and the properties of the worker-client relationship are interdependent. Doctors working in hospitals, for example, have more professional- autonomy within the organizational framework, and more authority in relation to their patients, than social workers have in public or even private agencies. However, the specific profession-bureaucracy relations in the case of social work are not due only to the semi-professional attributes of social work, but also to immanent structural properties of the administration of public assistance, a problem which will be dealt with in this chapter and in the following one.

To classify the nature and characteristics of the relationship between social work and the organizational setting in which it is performed, we shall first deal with some general ideas and concepts pertaining to the problem of profession-bureaucracy relationship. Then we shall analyze the typical traits which this relationship assumes in the case of a semi-profession as illustrated by social work in welfare agencies.

49

Contradiction and Compatibility between
Bureaucracy and Professions

One of the problems most often discussed in the sociology of
professions is the relationship between the professions and
bureaucratic structures. This is not surprising in view of the fact
that these two patterns of activity and organization are
becoming increasingly interwoven. The process is sometimes
described as the "bureaucratization of the professions," or, as
the "professionalization of bureaucracies." To quote Wilensky,
"It is not that organizational revolution destroys professionalism, or that the newer forms of knowledge . . . provide a
poor base for professionalism, but simply that all these
developments lead to something new. The culture of bureaucracy invades the professions, the culture of professionalism
invades organizations."[1]

It is important to bear in mind that certain general principles
of the professions as well as of bureaucracies are rooted in the
same developmental trends of modern Western culture, namely,
the growing division of labor, specialization, and rationalization.
Thus, Parsons in his analysis of the professions in modern
society concludes that the occupational sphere in general—the
professions, business, and bureaucratic administration—share
common elements of rationalty, functional specificity, and
universalism.[2]

Professionals in various fields acknowledge the fact that
nowadays it is almost impossible to carry out professional work
outside large and complex organizations, e.g. research institutes,
hospitals, business firms, welfare agencies, schools, and the like.
Various types of resources, and their management in organizations, are vital to the conduct of high quality professional work.
The student-professional in medicine, nursing, social work, and
teaching is partly trained in a bureaucratic framework—
hospitals, agencies, schools. The graduate student in social work
becomes familiar with agency structure through field training,
which is an integral and important part of his professional
education. This means that the student undergoes a process of
anticipatory socialization to the role of professional in a
bureaucratic organization. Also, in his later encounter with the

agency's rules and regulations, as a full-fledged professional, he may discover that in some areas the organization's requirements are in fact compatible with his professional ideology and standards; for example, the norm of treating the client with a certain amount of detachment and without emotional involvement coincides with the bureaucratic dictum of *sine ira et studio.*

Nonetheless, bureaucratic rules and authority are, more often than not, viewed as infringing upon the professional's freedom to apply his knowledge and skills according to his judgment and convictions.[3] The literature on this subject stresses the contradictions and inherent conflicts between bureaucratic organizations and professions rather than their points of congruity.[4] This may be so for a variety of reasons but, the most important is the distinctive control structure of the professions which is fundamentally different from bureaucratic control exercised in administrative organizations. Professional control is characterized by being exercised from "within" by an internalized code of ethics and special knowledge acquired during a long period of training, and by a group of peers, which is alone qualified to make professional judgments. This type of authority differs greatly from bureaucratic authority which emanates from a hierarchical position.[5] Gross writes, "A strong sense of competence is important because authority rests upon it. The professional in the last analysis has nothing else on which to base his authority. His authority is not charismatic, not based on tradition, nor on the occupancy of a formal position."[6]

The suggestion that professional authority is based solely upon knowledge and competence—even though this is so only "in the last analysis"—needs further qualification. First, the authority of the "established" professions, as the term itself implies, does rest to some extent on tradition. We may even detect some "magical" elements in the exercise of professional control, e.g. the doctor's treatment of patients with "awe-evoking" instruments whose function is not always scientific. Second, to some degree the professional's authority is charismatic, that is, based on the "extraordinary qualities of a person."[7] This can be demonstrated by comparing the performances of professionals with similar training, skills, and positions, who, nevertheless, exert diverse powers of personality. A good example would be provided by observing the performances of different lawyers in court. Finally, there is no doubt that the professional's authority is frequently combined with a high hierarchical position in the organization in which he is employed.

We do not intend to deny that professional authority is based mainly on knowledge and competence but wish to point out that "professional authority" and "bureaucratic authority" are ideal types. In reality, there are other components involved in the professional's authority, especially when he is engaged in service to people (the scientist in industry does not have "clients" in this sense). Furthermore, these other elements—traditional, charismatic, and official—come to the front specifically under those circumstances in which knowledge and technical skills are inadequate.[8]

Here we would like to deal briefly with two questions. First: what is the position of the semi-professions, particularly of social work, in regard to bureaucratic control? and, second: is a bureaucratic framework always "dysfunctional" for the conduct of professional work, or does it, under certain conditions, have some positive contribution?

Heteronomy and Semi-Professionalism

Semi-professions, such as teaching, nursing, librarianship, and social work are sometimes called "heteronomous professions."[9] However, these two concepts are not merely synonymous; they pertain to different elements in the characterization of the professions. Semi-professionalism denotes that the profession does not rest on a firm theoretical knowledge base; the period of training involved is relatively short; members cannot claim monopoly of exclusive skills; and the special area of their competence, i.e. their function, is less well defined as compared with the full-fledged established professions. Heteronomy, on the other hand, means that members of the profession are guided and controlled not only from "within"—that is, by internalized professional norms, expert knowledge and the professional community—but also by administrative rules and by superiors in the organizational hierarchy.

At first sight, the relationship between semi-professionalism and heteronomy seems clear and logical. Because professional authority rests basically on expert knowledge and technical competence, and because the semi-professions entail a shorter period of training, it follows that their members have less knowledge and less intrinsic commitment to professional norms. In short, they are less well "socialized" to perform their role without outside supervision. They will therefore be less able to insist on complete freedom from control whether by the public, special groups of laymen, or their administrative superiors.

Closer scrutiny, however, may reveal that the assumption of the intimate association between semi-professionalism and heteronomy, and between full-fledged professionalism and autonomy, is not a one-to-one relationship. To a large extent this assumption is a result of explicitly or implicitly comparing every profession with the stereotyped image of the "independent" physician in private practice. But we may raise the question of whether the doctor working in a state or municipal hospital or clinic is really completely autonomous in his daily conduct, or whether the lawyer employed by a large law firm is free from control by his superiors. The answer to these questions is obviously that members of established professions are sometimes controlled by their senior colleagues and their peers but not by nonprofessionals, at least not in the making of decisions and in the performance of tasks within their special sphere of competence.

It is true that teachers, nurses, social workers, librarians, and other members of semi-professions are more subjected to bureaucratic rules and regulations than physicians, lawyers, and scientists. Nevertheless, it is interesting to note that direct supervision in the semi-professions is always carried out by senior or ex-professionals who have "risen from the ranks"—the school principal, the head nurse, the social work supervisor, and the like.

It has also been noted that even semi-professionals are not

controlled to the same degree in the performance of all their different tasks and their various role relationships. To quote Lotrie,

> "Conventional concepts of hierarchical control usually assume that superordinate-subordinate linkages are marked by uniformity on all matters, i.e., that all of a superordinate's wishes carry equal initiatory power over his subordinate's actions. Yet, . . . it appears that decision areas are subjected to differential definition, and that 'variable zoning' exists in which, within the *same* dyad, initiatory power varies by topic."[10]

Thus, for example, the teacher is more autonomous vis-à-vis the school's principal with regard to in-class affairs than in respect to administrative matters, such as record keeping.

Similar differential zoning of control can be found in social work and other semi-professions. In particular, the actual encounter between practitioner and client is usually not observable (this includes the human-relation professions which do not enjoy the right of privileged communication), and is therefore not directly controllable. Exclusion from visibility allows the semi-professional a great degree of autonomy in his contact with the client, but it also implies the disadvantages of being judged by results rather than by the effort and skill invested in the process.

All this is not to deny the greater autonomy of the established professions, e.g. medicine and law. The relative lack of autonomy of social workers is indicated, for example, by the fact that there exists as yet no legal regulation in the form of licensure which restricts practice to those who hold a license (as in medicine), or certification which restricts the use of title to those who have a certain training (as in public accounting);[11] nor do social workers enjoy the right of privileged communication with their clients, which exempts the practitioner-client verbal interchange from any outside interference, including that of the courts (as in the practice of law).

However, by noting that social workers are not controlled to the same extent in the performance of their various tasks, we tried to emphasize that instead of labeling any profession as heteronomous, autonomous, or otherwise, we should ask:

which aspects of the professional's daily conduct are controlled, by whom, and how? If these aspects are specified, the description of any profession becomes more complex and realistic, and less ideal-typical. These problems will be taken up in more detail in the following chapter dealing with the operation of supervision in social work agencies.

In addition to the features directly associated with less scientific knowledge and exclusive skills of the semi-professions in general, there are other factors which increase the contingency of social workers upon bureaucratic control. The most elementary facts in this respect are, first, that almost all social workers are employed by bureaucratic organizations—public or voluntary agencies, schools, hospitals, prisons, and so on. Social work did not start as a "free" profession with "independent" practitioners; private practice in social work is only a recent development and for the time being quite marginal. Hence, the common distinction between "locals" and "cosmopolitans" is somewhat obscure in this case (in the sense of the employed social worker orienting toward an "outside colleague community" as a reference group and target of aspiration). Second, in public welfare agencies, workers are constrained by administrative regulations, owing to the primary function of these organizations, i.e. the dispensation of financial aid subject to state and federal laws and control. This fact is one of the major bases of the social worker's limited autonomy in welfare agencies, and will be further discussed in the subsequent chapter.

Certain demographic and structural elements that characterize social work, and the semi-professions in general, impairing their professional autonomy, should also be mentioned, notably, the proportion between the sexes among those comprising the profession, and their class and ethnic origins. It seems that these variables correlate with the type of knowledge and the degree of the socially legitimated autonomy that a profession commands.

Simpson and Simpson, for example, argue that the fact that semi-professions are more given to bureaucratic supervision is closely related to the prevalence of women in nursing, elementary school teaching, social work, and the like. They write,

"The public is less willing to grant autonomy to women than to men. Women's primary attachment is to the family role, and they are therefore less intrinsically committed to work than men and less likely to maintain a high level of specialized knowledge ... [and] less likely than men to develop colleague reference group orientations. For these reasons and because they often share the general cultural norm that women should defer to men, women are more willing than men to accept the bureaucratic controls imposed on them in semi-professional organizations, and less likely to seek a genuinely professional status."[12]

Social work is thus identified by the public as a feminine occupation; the helping, nurturant functions of the social worker are associated with the image of the traditional roles of women. It has also been noticed that in the professional literature there is a tendency to refer to a social worker of indeterminate sex as "she" rather than "he."[13] All of this constitutes a threat to the male identity as defined in our society, i.e. as being dominant, active, achieving, and so forth, and partially explains the fact that less than a third of all practicing social workers are men.[14] The relation between the existing sex-ratio, heteronomy, and the generally low prestige of social work is circular and cumulative: social workers are accorded less autonomy on the job, in part, because the majority of them are women; on the other hand, because of more bureaucratic constraints and less prestige, the profession finds it difficult to recruit more men into its ranks.

The stratificational origin of social workers affects and is affected by autonomy and status in a similar manner; it is at the same time a cause and a consequence. The majority of social workers have always come from middle-class families; in the past few decades they have been increasingly recruited from lower social strata and ethnic groups. This process may have a negative feedback on the profession's prestige by deterring people from higher classes or with upper mobility aspirations from choosing social work as a career.[15]

The Helping Professions and Bureaucratic Control

The attributes of semi-professions that have been mentioned so far tend to make their members more liable to organizational controls. Nonetheless, it seems that the very nature of these professions, particularly those dealing with the well-being of people, is incompatible with bureaucratic standardization. One of the main features of bureaucratic organization is that the work of its members is directed by a set of universalistic rules and generalized procedures. This can be maintained only if the work to be done is specific and routine; the helping professions, and in particular social work, are neither. First, the orientation toward the client is diffuse or "holistic," approaching him in his entirety and taking account of all his needs—physical, psychological and social. Second, each client is unique—there will always be "special circumstances" and "exceptions to the rule."[16] These two basic attitudes are expressed in the phrasing of the "Working Definitions of Social Work Practice" prepared by a committee for the Commission on Social Work Practice of the National Association of Social Workers in 1956.[17] Considering the values of social work, it says: "4) There are human needs common to each person, yet each person is essentially unique and different from others." And in the definition of the required knowledge for the performance of social work, we find "The practice of the social worker is typically guided by knowledge of: 1) Human development and behavior characterized by emphasis on the wholeness of the individual and the reciprocal influences of man and his total environment—human, social, economic and cultural."[18]

Our tentative conclusion is that social work, as well as other semi-professions, incorporate diverse attributes, some of which are conducive to organizational regulation and control, such as a relatively short training period, no developed theoretical knowledge base, feminization, and recruitment from the lower classes. Other characteristics, however, such as dealing with people and some of their most severe problems, are inherently incompatible with bureaucratic principles and make rigid categorization of clients and routinization of relationships with them extremely difficult.

The other question that was raised earlier concerns the positive functions of a bureaucratic setting for the conduct of professional work. We do not refer to the financial and organizational resources needed to discharge appropriate services to clients that can ordinarily be commanded only by an organization and not by an individual professional, but to the special structure of control in bureaucracies and its effects on the professional.

Some kind of strain, or even conflict, between line and staff seems to be unavoidable. However, sociologists have recognized that conflict may sometimes have positive functions for the parties engaged in it.[19] Gross writes, "Conflict can be a way of creatively solving problems if it takes place in a context in which it is institutionalized and in which the rules make certain the conflict is a fair one with the sides being permitted to make their case as strongly as possible."[20] He argues further, that a certain type and degree of organizational control of professionals will result in improvement of professional service to clients.

It has also been pointed out recently that the relationship between bureaucracy and professionalism is not necessarily a "battle" in which one will eventually dominate the other, but that through mutual adaptations new structures may emerge. Kornhauser, dealing with the position of scientists in industry, concludes that "the tension between the autonomy and integration of professional groups, production groups, and other participants tends to summon a more effective structure than is attained where they are isolated from one another or where one absorbs the others."[21]

In the human-relations and helping professions, and specifically in social work, the bureaucratic framework has still other functions for professional performance. It is true that rigid adherence to administrative regulations and categorization of clients in terms of abstract criteria are typical of what Merton calls "displacement of goals" or a "ritualistic orientation" which often interferes with the very goals the professional wants to achieve.[22] However, organizational rules and procedures sometimes serve as a restraining factor on a too-deep emotional involvement in the client's troubles, especially on the part of the young, idealistic, and inexperienced social worker.

Another function of the organizational setting for the holistic-helping professions is to make their services more impartial and fair. Formal impersonal rules are a yardstick for comparing and evaluating different clients' problems and needs. The positive functions of the bureaucratic organization for social work were commented on by Wilensky and Lebeaux: "Bureaucracy tends to minimize urgency, which may be counted a disadvantage. But the gains associated with it are clear: reliability, continuity, fairness."[23]

A less conspicuous function of organizational prescriptions, which has nevertheless been noticed in family service agencies,[24] is the use of administrative limitations as a defense against clients' demands, which either cannot be satisfied, or, in the social worker's opinion, should not be met. An extreme example of such use (or "abuse") of bureaucratic regulations would be the case in which the social worker tells his client, "Personally I would like to help you, but I am restricted by the agency's policy." The social worker is a typical "man (or woman) in the middle"; pressures in opposite directions are exerted on him by the organization on the one hand, and by the client on the other. Therefore, it is not surprising that under this strain he will sometimes justify his activities by claiming mere compliance with bureaucratic rules. "I am just following orders" is the typical justification of the bureaucrat faced with an overdemanding or complaining client. By contrast, the professional's ultimate legitimation of his actions is that "he is doing that which, to the best of his knowledge, will best serve the client's needs."

Thus it seems that the effects of the organizational framework on the social worker's role are not totally detrimental and do sometimes contribute to better service for clients. However, in practice, the problem still remains to achieve an optimal balance between ritualism, rigid adherence to rules, and indifference, and between complete freedom, ad hoc resolutions, and personal involvement. The conjunction of the semi-professional position of social workers and the task of eligibility determination cast upon them in public agencies, both of which tend to increase organizational controls, obstruct the attainment of such *modus vivendi.*

As mentioned previously, the attributes of semi-profes-sionalism and, in particular, the developmental stage of the knowledge base cannot be altered rapidly. However, the tension between the profession and the organization which emanates from the engagement in distributing welfare payments can be avoided by relieving the social worker of this duty, and carrying it out in differentiated administrative units. The implementa-tion of the Guaranteed Income proposal, for example, would automatically eliminate the present procedures of eligibility determination and checking by public welfare workers, thus allowing them to devote their time and skills to the provision of more professional services to clients.

In this chapter we have examined the relations between social work and the bureaucratic organization. The next chapter will be devoted to the analysis of the pattern of supervision currently exercised in social work agencies. Supervision may be regarded as the epitome of the worker-agency relations. The supervisor-worker relationship is the sphere in which the influence of organizational authority upon the professional worker is manifested, and its consequences can be most clearly observed. Different aspects and types of supervision, and the worker's attitude toward them, also affect his orientation and relationship with the client, thus furnishing one of the connecting links between the worker-client relationship and the structure of the organization.

Notes

1. Wilensky, "The Professionalization of Everyone?", p. 150.

2. Talcott Parsons, "The Professions and Social Structure," in Talcott Parsons, ed., Essays in Sociological Theory (New York: Free Press, 1957), pp. 34-49.

3. Referring to professionals in bureaucracies, Scott pointed out four areas of role conflict:

(1) the professional's resistance to bureaucratic rules,

(2) the professional's rejection of bureaucratic standards,

(3) the professional's resistance to bureaucratic supervision, and

(4) the professional's conditional loyalty to the bureaucracy.

W. Richard Scott, "Professionals in Bureaucracies—Areas of Conflict," in H. M. Vollmer and D. L. Mills, eds., Professionalization (Englewood Cliffs, N.J.: Prentice-Hall, 1966), p. 265.

4. Robert K. Merton, "Role of the Intellectual in Public Bureaucracy," in Robert K. Merton, ed., Social Theory and Social Structure (Glencoe, Ill.: Free Press, 1957), pp. 207-224; Joseph Ben-David, "The Professional Role of the Physician in Bureaucratized Medicine: A Study in Role Conflict," Human Relations 11 (1958): 255-274; William J. Goode, "Community within a Community: The Professions," American Sociological Review 22 (1957): 194-200; Alvin W. Gouldner, "Cosmopolitans and Locals," Administrative Science Quarterly 2 (1957-1958): 281-306, 444-480; Peter M. Blau and W. Richard Scott, Formal Organizations: A Comparative Approach (London: Routledge and Kegan Paul, 1963), pp. 60-74; William Kornhauser, Scientists in Industry: Conflict and Accommodation (Berkeley: University of California Press, 1962); Fred H. Goldner and R. R. Ritti, "Professionalization as Career Immobility," The American Journal of Sociology 72 (March 1967): 489-502; Peter M. Blau, Wolf V. Heydebrand, and Robert E. Stauffer, "The Structure of Small Bureaucracies," American Sociological Review 31 (April 1966): 179-191.

5. See Parsons' discussions of the differences between bureaucratic and professional authority in Max Weber, The Theory of Social and Economic Organization, A. M. Henderson and Talcott Parsons, trans., and Talcott Parsons, ed. (New York: Oxford University Press, 1947), "Introduction," Footnote 4, pp. 58-60.

6. Edward Gross, "When Occupations Meet: Professions in Trouble," Hospital Administration 12 (Summer 1967): 40-59.

7. Etzioni discusses the development and form that charismatic

elements assume in a variety of organizational positions, in Amitai Etzioni, *A Comparative Analysis of Complex Organizations*, pp. 201-209; see also Robert L. Peabody, *Organizational Authority* (New York: Atherton Press, 1964), pp. 117-131.

8. This problem is analyzed by Parsons in reference to the role of physician, in Talcott Parsons, *The Social System* (New York: Free Press, 1951), pp. 447-454.

9. See W. Richard Scott, "Reaction to Supervision in a Heteronomous Professional Organization," Administrative Science Quarterly (June 1965): 65-81. The term "heteronomy" is borrowed from Weber: "A corporate group may be either autonomous or heteronomous, . . . Autonomy means that the order governing the group has been established by its own members on their own authority. . . . In the case of heteronomy, it has been imposed by an outside agency." Max Weber, *The Theory of Social and Economic Organization*, p. 148.

10. Dan C. Lotrie, "The Balance of Control and Autonomy in Elementary School Teaching," in Amitai Etzioni, ed., *The Semi-Professions* (New York: Free Press, 1969). Italics added.

11. Voluntary registration exists at present in the state of California. The National Association of Social Workers has recently proposed a national voluntary registration plan as a step toward legal regulation.

12. Richard L. Simpson and J. H. Simpson, "Women and Bureaucracy in the Semi-Professions," in A. Etzioni, ed., *The Semi-Professions.*

13. Harold L. Wilensky and Charles N. Lebeaux, *Industrial Society and Social Welfare*, p. 323.

14. *Social Workers in 1950* (New York: American Association of Social Workers, 1952).

15. For a detailed analysis of the various factors responsible for the relatively low status of the profession, see Alfred Kadushin, "Prestige of Social Work—Facts and Factors," Social Work 3 (April 1958): 37-43.

16. These two characteristics, in their extreme form, conflict with the above-mentioned principles of specificity and universalism.

17. "Working Definition of Social Work Practice," Social Work 3 (April 1958): 2-6.

18. Ibid., p. 3.

19. Georg Simmel, "Conflict," in *Conflict and the Web of Group Affiliations*, Kurt H. Wolff, trans. (New York: Free Press, 1955), pp. 13-123, and Lewis Coser, *The Functions of Social Conflict* (New York: Free Press, 1956).

20. Gross, "When Occupations Meet," p. 50.

21. Kornhauser, *Scientists in Industry*, p. 197.

22. Robert K. Merton, "Bureaucratic Structure and Personality," in Robert K. Merton, ed., *Social Theory and Social Structure*, pp. 195-206.

23. Wilensky and Lebeaux, *Industrial Society and Social Welfare,* p. 243.

24. These observations are based on an unpublished study carried out by the author in Israel in 1964-1965.

Chapter 3

SUPERVISION IN SOCIAL WORK

Autonomy, as we have seen before, is one of the main features characterizing the well-established professions; namely, the professional community determines its own standards of training, recruitment, and performance. Once the professional becomes a recognized member of this community, he is relatively free from lay control and evaluation; the profession "becomes a monopoly in the public interest."[1] By comparison, the semi-professions are characterized by lower degrees of such self-determination; they are more exposed by administrative superiors and lay boards. Supervision is the institutionalized, built-in mechanism through which the attitudes and performance of social workers are controlled.

It was argued that it would be fruitful to specify which areas of the social worker's role are controlled and by whom, and in what manner is supervision implemented. Regarding the first question, that of differential authority in different role-sectors, it seems that of the two tasks distinguished above, that of financial aid is more strictly controlled than that of casework. In general, when tasks are more complicated and can be defined in advance only in broad terms, more authority will be delegated to the professional, since the details of performance have to be left to his own discretion. Eligibility determination is a routine and standardized procedure and is therefore easily prescribed and regulated by bureaucratic rules. Aside from this, the simple fact that the management and allocation of money which comes from public sources—federal, state, and local—is involved, by definition implies that these organizations will want to control the principles of its distribution. Boehm remarks that

> "In no other profession is the distinction between financial probity and professional prowess more difficult to establish. No other profession is less free than social work from being directed by the laity or from being deprived of self-determination regarding the nature of its professional functions and the manner in which it discharges them."[2]

The allocation of material goods is something which is indeed unique to social work; here the professional helps the client by giving him something which is not "his own." In other professions, or even semi-professions, the main resources at the disposal of the professional are "internalized"—specific knowledge and competence guided by a commitment to the ideal of service. It is true that the client of the physician, lawyer, psychiatrist, teacher, or scientist may profit materially as an indirect result of professional help, but in none of these cases is such profit the main or direct function of the professional. The point is that resources which are acquired by the professional in the course of socialization and training, such as knowledge, skills, and a professional code of ethics, will be less controllable by outside agencies than the dispensation and manipulation of "external" resources such as money or other material goods.[3]

The second question concerning supervision is who has authority over the professional in the conduct of his work and to whom is he accountable for his performance. The distinction usually made in this respect is that between control by colleagues and the professional community, and by extraprofessional individuals and groups.[4] However, the picture of supervision in social work is much more complex. The questions of what is supervised, in what manner, and by whom are interdependent and must be discussed simultaneously. If the social worker's adherence to the policy and regulations of the agency is to be controlled, it can be done by checking his performance against a set of abstract laws and prescriptions. If, however, his "capacity to help people" is to be supervised, another type of control is needed. The practitioner carrying out casework is engaged in a helping process which, to a greater or lesser degree, involves his values, intellect, and emotions. This kind of work can be supervised, if at all, only through a personal relationship between supervisor and supervisee.

The Purposes of Supervision

The use of different methods of supervision, personal or impersonal, depends to a large extent upon the goals one wants to achieve by their application. It is generally agreed that supervision in social work has a dual function: educational and administrative. The administrative function of the supervisory process is essentially the control of a subordinate (the worker) by a superior (the supervisor) in the organization's hierarchy. This includes the supervisor's right to plan the worker's job (caseload), to co-ordinate it with the work of others and with the overall objectives of the agency and program purposes, and to check the worker's performance against the "Manual of Regulations" or other institutionalized procedures.

The contents and methods of the educational function of supervision are more complicated and less well defined. Supervision developed initially as a master-apprentice relationship in the charity organization, in a period when social work practice preceded formal training.[5] Knowledge was based largely upon experience and was transmitted in a practical ad hoc manner. The new worker was supposed to be "learning by doing," under the watchful eye and guiding hand of the more experienced practitioner. During the first two decades of this century—a period in which the first schools of social work were established—tutorial teaching in agencies was rationalized and formalized. Its main goal was to help the trainee and inexperienced worker to bridge the discrepancy between theoretical knowledge and actual performance, and help him achieve intellectual and emotional integration of what he had learned in school. Thus, tutorial instruction in agencies was concomitant with classroom teaching. Beginning in the 1920s, with the emergence of the psychoanalytic school and the shift of emphasis from social reform to the individual client, the philosophy and techniques of supervision were modified. Attention was focused on the therapeutic function of the supervisor, that is, his task in helping the worker develop self-awareness and understanding of his motivations and feelings in an attempt to resolve his personality conflicts. All this, of course, was not an end in itself but was designed to advance the learning process of the trainee and to enable him to carry out more effective casework with his client.[6] During World War II, supervisory methods and definitions underwent yet another change. Emphasis shifted from the intrapsychic focus to the educational function of supervision.[7] This transition was influenced by the progress in educational theory and analysis of organizational structures. Towle writes:

> "We must be clear about the essential difference between re-educational help in social work education and therapy. A teaching situation differs from a psychotherapeutic session, in its heavy reliance upon the student's capacity to experience change in feeling and thereby change in thinking through an intellectual approach. In professional education, both in classroom and in field work, the initial approach or attack is upon the intellect."[8]

This does not mean that the trainee's feelings, especially those engendered by interaction with the client and with the supervisor, are not taken into consideration. Towle herself points out that "Supervision is a process in the conduct of which the supervisor has three functions—administration, teaching and helping. This mid-position has significance in the performance of each of these functions, and notably in helping."[9] These three elements of supervision are inter-related. The student and the new social worker need help because of the inevitable strains created by the process of learning, by the confrontation with the actual demands of practice (which include his encounter with the client, the agency, and the supervisor), and by the special nature of the profession. In turn, the learning process is facilitated by a positive-supportive relationship between supervisor and supervisee. The manifest goal of the education process is to help the practitioner become more competent and autonomous, to achieve effective integration of knowledge in order to be capable of rendering better service to clients.

Inherent Conflicts in the Established Pattern of Supervision

In reality, the administrative and teaching functions of the supervisor are often in conflict. When we allude to the supervisor as representing the agency's policy and regulations and as holding the supervisee accountable for his performance, we basically refer to the authority vested in a higher ranking position within the organization. When we refer to the teaching function of the supervisor, we mean the transmission of knowledge from the experienced to the inexperienced, the teaching of skills, the creation of positive identification—in short, something similar to professional authority. The imma-nent incongruity of these two types of authority has been recognized in social work literature; as Scherz says, "Adminis-trative leadership requires the use of one kind of authority; casework practice requires another."[10]

The debate about the effectiveness and advisability of this combining of administrative authority and the teaching and helping functions into one role has been going on in social work literature for more than a decade. One of the main arguments in this connection is that the administrative authority held and exercised by the supervisor interferes with the learning process of the supervisee. This argument derives from the conception that teaching is really the primary task of the supervisor, whereas his administrative duties are less important and somewhat "distasteful." Scherz critically observes that "As a teacher, the supervisor has been in conflict about discharging various administrative duties, including evaluation of workers, since these seem to intrude like a foreign body into the benign teacher-learner relationship."[11]

However, from an opposite point of view, which has been somewhat neglected, the question may be raised as to whether the personal-expressive relationship of teacher-learner does not infringe upon the maintenance of bureaucratic control by the supervisor. By now, it is an accepted proposition in sociology that roles in groups tend to differentiate along an axis of control-support, or authority-friendliness, and, in more general terms, along the instrumental-expressive axis.[12] When an individual has authority over another, the relationship between them will be characterized by restraint, respect, and the reduction of their interaction to the "necessary minimum" to carry out the common task in which they are engaged. On the other hand, the relationship between equals is characterized by intimacy, mutual liking, and the increase of interaction beyond that required for task performance.[13]

The supervisory role as it has been traditionally defined in social work includes both the "nurturant" and the "demanding" functions.[14] This definition introduces ambiguities into the relationship and creates problems of orientation both for the supervisor and the supervisee. The supervisor cannot exercise authority and give psychological support at the same time; the supervisee cannot acknowledge his duty to obey the supervisor and at the same time feel at ease in his company.[15]

Miller has attacked the "idyllic" picture which is usually presented of supervisor-supervisee relationships: "it would help a great deal to give up the sentimental sham that the worker-supervisor relationship exists between equals, or between professional colleagues who happen to have different functions and responsibilities. This kind of well-meaning distortion obscures the power and authority inherent in the supervisory functions."[16]

The potential sources of strain in the supervisor-worker relationship become clearer when we consider the main techniques of supervision: reviewing of records written by the worker, private conferences with him, and evaluation of his performance. These various techniques are interconnected; the weekly conference is based upon records of interviews with clients submitted by the practitioner; evaluation, in turn, is based upon both reviewing of records and case discussions.

Ideally, evaluation is an ongoing process which is to some degree a joint enterprise of supervisor and supervisee (student or practitioner), and which is periodically summarized in writing by the supervisor and submitted to either school or agency. The worker's skills and competence in performing his role are appraised, e.g. his capacity to establish and sustain helpful relationships with clients, his understanding and use of social work methods, the degree to which he has developed "self-awareness" and professional attitudes, and the like. In addition, the worker's administrative abilities may be evaluated, but this evaluation is of only secondary importance, since it is primarily regarded as an educational technique. Nevertheless, in-so-far as evaluation serves as a basis for promotion and salary changes (or for graduation in the case of students), the immanent conflict in the task is obvious. It is not easy to draw clear boundaries between the two tasks involved in evaluation. Austin notes that

"supervisors have tended to confuse the evaluation process and report by introducing educational concerns. An educational appraisal actually is quite a different matter from evaluation which carries a rating responsibility and implications for promotion or dismissal. There is ample experience to demonstrate that no matter how able the supervisor is in his teaching role, mixed feelings are aroused which affect the learning situation of the supervisee [sic] when the teacher is also the sole evaluator."[17]

Visibility and Supervision

The various supervisory techniques outlined above have a basic common feature: they attempt to supervise a set of relationships and activities which are not directly observable. Merton points out that the effective exercise of control requires superiors to be in a position to observe actual performance of subordinates in order to gain knowledge of their prevailing norms.[18] However, in some structures, such as the social work agency, individuals in positions of authority, being accountable for their subordinates' behavior and having the authority to mould it are, nevertheless, unable to observe the relevant activities. In cases like this, in which visibility is restricted by the practitioner's obligation to his clients, the supervisor has to rely chiefly on the worker's "attitudinal conformity."[19]

Professions, in general, try to assure conformity on the part of their members by careful screening of new recruits, and by a prolonged training process in which appropriate attitudes and norms are inculcated. Another method of controlling invisible performance is by evaluating its product and sanctioning the individual according to the proximity of the product to the expected norm. This, of course, creates the need for clear criteria of evaluation which are very difficult to establish in the human-relations professions. Ohlin describes the problem thus: "An extreme situation requiring a high degree of ideological conformity would exist if there were no clear criteria for evaluating successful work and the central activities of the job could not be observed or watched. There is no other profession which approximates this condition more than social work itself."[20]

But, even if these conditions were present in social work, that is, strong value commitment of practitioners, and definite criteria of evaluation, some kind of control of ongoing activities would still be necessary, since the emphasis, particularly in casework, is not only on results but also on the ways by which they could and should be attained.

The most original and distinctive feature of the supervisory methods of social casework, described above, is the attempt to reenact the unobservable interaction between worker and client, and thus to allow the supervisor to evaluate and regulate the worker's performance. This attempt creates many problems, the most obvious of which is the reliability of the worker's recording, especially if we take into account that first, the interaction with the client is sometimes strained and the practitioner may be emotionally involved no matter how much self-awareness he has gained, and second, that the reports to the supervisor serve as the basis of evaluation and the worker may, therefore, try to conceal his problems or failures.

Critiques of Supervision

In view of the numerous problems created by the prevailing supervisory practice in social work, some of which have been described above, it is comprehensible that the system has been strongly criticized by members of the profession. Almost every book and article that deals with social work supervision, written in the past two decades, points out its dysfunctions and puts forward some suggestions for change and modification.

Supervision is criticized on many grounds. It is claimed, for example, that emphasis on supervision impedes full acceptance of social work as a profession. Other professionals such as physicians, psychiatrists, scientists, and lawyers are not subjected to persistent, routine review; they conduct their work independently, and society accords higher status to autonomous practitioners. Another argument is that supervision is too costly, that the time and money spent for it could be used for more important purposes. Referring to the Hill and Ormsby cost study in the Family Service of Philadelphia, Wilensky and Lebeaux show that a total of 52% of all expenditures for casework services was spent on "maintaining communication" within the bureaucratic structure. This includes case recording (32.15%), supervisory conferences (13.17%), and case consultations (5.77%). Only 42% was spent for direct contact with clients.[21] Additional problems of supervision have been pointed out: for example, the "cultural lag" between the older experienced supervisor and the younger, recently trained, supervisee,[22] and the inadequacy of supervisory practice initially developed in casework, for other fields of social work, i.e. group work and community organization.[23]

The most crucial problems, however, with which much of the criticism of supervision is concerned, are those of role definitions and role relationships of supervisor and worker. Thus, Austin summarized the negative consequences of the existing supervisory system in four points: (1) the assimilation of knowledge and the internalization of standards by the worker are weakened by an emphasis on extreme controls; (2) the caseworker's professional contacts within the agency are too limited; (3) the assignment of two major functions—teaching and administration—tends toward a concentration of power in one person; and (4) the dual function leads to an overly complex assignment for the supervisor.[24]

Is the supervisor an administrator or a teacher? What kind of role conflict does the combination of these two functions in one role create for the supervisor? To what degree is the experienced worker independent? Is he subjected to the supervisor's bureaucratic control, or to his professional authority as well? All these are questions inherent in the debate about supervision that was "started off" by Babcock's article in 1953, in which the value of continuous supervision for the experienced caseworker was questioned.[25] Analyzing the phenomenon of "work inhibition" among social workers, she points to traditional supervision as one of its sources:

> "In many agencies, the social worker never becomes an independent person within the framework of agency administration. He must either remain a caseworker under supervision or try to become a supervisor. The opportunity to become an independent professional person within the agency, one who may or may not ask for consultation with the administration director or with the casework consultant as he feels he needs it, is rare. The gratification that comes from taking total responsibility for a task at hand is usually not attainable."[26]

The long-term goals of supervision, like those of any socialization process, are to develop the skills of the inexperienced worker, deepen his knowledge and understanding, and finally lead him to assume full responsibility as an independent professional. If, however, the supervisee is not allowed to "grow up" by continuous close supervision, the result will be that of general dissatisfaction with his work. Wax goes so far as to state,

> "Agency executives have but one course. If the profession wants to keep its professionals, it must treat them as professionals. Lifelong supervision is a vestige of the subprofessional past. Social workers do come of age. They can be proud of their training and confident of their skill. They must be accorded the respect, responsibility, and autonomy to which the professional is entitled."[27]

Imposed supervision, and special types of supervision, also affect the worker's relationships with different role-partners, i.e. his supervisor, his clients, and his colleagues.[28] If the net balance of consequences of supervision for the practitioner's role-performance is negative, then the very purpose of supervision, which is to render better service to clients, is not achieved.

The Unique Features of Supervision in Social Work

Still, it is reasonable to ask why supervision in social work is so much debated and so criticized, when after all, even in the most respected of professions, e.g. in medicine, the intern is supervised by the resident, and the resident by the staff physician, and so on. The major factors involved in the resistance and dissatisfaction with supervision in social work are precisely those attributes which distinguish it from, and are not shared by, supervision in other professions. The first is a "quantitative" element and pertains to the duration of supervision. There is as yet no formal time limit of the process, and the supervisor-trainee relationship carries over into the supervisor-practitioner relationship. This is not the case in other professions in which, once the independence of the fully trained member is established, he may consult more experienced colleagues, if he feels it necessary, but he is not obligated to report to them at fixed intervals and in a prescribed manner.

The second factor characteristic of social work supervision and one that contributes to the growing opposition to it, is a "qualitative" one. It has been mentioned before that the relationship between supervisor and supervisee is perceived as personal, with expressive overtones. Whereas the student-physician is guided and controlled by different specialists according to the problem at hand, the social work trainee has an individualized, diffuse relationship with only one supervisor. The relationship is diffuse in-so-far as the student's personal problems are probed and discussed, such as his feelings, conflicts, and projections. Again, this kind of psychotherapeutic technique is not part of supervision in medicine or in other professions, and is applied, if at all, only in extraordinary cases.[29] This special character of supervision in social work derives from the nature of the profession itself; since the social worker has to deal with the personal and psychological problems of the client, it is assumed that he must first be aware of and understand his own motivations and emotions. The prolonged and total nature of supervision is somewhat reminiscent of the "silver cord" by which a possessive mother ties the child to herself. Therefore, discussions of the problem in the professional literature use such terms as "maturity," "growing up," "emancipation," and "independence."

The third attribute that differentiates social work supervision from professional control is the administrative function of the social work supervisor. An integral part of his role is to see to it that the worker adheres to the regulations prescribed by the community and the organization, which are sometimes incompatible with professional ethics or the humanistic enthusiasm of the young practitioner. In contrast, an experienced physician, for example, when controlling the work of an inexperienced colleague, represents the profession or a specialty within it, but not the administrative structure.

The modifications suggested in the traditional supervisory system are related to the above points of criticism. The major changes proposed are "termination" and "separation." Termination signifies the assumption of autonomy by the practitioner after a stipulated number of years of supervised work, the proposals in this respect ranging from two to seven years of "internship," or "as best designed to meet the worker's developmental needs."[30] The second recommendation is to differentiate the administrative from the teaching function now combined in the supervisor's role. These two recommended changes are overlapping in certain aspects because it is the educational function of the supervisor which most social workers propose to limit, and not his administrative tasks. Alternative plans and experiments have been carried out, such as supervision of experienced workers by a group of peers,[31] and the establishment of administrative supervision with professional consultation available at the worker's request.[32] Thus, it is hoped to avoid the dysfunctions of traditional supervision for the professional role:

> "When the responsibility for continued growth is transferred to the worker himself, we can expect that his own motivation, creativity,

and interests, supplemented by available consultation, group meetings and opportunities for leadership within and outside the agency,
will ensure his continued professional development."[33]

These are some of the theoretical and practical arguments for
modifying the established supervisory pattern as they appear in
the professional literature of social work. In addition, the
perceptions and attitudes of workers and students toward
supervision should be considered.

Attitudes Toward Supervision

Data on attitudes toward supervision by those upon whom it
is exercised can be obtained only by systematic research.[34]
Interest in and empirical studies of the subject have been
growing constantly and have shown a diversity of orientations
toward supervision; different attitudes are held by different
groups of social workers toward different types of supervision.
Thus, for example, we would like to advance the hypothesis
that the attitudes of social work students as compared to the
attitudes of social workers, to organizational controls (administrative regulations), and to personal control (supervisory procedures), will progress in opposite directions in the course of
time. This seems theoretically plausible and is also indicated by
the data. The social work student, as he advances through his
years of training, becomes less critical of his supervisor but will
usually manifest strong resistance to the agency's rules and
constraints. On the other hand, the experienced social worker
tends to become less hostile to organizational demands and
regulations; at the same time, as he advances in years of
practice, he is likely to grow more resistant to close personal
supervision. The first part of the hypothesis, i.e. the student's
decreasing criticism of supervision in subsequent years of
training, is supported in a study by Rose, in which he found
that the intensity of this criticism is in part a function of the
phase of learning in which the student is involved.[35] In
regard to the worker's attitude to bureaucratic regulations, Blau
found, in a study of a public welfare agency, that the more

experienced workers were more adjusted to the organizational procedures and incorporated the official limitations in their thinking, whereas the new workers felt that these rules interfered with the implementation of the "service ideal."[36]

These and other studies may guide social workers in planning changes in the existing pattern of supervision, and may help them decide when to terminate which type of supervision, and what other mechanisms of control can be more effectively employed.

Scott, in his study of a public welfare agency, examined the influence of the degree of professionalism, of both supervisor and supervisee on the worker's attitude to supervision.[37] He found that when asked in general to evaluate the practice of persistent routine supervision, half of the respondents said that it was a "good arrangement," the other half stated that it had both "advantages and disadvantages," but none felt that it was "not a good arrangement." The degree of acceptance of the supervisory system in the agency was found to vary with the professional orientation of both workers and supervisors: (a) professionally oriented workers with longer formal training and stronger contact with the profession (the "cosmopolitans" in Gouldner's terminology) were more critical of the system than nonprofessionally oriented workers; (b) workers supervised by professionally oriented supervisors were less critical of the system than workers serving under less professionally oriented supervisors.

A NASW study of the problem reveals that social workers feel differently about the various functions of supervision.[38] Most social workers believe that supervision should change, according to the needs and progress of the supervisee, from a phase of direction and teaching to one of more permissive consultation. Evaluation was seen as a legitimate part of the supervisor's role. And none of the respondents objected to the supervisor's administrative authority and responsibility. These findings support the demand to limit the teaching role of supervision that was raised in the literature. They indicate that lack of autonomy in the performance of the professional core functions, such as diagnosis and treatment, creates strains in the supervisor-supervisee relationship, rather than the exercise of bureaucratic authority by the supervisor. Moreover, it seems that trained social workers are willing to concede administrative authority to their supervisors as part of the limitations imposed by the organizational framework; however, they resent and resist the teaching function of the supervisor which they perceive as encroaching upon their professional judgment, responsibility, and competence.

At the same time, we may assume that social workers would accept some degree of control of their professional conduct provided it were basically defined and perceived as "professional," such as the authority of the chief surgeon over his assistants. There are no available data to bear out this assumption in respect to social workers, but some support can be found in the study conducted by Goss of a hierarchically organized group of physicians.[39] She found that the hierarchical structure did not conflict with the individual professional autonomy, as expected, since the professional norms of the group did not require autonomy in every sphere of activity:

"but only that he will be free to make his own decisions in professional matters as opposed to administrative concerns. Nor even in the professional sphere, did the norms rule out the possibility of supervision; so long as supervision came from a physician and took the form of advice, it was within normatively acceptable bounds for physicians. Thus one of the organizational mechanisms for reconciling hierarchical supervision of professional activity with maintenance of individual authority in that sphere would appear to be the conception of supervision as a *formal advisory or consultation relationship.*"[40]

In conclusion, the autonomy of professionals within a bureaucratic framework is threatened only insofar as the organizational structure interferes either with the development and application of professional knowledge, or with the service orientation, i.e. with the professional commitment to place the client's interests above all others. If one or the other of these core qualities is impaired by organizational rules and procedures, the balance and consistency between them is disrupted, and in this lies the real danger of "bureaucratization" which salaried professionals may face. Semi-professionals are in this respect in a disadvantageous position relative to full-fledged professionals who possess esoteric knowledge and skills, high prestige in society, and the powerful backing of their professional associations.

Studies of the kind cited here, and further empirical research concerning the attitudes of social workers toward diverse types of supervision and control, point the direction in which the existing structure and role definitions within social agencies could be differentiated and reconstructed in order for social workers to render more effective service to their clients.

Concluding Remarks

In this first part we have identified social work as a semi-profession by evaluating its main features along the dimensions generally employed in the characterization of the established professions. We then examined the implications of the semi-professional nature of social work for the relations between workers and the organization, and suggested that semi-professionals are generally more subjected to bureaucratic control than full-fledged professionals. Social workers are further controlled in public agencies in which their role includes the dispensation of welfare payments. This source of tension between the worker and the organization can be eliminated by segregating the function of financial aid from casework, counseling, and therapeutic treatment.

The last chapter examined the distinct features of supervision which constitute the major mechanism through which organizational control is applied in social work. It was proposed in the Introduction that semi-professionalism and bureaucratic control are two of the main components responsible for the ineffectiveness of social work to improve the social functioning of their clients, to help them cope with their problems, and to promote their interpersonal competence.

The third and principal barrier for the achievement of these goals is posed by the structure of the worker-client relationship. The analysis of this relationship, and the effects of semi-professionalism and organizational structure on the interaction between social workers and their clients, are the central topics of Part II.

Notes

1. Gross, "When Occupations Meet," p. 47.

2. Boehm, "Relationship of Social Work to Other Professions," p. 644.

3. The distinction between internal and external resources is independent of the degree of functional importance or scarcity of resources. However, it is worth noting that in contrast to material goods the fund of knowledge does not diminish in the process of its application.

4. See, for example, Leonard Reissman, "A Study of Role Conceptions in Bureaucracy," Social Forces 27 (1949): 305-310; Gouldner, "Cosmopolitans and Locals"; and Goode, "Community within a Community."

5. See Charlotte Towle, *The Learner in Education for the Profession* (Chicago: University of Chicago Press, 1954); Lucille N. Austin, "An Evaluation of Supervision," Social Casework 37 (October 1952): 375-382, and "The Changing Role of the Supervisor," Smith College Studies in Social Work 31 (June 1961): 179-195, Margaret Williamson, *Supervision—Principles and Methods* (New York: Women's Press, 1950); Robert D. Vinter, "The Social Structure of Serice," in Alfred J. Kahn, ed., *Issues in American Social Work*, pp. 242-269; Mary E. Burns, "Supervision in Social Work," *Encyclopedia of Social Work* (1965), pp. 785-790.

6. It should be mentioned that supervision originally developed in the field of casework and although it was later taken over by group work and community organization, it never gained the same importance in these specialties as it did in casework. Strong criticism is directed, by group workers, against the adoption of supervisory methods used in casework because of the different contents and form of group work services. See Irving Miller, "Distinctive Characteristics of Supervision in Group Work," Social Work 5 (January 1960): 69-76.

7. Burns, "Supervision in Social Work."

8. Charlotte Towle, "The Place of Help in Supervision," Social Service Review 37 (December 1963): 405.

9. Ibid., p. 403.

10. Frances M. Scherz, "A Concept of Supervision Based on Definitions of Job Responsibility," Social Casework 39 (October 1958): 442.

11. Ibid., p. 437.

12. See, for example, Robert F. Bales, *Interaction Process Analysis* (Cambridge, Mass.: Addison-Wesley, 1950), pp. 153-154; Talcott Parsons

and Robert F. Bales, *Family, Socialization and Interaction Process* (New York: Free Press, 1955), pp. 259-306.

13. This analysis is based on Homan's hypotheses concerning the interrelationships among activity, sentiment, and interaction. If one of the interacting parties has authority over the other, i.e. he gives orders to which the other defers, then "the more frequently one of the two originates interaction for the other, the stronger will be the latter's sentiment of respect (or hostility) toward him, and the more nearly will the frequency of interaction be kept to the amount characteristic of the external system." G. H. Homans, *The Human Group* (London: Routledge and Kegan Paul, 1962), p. 247.

14. These two functions tend to be assigned to two different positions: that of "high status authority" and that of "high status friend." See Morris Freilich, "The Natural Triad in Kinship and Complex Systems," American Sociological Review 29 (August 1964): 529-539.

15. Relatively little attention has been focused in social work writings on the problems created for the supervisor himself by the traditional definition of his role. In addition to the problem of having to maneuver bureaucratic authority and a more collegial-advisory relationship with the supervisee, the supervisor is subject to orders and pressures from his superiors, and may in turn take a more or less autonomous stand toward them.

16. Irving Miller, "Distinctive Characteristics of Supervision," p. 76.

17. Lucille N. Austin, "Supervision in Social Work," *Social Work Yearbook* (1960), p. 584.

18. Merton, *Social Theory and Social Structure,* pp. 336-357.

19. See, Rose Laub Coser, "Insulation from Observability and Types of Social Conformity," American Sociological Review 26 (February 1961): 28-39.

20. Lloyd E. Ohlin, "Conformity in American Society Today," Social Work 3 (April 1958): 58-66. Another problem associated with such "invisible" relationships is the transmission of the knowledge and experience gained in them to others, as Freud once told his students: "in the strictest sense of the word, it is only by hearsay that you will get to know psychoanalysis." Sigmund Freud, *The Complete Introductory Lectures on Psychoanalysis,* J. Strachey, trans. and ed. (New York: W. W. Norton & Company, 1966), p. 18.

21. Wilensky and Lebeaux, *Industrial Society and Social Welfare,* pp. 241-242.

22. Burns, "Supervision in Social Work."

23. Irving Miller, "Distinctive Characteristics of Supervision," and Arthur L. Leader, "New Directions in Supervision," Social Casework 38 (November 1957): 462-468.

24. Austin, "An Evaluation of Supervision"; see also Scherz, "A Concept of Supervision."

25. Charlotte Babcock, "Social Work as Work," Social Casework 34 (December 1953): 415-422. Dr. Babcock, a psychiatrist, based her analysis on her experience with sixty social workers as patients in consultative and therapeutic interviews.

26. Ibid., p. 421.

27. John Wax, "Time Limited Supervision," Social Work 8 (July 1963): 43.

28. The repercussions of authoritarian supervision on the worker's orientation to the client, and on his performance, are examined in Blau and Scott, *Formal Organizations,* pp. 150-159.

29. Although some writers insist that the supervisor's goals are educational, many parts of the supervisory process, especially the conference with the worker, have a therapeutic character.

30. See Ruth E. Lindenberg, "Changing Traditional Patterns of Supervision," Social Work 2 (April 1957): 45; Esther Schour, "Helping Social Workers Handle Work Stresses," Social Casework 34 (December 1953): 423-428; Reva Fine, "Some Theoretical Considerations Basic to Supervisory Technique," Social Work 1 (January 1956): 67-71; Wax, "Time Limited Supervision"; and Leader, "New Directions in Supervision."

31. Ruth Fizdale, "Peer Group Supervision," Social Casework 39 (October 1958): 443-450.

32. The separation of teaching from administrative functions in social work in the U.S. Army was examined by Donald A. Devis, "Teaching and Administrative Functions in Supervision," Social Work 10 (April 1965): 83-89.

33. Leader, "New Directions in Supervision," p. 468.

34. See for example, Scott, "Reactions to Supervision in a Heteronomous Professional Organization"; Sheldon D. Rose, "Students View Their Supervisors: A Scale Analysis," Social Work 10 (April 1965): 90-96; and "Opinions on Supervision: A Chapter Study," by the Western New York Chapter, National Association of Social Workers Committee on Social Work Practice, Social Work 3 (January 1958): 18-25.

35. Rose, "Students View Their Supervisors."

36. Peter M. Blau, "Orientations Toward Clients in a Public Welfare Agency," Administrative Science Quarterly 5 (1960): 341-361.

37. Scott, "Reactions to Supervision."

38. NASW Committee on Social Work Practice, "Opinions on Supervision."

39. Mary E. W. Goss, "Influence and Authority among Physicians in an Outpatient Clinic," *American Sociological Review* 26 (February 1961): 39-50.

40. Ibid., pp. 49-50. Italics added.

The predominant type of interaction between professionals and their clients in current social work practice is the casework relationship. This relationship is designed to help clients cope better with their personal and interpersonal problems. For this purpose, the caseworker attempts to bring about certain desired changes in the client's perceptions, attitudes, abilities, and behavior.

The main argument in respect to the worker-client relationship that has been advanced here, is that its relative weakness as a vehicle of personal change is due to its structure as a one-to-one relationship. We shall first discuss what we regard as the main sources of inadequacy in casework to produce

Part II

THE RELATIONSHIP BETWEEN

SOCIAL WORKER AND CLIENT

significant and enduring change in clients. Next, the various elements of power inherent in the worker-client relationship will be analyzed, and the orientations of social workers to these aspects of their role will be explored. We shall then present some definitions and typologies of power and its mechanisms—advanced by social theorists—and apply them to the interaction between social worker and client. Finally, we shall try to show that some of the assumptions upon which the exertion of power of one person upon another are based, are not relevant to the worker-client relationship, thus curtailing the worker's ability to induce change in his clients through the casework relationship.

Chapter 4

THE CASEWORK RELATIONSHIP

The contention that the casework relationship is relatively ineffective as a change-inducing method is based on certain structural properties of this relationship which can be summed up in the following manner: The interrelation between the worker and his client is an isolated relationship. This isolation has several aspects:

(a) The interaction takes place in a dyadic setting; it does not involve other individuals, an immediate "audience," or a "third party,"[1] who might reinforce the advocated change, and thus contribute to its stability.

(b) The change in the client's behavior which the worker tries to induce is exercised, if at all, outside the client-worker encounter. In other words, the actual results of the process of influence are not directly observable by the worker.[2] Hence, according to the proposition of the relation between visibility and control, the worker is not in a position that allows him to regulate the client's behavior.[3]

(c) The social groups to which the client belongs (membership groups) and/or those groups whose values and norms he shares (reference groups)[4] usually lend no support to the worker-client relationship as such or to the normative and practical changes the worker tries to achieve through this relationship.[5]

Some Problems of Therapy and Socialization in Dyadic Settings

The only way to confirm or to disprove our proposition that the client-worker relationship, as it is structured at present, is not an effective medium for attaining attitude and behavior change in clients would be empirical research so designed as to compare the consequences of traditional casework performed in a dyadic setting with the effects of treatment which is not isolated from the client's other significant social interrelations.

Schwartz and Sample conducted an experiment that was designed to measure the amount of client-change produced by treating welfare clients by teams of social workers.[6] The team's supervisor assigned to each of his workers specific tasks rather than individual cases. The relevance of this study to our argument is not in its findings but in the general implication derived from the team model experiment:

> "Some people have seen in our experiment an assault on that most holy of holies in casework, the casework relationship. This, in the language of cognition, is a misperception. In our view, or in our perception, the team model has the desirable effect of helping supervisors to view the concept of relationship more selectively, to know when it is necessary, relevant, and useful, and what is likely to be achieved by its use."[7]

As can be seen, here too, the interpersonal relationship between worker and client, as the most fundamental and effective method for personal change, is challenged, though from a different viewpoint than ours.

Existing typologies and classifications of therapeutic or socializing relationships conceived in other fields of study, such as organizational research, group dynamics, juvenile delinquency, adult socialization and education, are not wholly satisfactory for analyzing the social worker-client relationship since they do not take into account its unique properties. Nonetheless, these studies provide some interesting insights that can help clarify the problem at hand.

In discussing the effects of psychotherapy, Frank was obviously aware of the problem that the patient encounters after the therapist-patient relationship has been terminated; he writes,

"The success of any form of treatment depends in large part on the extent to which the changes it has accomplished are supported by the patient's subsequent life experiences. A patient's attitudes must not only be changed, but the new ones must be 'frozen,' or he will slide back again. Little attention has been paid to this aspect of psychotherapy, apparently on the assumption that the changes produced by treatment will automatically be reinforced because they tend to lead to more gratifying experiences than the old patterns." [8]

It seems legitimate to interpret the "subsequent life experiences" that reinforce the change the patient has achieved as consisting, at least in part, of the positive responses, rewards, and approval he derives from interacting with other individuals or groups outside the psychotherapist-patient encounter.

The difficulties involved in maintaining personal change acquired in psychotherapy are described very clearly by Katz and Kahn:

"The return to the real-life organizational environment represents the weakest link in the therapeutic chain of assumptions. The individual, changed by therapy, returns to the organization, the family, and the neighborhood. The people with whom he must interact in those settings have not shared his explorations and experiences in therapy; they have undertaken no complementary changes. . . . As a result, the responses of family and colleagues are likely to urge the individual back toward the pretherapeutic condition." [9]

Kurt Lewin has reported the findings of several experiments showing the superiority of group discussions and decisions as compared with individual attempts to change food habits of housewives, and patterns of baby-care of young mothers, after leaving the socializing setting. [10]

However, other studies on the attempt to produce change in groups seem to contradict the argument that traditional casework is a relatively ineffective instrument for change induction, and that the group may be a more adequate framework in this respect. Some of these studies come to the conclusion that the fact that members of a group interact with one another, and develop a common identity and group culture, may be detrimental to the efforts of the therapist or socializing agent.[11] Becker, for example, distinguishes between collective and individual processes of adult socialization,[12] a classification adopted and elaborated by Wheeler in the construction of his typology of interpersonal settings in which socialization is carried out.[13] Becker points out that aside from the fact that decisions reached by a group are more effective in producing conformity than solutions proposed in individual settings, the group is also more likely to deviate from the standards set by the socializing agent than a single individual.

It is true that these studies are concerned with a situation which is basically different from that of casework. They all deal with the problem of producing change of attitudes and behavior of an individual while being a member of a group or an organization (a class of students, a family, a work group, a prison, a mental hospital, or the like). By contrast, the client of a social agency is accepted for treatment and socialized, on an individual basis, into roles he is supposed to perform at a time and place other than those in which the process of influence is exercised. Therefore, the problems created by the development of special group norms—a subculture, an inmate culture, and so forth—may not be relevant to the situation of individual casework. However, it seems possible to consider the welfare client's primary groups, his family, neighborhood, and community, as social frameworks in which most of his social relations and interaction take place, and whose norms and goals he shares.[14] Furthermore, both Becker and Wheeler note that successful or unsuccessful socialization outcomes depend on the initial commitment and the degree of organization among the socializees: "If initial commitment to the organization and its recruits is high, the peer group may be harnessed as an aid in socialization, thus intensifying the effects of the formal socialization program."[15]

We may assume that the welfare client is not initially committed to the norms and goals of the welfare agency; on the contrary, his attitudes and expectation are frequently incompatible with those of the agency and the social worker. If this is granted, namely, that the welfare client belongs to, and identifies with membership and reference groups whose norms differ from those of the agency, then some conclusions of research on collective and residential treatment institutions do not contradict, but support, our proposition that casework, as it is presently carried out in social agencies, is not the most effective possible tool to produce change in the client's norms and behavior.

Ohlin and Lawrence in their analysis of the problems involved in treating juvenile delinquents in residential treatment institutions argue that the clinical treatment approach which focuses on psychic disorders, and in which the main treatment instrument is the client-therapist relationship, proves ineffective "in residential institutions where an inmate culture and an informally organized system of social relationships compete with the official system for the allegiance of inmates."[16] In order to lessen the discrepancy between the formal norms and treatment goals of the institutions and those of the inmate subculture, the authors suggest restructuring the treatment process in various ways designed "to acquire the support of the basic inmate reference group and to incorporate treatment content as part of the inmate, everyday interactions of the peer-groups."[17] Generally, the same goal should guide the modification of the social worker-welfare client relationship, that is, to link it with significant social relationships of the client within the groups to which he belongs and with which he identifies.

We turn now to the definition of the functions and goals of casework as perceived by social workers, and to their conception of the problem of control entailed in the casework relationship.

The Purposes of Casework

As noted earlier, the establishment of a personal relationship with the client is regarded by social work theory as the basic functional prerequisite and mechanism through which the client can be helped to solve his problems. To quote Hollis, "Basic to all casework treatment is the relationship between worker and client."[18]

Perlman points out three major components of the casework
process: (1) the establishment of a therapeutic relationship
between the caseworker and his client, (2) the examination and
assessment of the nature of the problem, and of the possible
ways of dealing with it, and (3) the mobilization and provision
of the means by which the problem may be solved.

> "The first of these components, the therapeutic relationship, is basic
> to any effort to help a troubled person. At a time of helplessness,
> . . . people need and want acceptance, support, sharing, and release
> in a relationship with another person who has interest, compassion,
> strength, and potential help to offer. The caseworker, thus, begins
> and maintains his person-to-person contact by lending himself to his
> client with attentiveness, acceptance, warmth." [19]

Biestek expresses the same view in a more eloquent fashion;
he writes,

> "The importance of the client-worker relationship in social casework
> is almost impossible to exaggerate. Its importance can be sum-
> marized briefly in an analogy: it is the *soul* of casework while the
> process of study, diagnosis, and treatment may be considered the
> body. As the life-giving principle, it vivifies every part of casework
> and makes the whole a warmly human helping experience." [20]

It should be noted that the above descriptions of the
worker-client relationship present a somewhat misleading picture, partly because they are detached from their wider context
and thus reflect only the ideal-type image of this relationship.
Social workers usually admit that at the beginning of treatment
a client is liable to react to the worker's attempts to establish a
personal relationship with him with various degrees of anxiety
manifested in withdrawal, oversubmissiveness, or aggression,
and, of course, the endeavor is prone to fail completely in some
cases.[21] Nevertheless, the importance usually ascribed to the
casework relationship by traditional social work theory is hard
to exaggerate.

The purpose of the casework relationship has been defined as
a "problem-solving process."[22] The problems to be solved are
of two general kinds, generated by two types of sources—
external sources such as poverty, unemployment, and discrimi-

nation, and internal sources, i.e. intrapersonal disturbances leading to malfunctioning of the individual in his environment. The efforts of the social worker may be directed either at modifying the objective difficult circumstances in which the client lives, or at his ability to cope with them. Accordingly, the worker will employ different means—provision of financial assistance and other services in order to alleviate the burden of external conditions, and psychological-therapeutic means "by which the person's own powers can be released and constructively rechanneled."[23]

These classifications of the client's problems and of the various goals and techniques employed by the social worker are analytically useful distinctions. In reality, however, the internal and external bases of the client's problems are frequently interrelated in the form of a vicious circle in which severe social and economic problems of an individual, and his "deviant" perceptions, motivations, and behavior reinforce each other. Consequently, the distinctions between solving the client's "person-to-circumstance" problems in contrast to his "person-to-person" problems, by means of relief dispensation or by means of therapeutic casework, are useful mainly as analytical distinctions. In practice, they are frequently interwined, overlapping, or simultaneous.[24]

Casework as a Mechanism of Social Control

The crucial aspect from our point of view is that the social worker is engaged in an attempt to produce change, whether environmental or psychological, or both. To quote Perlman, "The aim of casework is to restore or reinforce or refashion the social functioning of individuals or families."[25] The terms applied in this definition, and in others which repeatedly appear in social work literature—such as improve, enhance, adjust—all signify some kind of modification of the status quo in order to increase the effectiveness of the client's functioning in his environment. Regarding the personal change-producing function of social workers, Taylor writes, "Thus every casework agency is charged, either explicitly or implicitly, with certain community functions relating to the modification of human behavior. The client is to be helped to alter his behavior in some respect or other, in order to conform more nearly to a pattern or model accepted as typical of one of his sex, age, social class, or other circumstance."[26]

Ensuring conformity of individuals to social norms entails the activation of social control mechanisms. It is interesting, though not surprising, that until quite recently social workers and social work writings tended to deny the social control function of their profession. This is expressed by emphasizing the helping role of the caseworker which is described as helping people to help themselves, encouraging clients to solve their own problems, protesting the client's right to self-determination, and the like. These formulae are value-laden, and clearly reflect the ideals and principles of an individualistic and democratic society, but they are, at the same time, based on empirical knowledge of the ineffectiveness of imposed change that is not accompanied by some inner conviction or commitment on the part of the client. Regarding this problem, Studt writes,

> "Out of unsatisfying experiences with the impotence of formal authority alone to effect significant changes in the lives of human beings, caseworkers developed the doctrine of the crucial importance of the *voluntary* request for help, since the client, by this act, gives the caseworker the right to help. A formal authority relationship has always been able to secure certain external conformities in behavior depending on the client's need to secure services. But a more meaningful influence relationship is achieved only when the client genuinely joins with the caseworker in dealing with a commonly acknowledged problem, and gives the caseworker temporary leadership responsibilities in this process."[27]

Studt argues that for the achievement of change in the client's attitudes and behavior the "social authority" which the worker commands, that is, the authority delegated to him by the community to administer resources and services, must be turned into "psychological authority" which she defines, following Erich Fromm, as "an interpersonal relation in which one person looks upon another as somebody superior to him."[28] According to Studt, the problem of transforming social authority into psychological authority is most difficult in correctional agencies in which the client "is held in the relationship by a legal obligation regardless of real need or psychological readiness." This may be so; nevertheless, similar problems obtain in public welfare agencies in which eligibility determination and casework are combined in the worker's role, and even in the more specialized agencies engaged only in casework and counseling. Taylor, analyzing the functions of control in casework, writes,

> "Our definition points to a distinction between 'coercive' and 'persuasive' control, but, aside from the function of the agency, this distinction, in most casework situations, may be one of degree. . . . Implicit, therefore, in the counselor-client relationship is the presence of power which induces the client to modify his behavior, since he requires what the counselor has to give." [29]

Thus social workers may be considered agents of social control whether they work in agencies that are defined as correctional settings or as nonauthoritative settings.

Leonard too, urges social workers to recognize the power element prevalent in the case worker-client relationship, whether it be coercive power or more "subtle ways" of persuasion:

> "This view of the social control elements in the casework relationship puts one further nail into the coffin of the myth of client self-determination. This has been a powerful and valuable myth, playing an important part in the ideological superstructure of social work, but its continuation unmodified may prevent a realistic appraisal of what actually happens in interviews." [30]

We may assume that there exists a deep-set ambivalence in the attitude of social workers toward the elements of control entailed in their role, associated with a liberal tradition and, in particular, with the principle of self-determination which is recurrently referred to in debates about the problem. Greenwood describes the dilemma thus:

> "Social work along with the other practices, is concerned with action and change; it therefore belongs among the controlling

agencies of society. Social workers, committed as they are to the principle of self-determination in the social work relationship, may conceivably resist this characterization of their profession. However, the plain fact is that social workers, by virtue of their technical knowledge and community sactioned status, possess a form of power which they exercise to reach certain ends."[31]

These scruples concerning the notion of power are produced by a commitment to certain fundamental values such as freedom and equality. The social worker, in particular, is troubled by such doubts; does he really know what is "right" or even "best" for the client? Questions of this kind usually do not plague the physician, for example, whose task in relation to the patient is more specific and whose knowledge, within this limited range, is more precise. Casework, however, includes an attempt to influence the perceptions and behavior of another individual, which directly involves social workers in the touchy problem of the "relativity" of norms and values. In Ohlin's words, "social work services are generally directed toward persons who in some fashion or other have failed to fulfill their expected roles in society. Consequently, social workers acquire a special sensitivity to the problem of values and the part which they play in inducing conformity or deviant behavior."[32] And to quote Spellman, "One of the main difficulties in discussing the matter in the context of social work is that the whole conception of authority and its application touches very deep emotions in all of us."[33]

As we have seen, the casework relationship has been generally highly valued among social workers, and its development and refinement have been regarded as one of the major professional achievements of social work. However, when attempting to specify the purposes, and particularly the various mechanisms operating in this relationship, the attitudes of social workers diverge. Some recognize the elements of power and control entailed in their relations with clients; others, who are strongly committed to the principle of self-determination, try to avoid the issue altogether.

Types of Power and Their Application in Social Work

After establishing, in general, that social control is an important component of the social worker's role in relation to his client, the main questions which present themselves are which types of power does the worker command and exercise, and how much power does he command. Let us deal first with the second issue. The formal, legitimate power of the worker, namely, his authority, is limited by the agency, the community, and their respective rules and laws. However, the more interesting problem is to examine the restraints on the actual exercise of control within the worker-client relationship itself. Basically, in every dyadic relation, the power of each partner over the other is restricted by the power the other has over him. The amount of power is determined by the dependence of one person upon another. Emerson writes,

"Social relations commonly entail ties of mutual dependence between the parties. A depends on B if he aspires to goals or gratifications whose achievement is facilitated by appropriate actions on B's part. . . . At the same time, these ties of mutual dependence imply that each party is in a position, to some degree, to grant or deny, facilitate or hinder, the other's gratification." [34]

The degree of dependence of one actor upon another varies according to the values of two variables: "The dependence of actor A upon actor B is (1) directly proportional to A's motivational investment in the goal mediated by B, and (2) inversely proportional to the availability of those goals to A outside the A-B relation."[35]

To begin with, the welfare client is not free to enter or to withdraw from the relationship with the worker for he is usually in great trouble and sometimes unable to help himself. In other words, he is dependent on the help (material, psychological, or other) that the social worker can provide. Second, it seems that the client is unable to resort to the two major "balancing operations" which are available to the parties in a mutual-dependence relationship. He cannot get what he wants (particularly financial aid) elsewhere, since welfare agencies have a monopoly over granting long-term support; nor can he reduce, to a significant extent, his need of the help he requests. Thus it seems that the social worker in his relations with the client is in the position of "A person who commands services others need and who is independent of any at their command, attains power over others by making the satisfaction of their need contingent on their compliance."[36]

Blau describes the extreme case in which a person has something to give that others need, and does not himself need anything which they could provide. This definition could be turned around to reflect the standpoint of the dependent party: A person who does not command any services that others need and who needs services that they command, is subordinated to their power, i.e has to comply with their orders so as to obtain satisfaction of his needs. The point is that the social power of one individual implies another individual's acceptance of this power, and is thus immanently restricted. As Etzioni remarks, "compliance relations are asymmetric (or 'vertical'). But it is not assumed that the subordinates have no power, only that they have less."[37]

The actual performance of control is a two-way process that includes the exertion of power by one person and its acceptance by another. To be effective, power has to be accompanied by compliance in some fashion or other. Weber distinguishes between *Macht* and *legitime Herrschaft* and writes, " 'Imperative control' [Herrschaft] is the probability that a command with a given specific content will be obeyed by a given group of persons."[38] A leader can be defined as such only if he has followers, i.e those who will carry out his orders. Homans describes the individual who holds a position of authority within a group as one who "tests his authority afresh every time he makes a new suggestion, and the results of the test may confirm his authority or undermine it."[39] This depends upon whether his suggestion (order) will be obeyed or not.

Although the access to means of control is unevenly distributed between social worker and client, the latter does have some resources at his disposal on which the social worker is dependent to a greater or lesser degree. Following the above discussion, the one thing the social worker cannot do without is the client's compliance. As such, compliance is a "generalized facility," and its use as a resource ought to be classified according to several criteria, such as its nature, duration, degree, and range. Here some illustrations will suffice; compliance on the client's part may range from his showing up for a subsequent interview with the social worker or giving correct information about eligibility requirements, to verbal acceptance of the worker's advice, and to change in attitudes accompanied by actual change in behavior in an important sphere of life.

Withholding compliance of any kind and to any degree will disrupt the successful performance of the social worker's role, and is thus a major source of power commanded by the client. Katz and Eisenstadt considering the relations between bureaucrats and clients write, "the bureaucrat teaches the client how to be a client so that he (the bureaucrat) can go on being a bureaucrat. This, seems to us, is a form of dependence, . . . it is dependence on the client to act in a way which makes it possible for the bureaucrat to do his job."[40] Following Parsons, the authors describe this type of power as the "ability to cause trouble by threatening to disrupt the system." Clients may also threaten or actually use physical force by going into a rage or by bodily attacking the worker. This is in fact part of the strategy of some clients to get what they want.

Aside from noncompliance and the use of force, clients may resort to more subtle ways of persuasion which can be roughly classified in two categories. The first is an appeal to the emotions of the social worker, to his general humanistic-helping orientation. Katz and Danet in their typology of clients' appeals call this type, appeals to the altruism of the official, "where one describes one's plight or throws oneself on the mercy of the official or the organization."[41] The second type of inducement is attempted through "activation of commitments." This type of power is usually mentioned in reference to the person who has authority to induce conformity. However, clients may employ the same type of power, and its concomitant strategies, by activating norms which are part of the social worker's credo, such as equality and the right to self-determination, or by referring to their "legal 'right' to the particular benefit, or, by the same token, to the official's 'duty' to provide it."[42]

These different types of power at the client's disposal were

mentioned only briefly as an illustration of the limits and
constraints upon the social worker's power to control the client.

The second question that has been raised earlier was what are
the different types of power at the social worker's command.
The professional social work literature, as we have seen, usually
posits a distinction between persuasive and coercive power.[43]
Some sociologists employ a triple classification of power:
remunerative, normative, and coercive.[44] The difference
between these two classifications is probably not substantial,
since it appears that social work authors view remunerative
power, e.g. withholding a client's check, as a kind of coercion.
In any case, it seems to us more useful to distinguish between the
two—control by means of physical force in its various
manifestations which is coercive power, and control by means
of material reward or deprivation, namely, remunerative or
instrumental power.[45]

The exercise of the social worker's remunerative or instrumental power is by way of money dispensation but includes, in
addition, other goods and services. This type of power is most
clearly defined by regulations and rules concerning eligibility;
however, as in many other instances, the formal regulations do
not completely reflect the concrete manipulations of this power
in reality. It is a well-known fact that social workers sometimes
use instrumental power in their attempts to influence the
client's behavior. The problems involved in this practice will be
discussed more extensively later.

Coercive power is exerted by social workers in the form of
"protective services" which involve increased surveillance by the
worker or by an agency detective who may enter the client's
home any time between dawn and midnight, by taking children
away from their parents, by sending a client to a mental
hospital or to jail. There is no doubt that the application of
coercive power is regarded by social workers as a last resort, to
be used only in those cases in which other means of inducement
are ineffective or impossible.

Normative power is much more complex than instrumental
or coercive power, and is therefore more difficult to define.
Before trying to do so, and before examining the applications
and implications of normative power in social casework, a

commonly neglected point should be mentioned. As long as a client is in great financial trouble, that is, his family does not have enough food, adequate housing, or medical care, and so on, we believe there is no ground upon which normative control can be exerted. It is true that change in the client's attitudes and behavior may in the end help to improve his objective conditions, but some minimum of physical and material "substratum" is necessary for normative power to have any significance at all.

Normative power can be divided into two subcategories according to the means employed by the individual who commands the power, or according to the rewards that are expected by the individual who is being controlled. Etzioni writes, "There are two types of normative power. One is based on the manipulation of esteem, prestige, and ritualistic symbols (such as a flag or a benediction); the other, on allocation and manipulation of acceptance and positive response."[46] He calls the first kind "pure normative power," and the second, "social power."

Parsons distinguishes among four types of power (though he uses the term "influence"): (a) "inducement," and (b) "deterrence" (which correspond to the above instrumental and coercive types of power), (c) "persuasion," and (d) "activation of commitments" (which are roughly equivalent to the two types of normative power noted above.) "Activation of commitments is ego's attempt to get compliance by offering reasons why it would, from alter's own point of view, be 'wrong' for him to refuse to act as ego wishes."[47] Thus, activation of commitments is an attempt to influence a person to conform to norms to which he is basically committed, but which are at the time "dormant" or overshadowed by other conflicting norms. "Persuasion is ego's attempt to get compliance by offering reasons why it would from alter's own point of view, independent of situational advantages, 'be a good thing' for him to act as ego wishes."[48] This definition of persuasion is not directly relevant to our purpose, for Parsons' main emphasis in distinguishing persuasion from activation of commitment is on the type of sanctions ego employs in attempting to influence alter, whether positive sanctions, that is, showing alter that it will "be a good thing" for him to comply, or negative sanctions, i.e. offering alter reasons why he is "wrong" in not complying.

From our point of view, the important distinction between activation of commitments or pure normative power, and persuasion or social power is that the former is an attempt to control another person's behavior by manipulating value-orientations and norms, while the latter is an attempt to influence by manipulating interpersonal relationships. This distinction becomes clearer when attention is shifted from static factors such as the source, the aims, or the amount of control, to the different mechanisms through which influence is exerted or accepted. Kelman, for example, distinguishes three processes of influence: acceptance, compliance, identification, and internalization.[49]

> "*Compliance* [the individual] . . . adopts the induced behavior not because he believes in its content but because he expects to gain specific rewards or approval and avoid specific punishments or disapproval by conforming. Thus, the satisfaction derived from compliance is due to the social effect of accepting influence.
>
> "*Identification* . . . an individual accepts influence because he wants to establish or maintain a satisfying self-defining relationship with another person or group. . . . He adopts the induced behavior because it is associated with the desired relationship. Thus the satisfaction derived from identification is due to the act of conforming as such.
>
> "*Internalization* . . . an individual accepts influence because the content of the induced behavior—the ideas and actions of which it is composed—is intrinsically rewarding. He adopts the induced behavior because it is congruent with his value system. . . . Thus the satisfaction derived from internalization is due to the content of the new behavior." [50]

There are other, more or less similar classifications of the processes leading to conformity, for example Asch's "conviction," "what-everybody-does," and "it-is-dangerous-not-to-conform,"[51] and Jahoda's "consentience," "conformance," and "compliance" (she distinguishes a fourth process, "convergence," which does not correspond to any of Kelman's or Asch's terms).[52]

The purpose in presenting the different definitions and typologies of power and the processes through which it is exerted and accepted is to try and see what the significant theoretical problems and questions for research are that emerge by applying them to social work practice.

Possible Obstacles to the Exercise of Normative Power

The present analysis will be focused mainly upon the problem of normative control in social casework. As we have seen, the attempt to change an individual's behavior[53] by employing normative power is mediated by personal influence or by activation of value commitments. From the viewpoint of the individual toward whom this power is directed, compliance is associated with the expectation that his behavior will be rewarded; noncompliance will evoke negative sanctions. Rewards are gained by attaining or maintaining approval and liking, or by the satisfaction acquired by conforming to a norm "for its own sake."[54] This presupposes that social approval of another person or group is conceived as a valuable reward for the individual in question and/or that he shares, to some extent, the norms which this person or group tries to activate.

Considering now the social worker-client relationship we must ask, does the client share the norms that the social worker wants him to conform to? And, does the worker's approval or liking furnish a significant reward for him?

Regarding the first question, it has been noted that welfare clients and social workers belong to different subcultures or subgroups and adhere, therefore, to different norms. The social worker in his interaction with the client is explicitly or implicitly referring to models of man or role-models, against which he evaluates the client's behavior, and toward which he tries to direct him. For example, "A good father provides for his children," "A man has to work," "A person should be honest," "A responsible mother does not neglect her children," and so on. Although we may assume that persons from lower classes, including welfare clients, share, to some extent, the universal values of the society they live in,[55] it is doubtful whether they are committed to them to such a degree that mere moral prescriptions will have any impact on their behavior. In exchange-theory terminology we would say that conformity by clients to these norms just does not "pay off"; they have very little to gain by modifying their behavior and very little to lose by persisting in the present pattern.[56] Moreover, under such circumstances, it is proposed that "pure" normative control through the manipulation of symbolic rewards will not only be ineffective but actually alienating and frustrating for the client. Nobody likes to be constantly reminded of his inadequacies and reprimanded for his failures. Taylor comments that

> "It is not true that 'no one talks of sin anymore,' but social workers rarely talk of sin. Today a new language has evolved. . . . Whether jargon or scientific terminology, the new language has a strong emotional content. Behavior is still labeled as 'good' or 'bad.' 'Good' may be termed 'wholesome personality,' 'adjustment,' or 'normal'; 'bad' may be 'maladjustment,' 'neurotic' or 'abnormal'. . . . In other words, 'bad' behavior is behavior that does not conform with the community models. Sin is now 'deviant behavior.' "[57]

In any case when a person is repeatedly accused of deviance from norms, he is likely to resort to defense mechanisms such as evasion, withdrawal, aggression, or even accepting the stigma, thus giving rise to a process of "self-fulfilling prophecy."[58]

The other type of normative power, namely, social power, is mediated through interpersonal relations; a person may conform to a norm not for its own sake, but in order to gain social approval. What is known about this mechanism of influence is based mainly on research in small experimental groups.[59] The general conclusion of these studies is that a person within a group will behave in such a manner as to maximize favorable attitudes from other group members; this is the so-called "motivational theorem" in sociology.[60] To be able to apply this theorem to the social worker-client dyad, one basic condition is necessary: the worker must constitute a "significant other" for the client; in other words, the client feels rewarded by the worker's favorable evaluations of his behavior, and he regards his disapproval as depriving or punishing. For this to be so, the worker-client interrelation must have a certain degree of attraction for the client (we refer only to the client since he is the one who is supposed to modify his attitudes and behavior). This can by no means be taken for granted. As long as the client is dependent on the social worker for welfare payments, it is very difficult to decide whether the client derives satisfaction from his personal relationship with the worker, or whether he perceives the contact with the worker as a necessary "investment" for getting material rewards. Thus, it seems that if anything more than mere promises to comply, or lip service, is to be attained, the first step needed is to enhance the attractiveness of the personal interrelation with the worker for the client. The other process of influence, that is, increasing the relevance of the norms that guide the worker's demand, is after all a goal rather than a means in the context of the worker-client relationship.

To make the worker-client interaction more salient and rewarding for the client, it is necessary to break through the isolation of this relationship by attaching it to wider and more meaningful social relations of the client. The worker's approval expressed in the interview with the client in verbal communication and in so-called "grunting techniques" is not enough. As long as the worker-client relationship is detached from group norms and interactions, the position of the worker will be that of a "counternorm communicator" who proposes opinions and standards of behavior that are at odds with those approved and practiced by the groups in which the client holds membership.[61] In short, for the change in attitudes and behavior to be accepted by the client, it must be reinforced in interaction with individuals who constitute his membership groups, and supported by his reference groups.

In conclusion, it should be noted again that the analysis of various forms of normative power alone does not take into account other types of power which are sometimes operating in combination with it. However, it seemed useful to focus attention upon the inherent problems of the social worker's normative power as the most complex, and probably the most effective means of control, in the long run, that the social worker commands.

Let us now consider in more detail the consequences of the

use of different kinds of power for the major manifest goals of casework—the improvement of the client's functioning in his environment.

Different Types of Power and Their Consequences

So far, the available types of power of the social worker in interaction with the client have been discussed. It is now necessary to assess the outcomes of the exercise of various types of power for the intended goals which the worker aims to achieve, and to specify the conditions under which these outcomes are functional or dysfunctional in terms of these goals.

We have noted that in general a worker engaged in casework attempts to change the client's attitudes and behavior in such a way that he will conform more closely to role-models assigned by social norms to individuals in certain positions. Specifically, a man should support his family, a woman should not have children out of wedlock, a young child should attend school, and so forth.

From another viewpoint, the ultimate goal of casework, and for that matter of any therapeutic relationship, whether mental, social or physical, is the termination of this relationship. Ideally, the patient of a physician or psychotherapist is released from the relationship when he is well again, and the social worker closes the case when the client is self-supporting and able to handle his problems independently. However, in the instance of social work, the fact that a case has been closed provides a very unreliable indicator of success of the casework process. To give an obvious example, cases may be closed not because the goal of "improved functioning" on the client's part has been achieved, but because cuts in the agency's budget, or a redefinition of eligibility requirements have been decreed.

All along we have avoided a distinction usually made in the analysis of personal change, that is, whether the processes of control, socialization, influence, and the like, produce change in the values, norms, beliefs, and attitudes of an individual, or whether change in patterns of behavior, performances, and activities occur. It seems that this distinction per se is not very significant, especially when applied to the welfare client. As Rosow states,

> "socialization always has the same objectives: to inculcate in the novice both values and behavior, or beliefs and action. Our basic premise is that conformity is invariably sought on both dimensions. . . . In any context, the fully socialized person internalizes the correct beliefs and displays the appropriate behavior." [62]

This is not to deny that people sometimes behave in ways which are not compatible with their value commitments. Nevertheless, if a welfare client declares that she realizes that it is bad to have transient relations with different men, and then does not adhere to the norm of monogamous marriage in practice, it cannot be directly inferred that a change on the normative level took place without parallel modifications in behavior. Or conversely, if behavior is changed it does not imply, by definition, that a transformation of perceptions and beliefs preceded.

Therefore, it seems that in the case of welfare clients the distinction between "public conformity" and "private acceptance," [63] and the specific conditions under which they occur, are more relevant than distinguishing between attitude change and behavior change. Compliance with the directives of a controlling agent may occur with or without private acceptance. A change in a person's attitudes and behavior is called public conformity if it disappears on removal of the source of induction; private acceptance is the case in which the induced behavior or attitude persists even if the "power field" of the influencing agent is removed. [64] This factor of the presence or absence of the influencing agent has direct significance for the analysis of the consequences of casework. It was previously noted that the day-to-day activities of the client are performed outside the worker's range of visibility: thus, the client may tell the worker that he will comply, but the fulfillment of this promise is or is not carried out when the social worker is not present. The worker may employ some methods which are intended to check on the client's behavior, such as home calls, conversations with other members of the family or neighbors, and in more extreme cases, close surveillance. Nevertheless, this kind of "remote control" can hardly be compared with the pressures toward conformity that a group exercises upon its members, or with the control one person exerts upon another with whom he has a continuous relationship (e.g. marriage), or during face-to-face interaction (foreman-worker). There are many technical difficulties involved in the ability of the social worker to observe the client's behavior outside the agency; in other words, it is relatively easy for the client to evade being observed by the worker in performing those activities that he does not want him to witness.

The question is, under what conditions is it likely that public conformity without private acceptance will occur? This question is related to the various types of power exercised: different types of change tend to ensue when different bases of power are activated.

Kelman views the three processes of influence-acceptance which he distinguishes—compliance, identification, and internalization—as mediating between a set of antecedent conditions—the source of power of the influencing agent—and between a set of consequences—the conditions under which the adopted behavior is performed. His hypotheses concerning the relations among these variables may be presented in the following manner: [65]

Source of Power	Process of Acceptance	Conditions of Performance
means-control	compliance	surveillance
attractiveness	identification	salience of relationship
credibility	internalization	relevance of issue

These hypotheses were confirmed by Kelman's study designed to change the attitudes of a group of Negro college freshmen in relation to the impending Supreme Court decision on desegregation in public schools in 1954.[66]

Different authors differ as to the extent of importance they ascribe to the different conditions that produce public adherence as against private acceptance. Festinger, for example, emphasizes the degree of attractiveness of group membership or interpersonal relations as the main factor effecting different types of change. The major points in his theory of compliance are

"1. Public compliance without private acceptance will occur if the person in question is restrained from leaving the situation and if there is a threat of punishment for noncompliance.

2. Public compliance with private acceptance will occur if there is a desire on part of the person to remain in the existing relationship with those attempting to influence him." [67]

Jahoda, on the other hand, attributes crucial importance to the "emotional and intellectual investment in the issue" as determining conforming or independent behavior.[68] She proposes that the distinction between public and private acceptance is significant, "but its importance derives more from viewing it in conjunction with cathexis to the issue than in conjunction with group membership."[69] Considering the attraction to a person for upholding an existing relationship, she argues that public compliance without private acceptance may depend on the individual's wish to remain in the existing relationship with those attempting to influence him (in the case of friendship, for example), and not only upon the forces restraining him from leaving the relationship.

Private acceptance will accompany public conformity, it seems, under the conditions that normative power is success-fully exercised, namely, if the person either identifies with the individual or the group who exerts this power, or if he internalizes the values and norms which guide the induced behavior. Under these circumstances the presence of the source of power is not the determining factor of conformity because the individual's behavior is regulated "from within" by his desire to continue his relationship with a person or a group, or by integrating their values with his own value-system (in psychoanalytic terms, these values become part of his super-ego). Of course, normative power may fail to produce behavior and attitude change in much the same way as coercive or instrumental power (which in Kelman's typology are both included in the category of "means control"). The attractiveness of the relationship with the person who commands the power, or his credibility may be eroded for some reason or other. Nevertheless, attractiveness and credibility as sources of power, and their mediating mechanisms of influence acceptance are more likely to produce conformity accompanied by private acceptance, that is, change of a more enduring and stable nature, than does power which is based on control of instrumental means. This can be seen by looking at the third row of the above table; compliance occurs under conditions of surveillance, which corresponds to what we have called conditions of observability or close supervision. Identification operates as a mechanism of influence acceptance so long as the relationship with the person who exerts power is salient for the person toward whom influence is directed; internalization takes place if the issue in question has relevance for the person influenced.

When coercive power is exerted, it is possible to predict that if the source of force is not present the person toward whom it has been directed will not adhere to the enforced behavior, for example, the prisoner will escape if the bars are removed. A less extreme example is provided by a study which has been conducted to evaluate the effects of a training program for housekeepers rated as poor by housing personnel and social service staff. Clear improvement was found in the group that received training, as against a control group whose only stimulus for change was the threat of eviction.[70] Instrumental power may have similar effects, that is, if the provision of rewards is discontinued; or if their value diminishes for some reason, the individual will not persist in that behavior to which he resorted in order to gain the desired rewards.

Some reservations concerning the pertinence of these theories of normative and behavioral change, and their practical implications for social work practice, must be noted. The situation of the welfare client is frequently a result of a combination of various circumstances and events: poverty, lack of education, unemployment, and so forth. Often, this type of vicious circle cannot be broken merely by an act of will as a response to normative induction. On the other hand, improving the material conditions of a client may promote his adherence to accepted social norms, as, for example, the provision of better medical services, better housing, and steady employment.

Thus, the advantages usually attributed to normative power over instrumental power do not apply to all attempts to produce personal change, and depend among other things upon the objective circumstances of the individual toward whom they are directed.

Some Research Problems and Findings

Predicting the kind of conformity that is likely to ensue is very difficult in the case of the welfare client since the social worker commands and usually administers more than one type of power. Which of the various sources of power—coercion, instrumental rewards, the attractiveness of the relationship with the worker, or the relevance of the issue—are most effective in producing change? And which type of change? It seems almost impossible to measure the relative strength of each type of power and to evaluate its independent effects in real-life situations. It must be remembered that in practice, even specialist social workers in closed institutions (prisons or mental hospitals), in welfare agencies, and in psychiatric clinics, usually employ more than one type of control, though to varying degrees. Nevertheless, an experiment could be conducted with different groups of clients, matched on all the relevant aspects, varying only the mode of intervention. In the first group, the worker would employ coercive power; in the second, instrumental sanctions; and in the third, normative power. The degree of change of clients' behavior and its direction should be measured, and then compared for each of the three groups. A follow-up would be needed to determine the durability of change.[71]

To return to nonexperimental situations of worker-client interaction, several empirical problems present themselves. First, it must be mentioned that the exertion of power does not exhaust the whole range of the worker-client relationship. In other words, the worker sometimes does not apply any of the various types of power in his encounter with the client. Power is used only in those instances in which the intentions of the person who possesses power, and those of the person who has less power at his command, diverge; power will then be applied to overcome resistance and opposition.

Second, if we consider only those aspects of the worker-client interaction in which the worker attempts to control the client's attitudes and behavior according to his intentions which are resisted or opposed by the client, it still remains for the researcher to decide which type of power is exercised in specific instances. This is particularly difficult when the worker's suggestions are not accompanied by "persuasive appeals"[72] or by an explicit reason why the client should act in the prescribed manner. This category includes plain orders—do so and so—that are either based upon the worker's "expert power,"[73] i.e. his knowledge and information, for example, "Go to the city's department of housing," or on the worker's general authority, i.e., his legitimate power by virtue of his position, for example, "Next time, bring me your license for the store." Usually this kind of command, advice, instruction, suggestion, and demand implicitly includes the promise of a reward for compliance, or the threat of some deprivation for noncompliance, such as becoming or not becoming eligible for financial assistance, getting or not getting a better apartment, or gaining the worker's approval or disapproval.

Authority—"the ability based on the right accrued to an occupant of a certain elevated position, to make people do things that they do not wish to do"[74]—cuts across the typology of power. In other words, instrumental, coercive, social, and normative power may or may not be legitimate under different conditions. Thus, for example, the policeman's coercive power is part of his authority, whereas this kind of power is not legitimate in the case of the school teacher. Formally, the social worker's authority includes all four types of power though the actual relative use of each is more or less determined by ad hoc circumstances.

Rosenberg and Pearlin, in their study of power orientations of nurses in mental hospitals, asked the respondents what they would do in case a patient refused to go to bed at the prescribed time.[75] The question was followed by several alternative answers. One of these was, "Since a nurse or nursing assistant has the right to tell a patient what to do, I would simply tell him to change his sleeping habits." The selection of this answer was regarded as an indicator of the use of authority in contrast to the other alternatives which were coercive power, contractual power, persuasion, or manipulation.[76] Although the authors were not specifically concerned with the problem, this statement implies that the compliant patient will be rewarded (by approval, cigarettes, candy, or other privileges), and the noncompliant patient will be punished (coerced to go to bed or deprived of privileges). The implicit sanctions of the nurses' authority could be exposed by asking them what they would do after a patient obeys their order, or after he refuses to comply.

Obviously it is easier to decide which type of power the official or professional thinks he would use when, as in the Rosenberg-Pearlin study, a hypothetical situation is described, and the respondent is asked to choose among a fixed number of alternative answers. If, however, the worker-client interaction is actually observed, as it was in the study of "Family Agencies,"[77] the determination of which type of control is being exercised, is complicated. This study was designed to examine the nature of the workers' efforts to inculcate values, socialize the client to social roles, and direct his behavior. One of the questions which the analysis of data attempted to answer was: Which kinds of strategies do social workers employ to attain these goals? Since the study was initially based on somewhat different premises than the theory of power relations, the categories of analysis do not correspond exactly to the classification of power presented earlier, but they are near enough in order to supply some empirical evidence bearing upon the nature of control exercised in welfare agencies. The ways in which the worker attempted to induce compliance with his demands were classified in the following categories:

(1) *Reference groups*—referring to persons or groups who are in the same position as that of the client, for example, "Your neighbor has five children too, and she manages to go to evening classes twice a week."

(2) *Advice*—for example, "I am sure something can be done about your son, I suggest that you take him for examination to the psychiatric clinic."

(3) *Command*—for example, "Tell your husband to come here with you next time," or, "You have to send some money to your mother."

(4) *Instrumental manipulation* (reward/punishment)—for example, "If you and your husband are willing to go to a development area, I will try to get you an apartment for a reasonable price."

(5) *Approval* (disapproval)—for example, "I think you did very well by bringing your sick mother-in-law to live with you," or disapproval, "I was shocked by your wife's story of how you treat her and the children."

(6) *Normative inducement*—for example, "This is a young developing country, everybody has to work and do his share." [78]

The following table indicates the various modes of control employed by the workers ranked according to their frequency:

Strategies Employed by Social Workers to Induce Compliance

Strategy	Number*	Percentage
1. Approval/Disapproval	171	29
2. Reference Groups	118	20
3. Commands	103	18
4. Instrumental Rewards/Punishment	66	11
5. Advice	63	11
6. Normative Inducement	62	11
Total	583	100

*Numbers refer to the instances in which the worker attempted to induce change in the client's behavior or motivation by verbal communication.

The table shows that the control mechanism most frequently used by social workers (29%) is based on the interpersonal relationships between them and their clients, and is exercised by praising or reproving the client for past, present, or future behavior.

It is now possible to classify the various mechanisms of control exertion listed in the table according to the source of power on which they are based, and relate them to the concomitant mechanisms of control acceptance.

First, manipulation by way of approval or disapproval of the worker (1), and of the client's reference groups (2), may be collapsed into one category. They are both based on social power, that is, on the desire of the individual toward whom they are directed, to establish or maintain a positive relationship with the worker or with his reference and/or membership groups. Acceptance of this type of control is based on the process of identification.

Second, instrumental rewards (4), and advice (5), can be combined into one category since they are both based on instrumental power. We include advice in this category because the data suggest that a material reward for following the worker's advice was usually implied, and by the same token, not getting this reward was associated with refusing to implement the worker's suggestion. The concurrent mechanism of acceptance of this source of power is compliance.

Normative inducements (6) are based on normative power and mediated through internalization. Commands (3), with no accompanying reason or "justification," are based on the worker's formal position, i.e. his authority, as defined earlier. It may be accepted or rejected by the client depending on the client's perception of the legitimacy of this type of control. Because of the generalized nature of this source of power, and the inability to decide on the basis of the available data, whether it overlaps any of the other types of power (social, normative, instrumental), it is regarded as a special category.

The distribution of the different mechanisms of control employed by workers, as revealed by the study, can now be summarized in the following table:

Distribution of Sources of Power and Mechanisms of Control

Source of Power	Mechanism of Control	Number	Total Percentage	Percentage Excluding Commands
Social	approval/disapproval reference groups	289	50	60
Instrumental	reward/punishment advice	129	22	27
Normative	normative inducement	62	10	13
Subtotal		480		100
Authority	command	103	18	
TOTAL		583	100	

Half of the total control attempts directed from worker to client are through manipulation of interpersonal and social relationships. This finding is quite surprising in view of the fact that the study was conducted in a public welfare agency in which the worker can easily employ instrumental power in his attempts to change the client's behavior (which amount to only 22%).[79] The other interesting finding is the low frequency of the activation of "pure" normative power (10%).

The high frequency of relational manipulation seems to be based not on theoretical considerations, but rather on the workers' experience that this method is relatively effective. This notion is supported by a descriptive study of former AFDC clients of the Pasadena District Office, Los Angeles County Bureau of Public Assistance.[80] Clients were asked to express their opinion about their caseworkers in general, to say what they expected of their workers, and what they thought the workers expect of them. The researchers came to the conclusion that

"Perhaps a new concept of helpful activity, related to ego-model, has been found in this study. Clients found 'personal examples' helpful. Clients recalled workers telling of personal experiences related to problems similar to those of clients. These accounts seemed to make the workers more human, less distant and easier to identify

> with. . . . The use of personal examples does not appear to be currently emphasized in the teaching of casework methods. This activity conflicts with one of social work's oldest ideals, namely that a professional relationship is an impersonal one. We were impressed and surprised by the emphasis respondents placed on helpfulness when the workers shared their similar life experience in problem solving efforts with the clients."[81]

The technique of "personal examples" (whether real or fictitious), given by the worker to the client, is related to one of the main processes of influence acceptance, that of identification of the client with the worker. Although it is true that this mode of help or influence is not part of formal casework techniques studied in schools of social work, we know from the study on welfare agencies mentioned above that workers employ this method extensively, i.e. they try to evoke the client's identification with them by showing him that they are, or have been in the same situation that troubles the client. For example, "I understand your problem because I have a teen-aged daughter too, therefore I think you should . . .," or "When my husband and I were your age we did not have any money, we both worked very hard to achieve what we have now." In the Family Agency study, verbal communication of this kind was classified in the category of "reference groups" or in that of "approval/disapproval" in case they included explicit praise or reprimands.

We also know from this study that each worker employs more than one type of control mechanism. Therefore, it is hypothesized, though this will have to be tested by further, more detailed analysis, that the relative frequency of various types of power and control mechanisms may present a certain pattern or sequence of the application of control mechanisms. Thus, the worker will first try to induce change in the client's behavior by drawing upon their interrelationship (approval/disapproval), or by evoking other salient relationships of the client (reference groups). If this proves ineffective, i.e. the client does not respond or does not accept the content of influence, the worker will use the instrumental power at his command. Finally, if this method does not produce the intended effects, the worker will attempt to activate the assumed relevant commitments of the client.[82] Although mechanisms of coercion were not part of the data analysis, we suggest that threats to use force or actual coercion could be included as the last step in the sequence, that is, after the possibilities of the first three modes of control have been exhausted, the worker may resort to coercive power.

This seems to be the logical pattern of the use of different types of control. However, we know from observations of worker-client interaction and from reading of records that those social workers who attempt to do more than establishing and checking clients' eligibility tend to employ different modes of control in the same interview or even in the same sentence, such as, "You shouldn't send your son to work, you know how important an education is nowadays. Besides, the law holds parents responsible for their children's education, and you may even be jailed for taking him out of school." This kind of combined control mechanism may prove to be ineffective in achieving the designated goal due to the "neutralizing effect" that different types of power have upon each other.[83] Merton, for example, has shown that the combination of utilitarian and normative appeals during a war bond drive proved less effective than the appeal to patriotic values alone.[84]

In casework, a threat by the worker to use force will undermine the effect of normative and social inducements because the resentment evoked by such threats is incompatible with the mechanisms of influence acceptance by way of identification or internalization. The same is true for the combination of normative or social controls with instrumental manipulations. This is so mainly because such manipulations will lower the social worker's credibility or the attractiveness of the relationship with him as perceived by the client. The types of acceptance associated with these different types of power are inherently incompatible. For example, if the worker tries to activate certain value commitments of the client and at the same time withhold instrumental rewards, such as, "You are healthy now and not eligible for welfare. If you start working you will feel much better and independent," the client is liable to disregard the normative message, for he will not believe that it is sincere. If however, the worker promises financial aid while using normative power, the client will also tend to pass by the normative implications, though for different reasons. In this case, the client may comply with the worker's demands but his compliance is likely to be of the type previously called "public compliance." Thus, the deeper and more enduring change that the worker attempts to induce by normative means will not be attained.

But, as we have noted earlier, conformity is not a purely motivational problem.[85] The implementation of expected patterns of behavior requires the access to certain resources or opportunities which the welfare client usually lacks, to a greater or lesser degree. The point, therefore, is not that clients should not be provided with these necessary means, but that remunerative and normative power should not be combined in the same relationship.

Two types of power which may produce compatible modes of compliance, and hence have accumulative effects on the recipient of influence, appear to be social and normative power. It is known from psychological and sociological theories concerning the socialization of children, that this process is mediated by the identification of the child with the socializing agents (parents), and the internalization of their norms and values. However, in contrast with the child's interrelations with his parents, the client's relationship with the worker is of a more transient and specific nature. Under these circumstances, the effectiveness of manipulating the worker-client relationship as far as modifying the client's behavior is concerned, depends to a large extent upon the support of these changes by the client's reference and/or membership groups (and, of course, upon the adequate means at the client's disposal to implement these changes). This may be the reason why, as the data indicate, social workers frequently refer to the client's identification, responsibility, and loyalty to these groups.

Two major practical conclusions may be drawn from the analysis of the power elements in the casework relationship; first, that social workers should be made aware of the specific implications and problems involved in using different types of power at their command, and of the possible neutralizing effects of applying mixed modes of control in the same relationship with one client. This would enable them to decide which type of control mechanism to activate according to the effects they wish to produce. Second, the argument in favor of a complete segregation of income maintenance from the therapeutic or socializing functions of casework suggested in the preceding discussions of the profession-organization and supervisor-supervisee relationships, gains further support from the analysis of the various types of power and their operation within the worker-client relationship.

Notes

1. See William J. Goode, "Illegitimacy in the Caribbean Social Structure," American Sociological Review 25 (February 1960): 21-30.

2. This does not imply that certain patterns of behavior of clients which social workers attempt to modify, such as neglect of children, unwillingness to work, or heavy drinking are invisible—only, that they usually occur outside the worker-client encounter.

3. Merton, *Social Theory and Social Structure,* p. 350, and Coser, "Insulation from Observability."

4. The concept of "reference group" was systematically introduced by Herbert H. Hyman, in "The Psychology of Status," Archives of Psychology 269 (1942): 47-57.

5. The power of membership and reference groups as an explanatory factor of the individual's tendency to conform to group norms has been established by evidence from many studies. For example, see Carl I. Hovland, Irving L. Janis, and Harold H. Kelley, *Communication and Persuasion* (New Haven: Yale University Press, 1953), Ch. 5, and Elihu Katz and Paul F. Lazarsfeld, *Personal Influence* (New York: Free Press, 1964), Part I.

6. "First Findings from Midway," consists of two parts: (1) Edward E. Schwartz, "The Field Experiment: Background, Plan, and Selected Findings," and (2) William C. Sample, "The Findings on Client Change," Social Service Review 41 (June 1967): 3-24, 25-39.

7. Ibid., p. 39.

8. Jerome D. Frank, *Persuasion and Healing* (New York: Schocken Books, 1963), p. 146.

9. Robert L. Kahn and Daniel Katz, "Social Work and Organizational Change," in *The Social Welfare Forum,* Proceedings of the National Conference on Social Welfare (New York: Columbia University Press, 1966), pp. 166-167.

10. Kurt Lewin in *Field Theory in Social Science,* Dorwin Cartwright, ed. (New York: Harper and Row, 1964), pp. 229-231.

11. See, for example, Albert K. Cohen, *Delinquent Boys: The Culture of the Gang,* (New York: Free Press, 1955), and Erving Goffman, *Asylums* (New York: Anchor Books, Doubleday and Company, 1961).

12. Howard S. Becker, "Personal Change in Adult Life," Sociometry 27 (March 1964): 40-53.

13. Stanton Wheeler, "The Structure of Formally Organized Socializa-

tion Settings," in Orville G. Brim and Stanton Wheeler, eds., *Socialization after Childhood* (New York: John Wiley and Sons, 1966): 53-113.

14. It is realized that these groups to which the client belongs are not "closed" groups like the ones of inmates of "total" institutions such as prisons or mental hospitals.

15. Ibid., p. 64.

16. Lloyd Ohlin and Williams C. Lawrence, "Social Interaction Among Clients As a Treatment Problem," Social Work 4 (April 1959): 4.

17. Ibid., p. 12.

18. Florence Hollis, *Casework: A Psychosocial Therapy* (New York: Random House, 1964), p. 149.

19. Helen H. Perlman, "Social Casework," in Harry L. Lurie, ed., *Encyclopedia of Social Work* (1965), p. 706.

20. Felix P. Biestek, "An Analysis of the Casework Relationship," Social Casework 35 (February 1954): 57. Italics added.

21. The empirical problem in this connection is the development of criteria to measure the outcomes of the worker-client interaction by which success or failure can be evaluated.

22. Helen H. Perlman, *Social Casework: A Problem Solving Process* (Chicago: University of Chicago Press, 1957).

23. Helen H. Perlman, *Social Casework*, p. 705.

24. See the brief reference in Chapter 1 to the worker's tendency to manipulate material rewards to persuade the client to comply with accepted norms and patterns of behavior.

25. Ibid., p. 704.

26. Robert K. Taylor, "The Social Control Function in Casework," Social Casework 1 (January 1958): 17-21.

27. Elliott Studt, "An Outline for Study of Social Authority Factors in Casework," Social Casework 35 (June 1954): 233. Italics added.

28. Erich Fromm, *Escape From Freedom* (New York: Farrar and Rinehart, 1941), p. 164 (quoted in Studt, ibid.).

29. Taylor, "The Social Control Function," p. 18.

30. Peter Leonard, "Social Control, Class Values and Social Practice," Social Work (U.K.) 22 (October 1965): 10. See also Elliott Studt, "Worker-Client Authority Relationships in Social Work," Social Work 4 (January 1959): 18-28, and Herschel A. Prins, "Authority and the Casework Relationship," Social Work (U.K.) 19 (April 1962): 21-26.

31. Ernest Greenwood, "Social Science and Social Work: A Theory of Their Relationship," Social Service Review 29 (March 1955): 25.

32. Ohlin, "Conformity in American Society Today," p. 58.

33. Eileen Spellman, "Authority and Social Work," Case Conference (December 1954). See also Mary J. McCormick, "The Role of Values in the Helping Process," Social Casework 42 (January 1961): 3-9; Shirley C.

Hellerbrand, "Client Value Orientations: Implications for Diagnosis and Treatment," Social Casework 42 (April 1961): 162-170; Irving Weisman and Jacob Chwast, "Control and Values in Social Work Treatment," and Editorial Notes, "The Question of Relative Values," Social Casework 41 (November 1960): 451-456, 478-482; and Irving Svarc, "Client Attitudes Toward Financial Assistance: A Cultural Variant," Social Service Review 30 (June 1956): 136-146.

34. Richard M. Emerson, "Power-Dependence Relations," American Sociological Review 27 (February 1962): 32.

35. Ibid., p. 32.

36. Peter M. Blau, *Exchange and Power in Social Life* (New York: John Wiley and Sons, 1964). Also see Edmund Dahlström "Exchange, Influence and Power," Acta Sociologica 9 (1966): 237-284.

37. A. Etzioni, *A Comparative Analysis of Complex Organizations,* p. 4. An additional way in which this problem can be analyzed is the notion of "intercursive power relations" in which individuals control others in some scopes and are controlled by them in other scopes; see Dennis H. Wrong, "Some Problems in Defining Social Power," American Journal of Sociology 73 (May 1968): 673-681.

38. Max Weber, *The Theory of Social and Economic Organization,* p. 152.

39. George C. Homans, *Social Behavior: Its Elementary Forms* (New York: Harcourt, Brace and World, 1961), p. 293.

40. Katz and Eisenstadt, "Some Sociological Observations," p. 124.

41. Elihu Katz and Brenda Danet, "Petitions and Persuasive Appeals: A Study of Official-Client Relations," American Sociological Review 31 (December 1966): 813.

42. Ibid., p. 811.

43. Taylor, "The Social Control Function"; Leonard, "Social Control, Class Values"; and Studt, "Worker-Client Authority Relationships."

44. Etzioni, *A Comparative Analysis,* pp. 4-6.

45. For other, more or less overlapping typologies of power, see, for example, John R. P. French, Jr. and Bertram Raven, "The Bases of Social Power," in Dorwin Cartwright, ed., *Studies in Social Power* (Ann Arbor: University of Michigan, 1959), pp. 150-167, and Morris Rosenberg and Leonard J. Pearlin, "Power-Orientations in the Mental Hospital," Human Relations 15 (1962): 335-349.

46. Etzioni, *A Comparative Analysis,* p. 5.

47. Talcott Parsons, "On the Concept of Influence," pp. 37-62.

48. Ibid., p. 43.

49. Herbert C. Kelman, "Compliance, Identification and Internalization: Three Processes of Attitude Change," Journal of Conflict Resolution 2 (1958): 51-60.

50. Ibid., p. 53.

51. Solomon E. Asch, *Social Psychology* (New York: Prentice-Hall, 1952).

52. Marie Jahoda, "Psychological Issues of Civil Liberties," American Psychologist (May 1956).

53. For the time being, we do not distinguish between change of behavior and change of attitudes and beliefs, but consider normative control as an attempt to change behavior via change in perceptions and attitudes.

54. Homans, *Social Behavior,* pp. 116-117.

55. Robert K. Merton, "Social Structure and Anomie," in Merton, ed., *Social Theory and Social Structure,* pp. 125-150.

56. It should be mentioned again that conformity does not depend on intention or motivation alone. The nonconformer sometimes simply lacks the adequate means or assets to behave in accordance with accepted social norms. See for example Merton's analysis of "anomie" in Merton, ed., *Social Theory and Social Structure,* pp. 125-150, and Amitai Etzioni, *The Active Society* (New York: Free Press, 1968), ch. 13.

57. Taylor, "The Social Control Function," p. 19.

58. Robert K. Merton, "The Self-Fulfilling Prophecy," in Merton, ed., *Social Theory and Social Structure,* pp. 179-195.

59. See, for example, Muzafer Sherif, *The Psychology of Social Norms* (New York: Harper and Row, 1936); Solomon E. Asch, "Effects of Group Pressure upon the Modification and Distortion of Judgements," in Guy E. Swanson et al., eds, *Reading in Social Psychology* (New York: Holt, 1952), pp. 2-11; Muzafer Sherif and Carl I. Hovland, *Social Judgement: Assimilation and Contrast Effects in Communication and Attitude Change* (New Haven: Yale University Press, 1961); Terence K. Hopkins, *The Exercise of Influence in Small Groups* (New Jersey: Bedminster Press, 1964); and Leon Festinger et al., "Theory and Experiment in Social Communication" (Research Center for Group Dynamics, Institute for Social Research, University of Michigan, 1950).

60. See, for example, Hans L. Zetterberg, "Compliant Actions," Acta Sociologica 1 (1956): 189.

61. Harold H. Kelley and Christine L. Woodruff, "Members' Reactions to Apparent Group Approval of a Counternorm Communication," Journal of Abnormal and Social Psychology 52 (1956), and Harold H. Kelley and Edmund H. Volkart, "The Resistance to Change of Group-Anchored Attitudes," American Sociological Review 17 (1952): 453-465.

62. Irving Rosow, "Forms and Functions of Adult Socialization," Social Forces 44 (September 1965): 35.

63. Leon Festinger, "An Analysis of Compliant Behavior," in Muzafer Sherif and M. O. Wilson, eds., *Group Relations at the Crossroads* (New

York: Harper and Bros., 1953), pp. 232-256; Kelman, "Compliance, Identification and Internalization," p. 31; Marie Jahoda, "Conformity and Independence: A Psychological Analysis," Human Relations 12 (1959): 104; and Rose Coser, "Insulation from Observability." Public versus private acceptance should not be confused with the distinction between value change and behavior change.

64. Festinger, "An Analysis of Compliant Behavior," p. 234. Festinger's distinction is based on earlier research by French; see J. R. P. French, Jr., "Organized and Unorganized Groups under Fear and Frustration," *Studies in Topological and Vector Psychology, III.* (Iowa City: University of Iowa, 1944).

65. Kelman, "Compliance, Identification and Internalization."

66. Ibid., pp. 57-58.

67. Festinger, "An Analysis of Compliant Behavior," p. 235.

68. Jahoda, "Conformity and Independence."

69. Ibid., p. 111.

70. Harold Lewis, "Implications of Evaluation," in Housekeeping—A Community Problem: Summary of Workshop (Philadelphia: Friends Neighborhood Guild, 1961, mimeographed).

71. Studies concerning different approaches toward clients and different types of intervention have been carried out; these, however, were not related to consequent effects upon the client. See, for example, Henry S. Maas, "Group Influences on Client-Worker Interaction," Social Work 9 (April 1964): 70-79, and Blau, "Orientations Toward Clients."

72. See Katz and Danet, "Petitions and Persuasive Appeals."

73. See French and Raven, "The Bases of Social Power." They distinguish between expert power based on the credibility of the influencer, and informational influence, based on "self-evident facts."

74. Warren G. Bennis, N. Berkowitz, M. Affinito, and M. Malone, "Authority, Power and the Ability to Influence," Human Relations 11 (1958): 144.

75. Rosenberg and Pearlin, "Power Orientations in the Mental Hospital," pp. 335-349.

76. Ibid., p. 336.

77. This study was carried out by students of the School of Social Work in Israel and was mentioned previously.

78. Control by threats to use force or by actual coercion was not included in the study because it appeared only in very few cases and only when the worker had to control the client's behavior in the immediate encounter, for example, when a client broke a window, or when another threatened to leave her children in the worker's office.

79. Of course, this "friendly persuasion" may have been interpreted by the client as implying remunerative sanctions. The data, nonetheless, show

that social workers in this study did not frequently employ instrumental power in an explicit fashion.

80. Hugh McIsaac and Harold Wilkinson, "Clients Talk About Their Caseworkers," Public Welfare 23 (July 1965): 147-154.

81. Ibid., p. 152.

82. This analysis, as can be noticed, excludes the category of "commands" for reasons mentioned earlier.

84. A. Etzioni, *The Active Society,* pp. 366-367.

84. Robert K. Merton, *Mass Persuasion: The Social Psychology of a War Bond Drive* (New York: Harper and Row, 1946), pp. 45-47. The effects of mixed inducements could be studied in different spheres, such as in advertising. Automobile companies sometimes attempt to influence people to buy a certain car that they produce claiming that it confers prestige and that it is economical. It is easy to see that the contents of these two arguments neutralize each other. The potential customer will feel somehow that a car can either be a symbol of high status or economical, but it cannot be both at the same time.

85. R. K. Merton, "Social Structure and Anomie," and Richard A. Cloward and Lloyd E. Ohlin, *Delinquency and Opportunity: A Theory of Delinquent Gangs* (New York: Free Press, 1960).

Chapter 5

THE EFFECTS OF THE NATURE OF THE PROFESSION AND THE ORGANIZATIONAL SETTING ON THE WORKER-CLIENT RELATIONSHIP

The preceding chapters were mainly concerned with the problems created by the structure of the worker-client relationship in casework. The consequences of the isolation of the one-to-one relationship from other interpersonal relations for the process of influence were noted.

As mentioned earlier, the particular structure of the casework relationship should be analyzed in conjunction with the two other principal sets of factors: the semi-professional nature of social work, and the bureaucratic setting in which it is practiced. These factors exert a significant impact upon the worker-client relationship and strengthen the barriers inhibiting the workers' ability to produce change in clients' patterns of behavior and attitudes.

Prestige and Control

We shall first discuss the degree of prestige imputed to a profession, which is a general attribute derived from the particular components of the profession (knowledge, competence, autonomy, organization, and ideology) and its consequences for the ability of the professional to produce change in the client in a designated direction.

It is generally accepted that the ability of an individual to influence another is positively correlated with the amount of prestige ascribed to him by the influencee.[1] This relation has been demonstrated by many studies in small, face-to-face groups; the higher the prestige of a group member, the more influence he wields upon other members.[2]

It is also known that social workers are accorded relatively low prestige by the general public and by their clients. In 1947 North and Hatt carried out a survey of a nationwide cross-section of the U.S. population to explore the basic public attitudes regarding occupations.[3] People were asked to evaluate 90 different jobs. From among them, Supreme Court Justice got the highest rating; physician and state governor tied for second place. The lowest public evaluation was given to shoe-shiner and street-sweeper. Welfare worker for a city government ranked forty-sixth in this list of 90 occupations. We may assume that if the job of professional social worker would have been included it would have fared better than that of welfare worker, though probably not much better.

Each of the occupations was given a single general score with a theoretical maximum of 100 points and a minimum of 20 points. The average score for professional and semi-professional workers was 80.6. Within this group of occupations, physicians had a score of 93; college professors, 89; lawyers, 86; public school teachers, 78; and welfare workers, 73.

A less systematic picture of the public evaluation of social work is reflected in such stereotyped epithets as, "do-gooder" or "cold snooper." White notes that "The very name 'social worker' is a semantic curiosity. 'Worker' is a term associated with occupations which require little erudition. . . . Then, 'social' is vague: does it mean existing and behaving in a human group . . . or does it mean concern for human ideals and human weal?"[4]

Studying the image of social work in the eyes of students who face selecting it as an occupation, Meyerson writes, "Our conclusion is that they have adopted a distorted picture of an unattractive—or at best—plain, middle-aged, nosy, and officious do-gooder, with her head in the clouds and her hand in the public purse."[5]

More systematic data on self-evaluation of social workers is provided by a 1951 Detroit metropolitan area study of the status of social workers.[6] The subjective position of the social worker was examined by asking a sample of social work students at Wayne University to rank a list of occupations according to their prestige in the community. The ratings were as follows:

Relative Prestige of Social Work as an Occupation[7]

Occupation	Mean Rank, N=75	Rank Order
Doctor	1.6	1
Lawyer	2.5	2
Plant Executive	2.3	3
School Teacher	4.6	4
Store Owner	5.0	5
Social Worker	6.1	6
Plant Foreman	7.1	7
Salesman	7.4	8
Clerical Worker	8.8	9
Carpenter	9.1	10

As in the NORC public evaluation study, social workers were ranked below doctors, lawyers, and school teachers. The distinctive finding of the Polansky study was that social work students placed the ten occupations listed, including social work, in exactly the same rank order as did three other student samples that were drawn from two classes in Introductory Psychology, and a graduate class in Education at the same university.

Reviewing the available research on relative prestige of occupations, Kadushin draws two general conclusions:

"First, the prestige level of social work in the hierarchy of occupations has not as yet been clearly 'positioned'; the level of the profession in the traditional structure of occupational prestige relations has not as yet been clearly, and firmly, institutionalized. . . . Secondly, there is considerable consistency with which social work repeatedly ranks high on the occupational prestige scale of the *total range of occupations* but among the lowest of the professions listed ... on the basis of research available it would appear that, in the image of the public, social work is a minor, if not a marginal, profession."[8]

He then lists a variety of reasons for the relatively low position of social work as a profession: (1) social work is a feminine profession, seventy percent of all social workers being women; (2) since social work, by and large, serves the least prestigious members of the community, its own prestige is adversely affected; (3) social workers are not independent professional entrepreneurs; they are employees of an organization which is not itself independent. This negatively affects the evaluation of social work, especially by other professions with which they work in close contact; (4) the prestige level of social work is in part a function of the "projected hostility and criticism of anxious, sick people and a frightened and immature society";[9] (5) the low wages of social workers tend to reinforce their depressed prestige rating as compared to more lucrative occupations; (6) social work, and social workers, very often articulate the unpopular point of view; for example, they display an accepting attitude toward deviates, they demand far-reaching social legislation, and so forth—"As a result, we are less than wholeheartedly accepted by the public and our prestige rating suffers";[10] (7) the social worker is concerned with problems at which everyone works, thus narrowing the distance between the professional and lay-knowledge; (8) the amount of training required for entering the profession is a major factor determining prestige—"In this sense we are only nominally professionalized since only a small percentage of social workers actually meet full educational qualifications";[11] (9) the function of social work is not regarded as indispensible to the maintenance of the ongoing life of a society; furthermore, it is not clear what function the profession serves, and hence it is difficult to evaluate the importance, and prestige, of the profession; (10) prestige is closely related to power, and "Because we do not have clear control or access to any kind of goods and/or services highly valued by a large and influential segment of our society, our prestige is necessarily limited."[12]

This list of factors, corrosive to the prestige of social work as a profession, refers to the main features which account for the semi-professional position of social work: (a) the nature of the profession's knowledge-base, skills, and training; (b) the type of its organization and the consequent limited autonomy of the individual worker; (c) its ethic or ideology, which according to Kadushin makes the profession unpopular in the public view; and (d) the "halo affect" of the inferior status of the clientele that is served by the profession.

Concerning the problem of control, the general conclusion is that a profession that is evaluated relatively low on the scale of prestige by the public, its clients, and other professions, and whose members are themselves "status-conscious," will not be able to control the behavior of its clients to the same degree as the more prestigious professions; people will submit more readily to the directions of their physicians and lawyers than to those of their social workers.

In addition, the general social status achieved by professional standing reacts upon the professional's authority over the client. Analyzing the doctor-patient relationship, Freidson writes,

> "In the consulting room the physician may be said to have the manifest status of expert consultant and the latent status of his prestige in the lay community. His latent status has no necessary relationship to his technical qualification to be an expert, but obviously impinges upon his relation to his patients. Indeed, latent status seems crucial for sustaining the force of manifest or professional status, for while many occupations possess expert knowledge, few have been able to control the terms of their work."[13]

It should be mentioned that the previous discussion, following the tradition of research in "prestige suggestion,"[14] is limited to control as related to prestige, i.e. the distance between the expert knowledge and social position of the professional and his client. We have, so far, ignored the opposite proposition that the degree of influence may be positively related to the proximity, or similarity in status and life-experiences between interacting individuals. Comparing the effects of social distance between ministers, physicians, psychotherapists, and their clients, Kadushin writes,

"Closeness and understanding, on the one hand, and objectivity and detachment, on the other, are essential to satisfactory client-professional relationships. In the distant relationship understanding is lost; in the close relationship the professional loses his objectivity. . . . Attention is confined to professions in the mental-health fields; the nature of their clients makes the problems of distance and instability more dramatic."[15]

Stable interaction between client and professional is more likely when similar internalized norms, common expectations, and optimum cathexis exist among the role partners. Social proximity and distance each have advantages and disadvantages in maintaining the conditions of stable interaction.

The problem will be considered later in reference to influence within groups of clients.[16] One point, however, should be made here; a certain degree of social and cultural closeness between professional and client seems to be particularly important in the case of professionals, such as social workers, whose range of influence is potentially very wide, though its intensity may not be great. A physician who deals almost exclusively with physical symptoms may "keep his distance" from the patient without impairing the limited relationship with him, or his strong, though specific, authority and control over him. The social worker, by comparison, attempts to influence a wide spectrum of the client's life, and deals with problems which are often emotionally charged. Under these circumstances, it is more difficult to confine the relationship to its specific and affectively neutral limits. A certain degree of nearness may enhance the susceptibility of the client to accept the worker's influence. One bridging mechanism that is sometimes utilized in social work agencies to overcome the distance between professional and client is the employment of indigenous, nonprofessional workers,[17] (in the medical practices, the nurse partly fulfills a similar function).[18]

As mentioned before, the prestige level of a profession is a general characteristic based upon a number of specific properties. Let us now see how the semi-professional qualities of social work affect both the social worker and his client, in particular, the ability of the worker to control the client and to produce change in his behavior, and in his tendency to comply.

The Knowledge-Base

The very nature of the knowledge upon which social work is based is an obstacle to the establishment of a clear-cut asymmetric control relationship between worker and client. One aspect of this knowledge that has already been mentioned is its weak theoretical or scientific base, a quality which hinders its monopolization by any professional group. An individual is more apt to follow the doctor's prescriptions than those of the social worker, in large part, because the patient lacks medical knowledge and the doctor has it all. Describing the institutional situation of the sick person, Parsons writes,

> "He is not only generally not in a position to do what needs to be done, but he does not 'know' what needs to be done or how to do it. . . . Only a technically trained person has that qualification. And one of the most serious disabilities of the layman is that he is not qualified to judge technical qualifications, in general or in detail."[19]

On the other hand, most people regard themselves as having some knowledge, understanding, and experience in human behavior and interpersonal relationships. Therefore, they are less inclined to concede absolute supremacy to any professional trying to influence these aspects of their lives. This type of resistance is the more pronounced the more the claimed superiority of the human-relations expert is characterized by lack of esoteric knowledge and skills, by short training,[20] and consequently, by low prestige in the wider community. Thus, other things being equal, a psychiatrist will be able to wield more control and influence over his patient than a marriage counselor or a social worker.[21] In addition, the welfare client, as compared to the sick patient, not only feels that he knows what his problem is, but also thinks that he knows the remedy for it.

In most cases the social worker does not have a strictly technical job. Even if he is engaged in eligibility investigation, this involves probing various diffuse and expressive spheres of the client's life. The very comprehensiveness of the worker's task lessens his power to influence the client, first, because people tend to resist the management of their lives by external interference, and second, because the tools and procedures for the accomplishment of such a task are less well defined and, in most cases, are unable to produce immediate improvement.

In this relation it is worth mentioning that social workers, as compared to the more technically specialized professions, lack some of the status symbols attached to the established practicing professions. Not only do they lack "awe evoking" tools, such as highly sophisticated instruments as in the doctor's case (which often do have instrumental, not only symbolic significance), they also do not wear uniforms, and have no titles preceding their names. Commenting on this point, Kadushin writes, "Unlike the psychologist, we do not even have the mysterious Rorschach or T.A.T. which can be employed to establish and maintain high prestige. The interview, as our most highly developed skill, is seen as something in which everyone can, and does, engage."[22]

This leads us to consider the effects of the personal relationship between worker and client, so highly valued in social work theory and practice, upon the worker's authority over his client. As Rogers states, "To withhold one's self as a person and to deal with the other person as an object does not have a high probability of being helpful."[23]

It seems that this reliance of social work in general—and of casework in particular—on establishing and maintaining an interpersonal relationship with the client, limits, in certain respects, the worker's power and ability to influence the client. This is not to deny that for psychological and moral reasons, the one-to-one relationship is still regarded as one of the most important bases for producing change in the client's behavior and attitudes. Nevertheless, this technique makes the worker more dependent on the client, his good-will and cooperation, than do more impersonal means and procedures employed by other professions, for it involves the worker personally and emotionally.

Though social work writings stress the professional attitude of "detached concern" in relations with clients, and caution inexperienced workers about getting "too involved" in their clients' troubles and misery, the point at which empathy is necessary and functional for the purpose at hand, and at which it becomes dysfunctional, is not clear. Kuhn, interpreting the social work interview in the symbolic-interaction tradition, claims that the interviewer is not a neutral agent, but must occupy an active role in an interactional situation which is a prerequisite for effective casework. However, he is aware of the inherent paradox between authority and rapport: "The interview will fall apart without control and will be meaningless without rapport. But the social distance between client and worker results in secrets on both sides, especially on the side of the client."[24]

It is true that other professionals sometimes attempt to establish some kind of personal relationship with their clients. Doctors, especially those in private practice, may develop a "bedside manner" to alleviate the patient's fear and anxiety. However, the doctor's kindness and understanding are never the main instruments of treatment. Furthermore, a patient is willing to accept a detached and impersonal attitude on part of his doctor as long as he believes him to be technically highly qualified. In the social worker's case, the crucial position of the personal relationship with the client has a leveling effect, undermining the worker's authority, and rendering him more vulnerable to the clients moods and attitudes.

The Code of Ethics

Beside knowledge and skills, the other crucial element of any profession is its special code of ethics. The code, adopted by the Delegate Assembly of the National Association of Social Workers, October 13, 1960, includes the following statements:

"I regard as my primary obligation the welfare of the individual or group served which includes action for improving social conditions.

"I give precedence to my professional responsibility over my personal interests.

"I hold myself responsible for the quality and extent of the service I perform.

"I respect the privacy of the people I serve.

"I use in a responsible manner information gained in professional relationships.

"I treat with respect the findings, views and actions of colleagues, and use appropriate channels to express judgment on these matters.

"I practice social work within the recognized knowledge and competence of the profession.

"I recognize my professional responsibility to add my ideas and findings to the body of social work knowledge and practice.

"I accept responsibility to help protect the community against unethical practice by any individuals or organizations engaged in social welfare activities.

"I stand ready to give appropriate professional service in public emergencies.

"I distinguish clearly, in public, between my statements and actions as an individual and as a representative of an organization.

"I support the principle that professional practice requires professional education.

"I accept responsibility for working toward the creation and maintenance of conditions within agencies which enable social workers to conduct themselves in keeping with this code.

"I contribute my knowledge, skills, and support to programs of human welfare."[25]

This code applies only to qualified social workers, with two years of graduate social work training and who are members of NASW. One of the conditions of membership in NASW is "agreement to abide by the Code of Ethics of the Association and to submit to proceedings for any alleged violation of the same."[26]

The phrasing of this code was obviously influenced by the codes of ethics of established professions, and asserts service to the client in a "disinterested" manner.[27] However, there is no reference to the restrictions on the social worker's dedication to the norm of service by the institutional framework of the profession, except the allusion in the code's introduction that social work is a "public trust."

Social work is conducted in private and public agencies, and "what is too often overlooked is that the social work profession's commitment to maximum service is not and never has been fully shared by social agencies. . . . for serving the client is not the sole, perhaps not even the major, concern of social agencies."[28] Private agencies are controlled by lay-boards that usually provide the funds, and decide how they should be distributed and which services should be supplied to which clients. Wilensky and Lebeaux call these decisions "big policy."[29] "Small policy" of daily conduct in the agency is made by the rank-and-file workers. In public agencies, big policy decisions are made by local or state welfare commissions, and by public officials, within the limits of the existing legislation.

These are typical structural features of the operation of social work; they are, nevertheless, incoporated in the profession's ethic and in the training of its members. This fact finds expression in the "Working Definition of Social Work Practice," which states,

"Social work is not practiced in a vacuum or at the choice of its practitioners alone. Thus, there is a social responsibility inherent in the practitioner's role for the way in which services are rendered. The authority and power of the practitioner and what he represents to the clients and group members derive from one or a combination of three sources:

"1. Governmental agencies or their sub-divisions (authorized by law).

"2. Voluntary incorporated agencies, which have taken responsibility for meeting certain of the needs or providing certain of the services necessary for individual and group welfare.

"3. The organized profession, which in turn can sanction individuals for the practice of social work and set forth the educational and other requirements for practice and the conditions under which that practice may be undertaken, whether or not carried out under organizational auspices."[30]

Thus, the concrete help and service that the social worker can supply to his clients do not derive only from technical skills and ethical commitments, but depend on the decisions of social groups outside the profession who do not share the worker's specific knowledge and general selfless orientation. Consequently, the social worker's responsibility is not confined to the welfare of the client as dictated by the professional code; he is also responsible to the community and the broader society. His obligation and loyalty have, at least, a double focus: the client and the community, as represented by the policy and rules of social work agencies.

This special position of social work affects worker-client relationships. We have already discussed at some length the problems of bureaucratization in social work and the subsequent bureaucracy-profession conflict.[31] However, it should be noted that we cannot simply apply this term, conceived in the analysis of full-fledged professions in bureaucratic organizations, to social work. The social worker is, by definition, committed to abide by bureaucratic rules and procedures, which prescribe not only certain administrative regulations but the essential contents of his role. To quote Briar,

> "The organizational requirements of social agencies generate pressures to substitute routinization for innovation and rules for the exercise of professional discretion. As a result, in many social agencies certain of the crucial conditions that caseworkers should be able to vary in order to help their clients are normatively prescribed, including the methods of intervention he is to use; and even the very language he is to use to describe his clients and the theory that is to inform his practice."[32]

The worker may be more or less opposed to established legislation and rules, and may feel that his service ideal is restricted by bureaucracy; he is, nevertheless, basically obliged to conform to these rules, and perform his helping role within their limits.

The client too, is aware of this special situation. Therefore, he may not be sure that the social worker is concerned primarily with his welfare, and he will trust him less than he does other professionals with whom he might be in contact. Hence, we conclude that the client will be less motivated and less willing to accept the worker's advice, suggestions, and orders, as compared with those of other professionals.

Thus, the code of ethics of social work, though it puts very great emphasis upon help and service to clients, is nevertheless shaped by other values and their constraints which govern the formal structure of the profession.

Professional Autonomy

The bureaucratic nature of social work's organization has been discussed in the previous section for it was argued that it is inseparable from the profession's code of ethic. We shall, therefore, deal here with the manifestations of bureaucratization on the role level, i.e. the practice of supervision and the consequent relative lack of professional autonomy of the individual social worker.[33]

Though the client may not be initially acquainted with the administrative regulations that restrict the worker's autonomy, or with the methods of supervision exercised in agencies, he will soon realize that the worker is not "omnipotent." Workers often tell their client that they will have to consult their superiors in relation to a certain matter, or that they are bound by agency, community, or state rules. Recently, leaders and groups of clients have been engaged in an attempt to bring these rules, especially those pertaining to the client's legal rights, to the clients' attention.[34] In any case, the worker is aware of the various controls limiting his professional freedom. The intensity of the conflict instigated by these controls varies with the type of the organizational setting, the type of supervision, the quality of the worker's training, the length of his experience, and his basic orientation whether mainly professional or bureaucratic. Peabody, in his study of organizational authority, asked workers of the welfare department in Orchard County whether they received instructions from above which seemed to conflict with their own views, and if so, what was the frequency of such instructions.[35] The data show the following distribution:

Extent of Conflict-Producing Instructions (Percentage) [36]

Frequently	27
On occasion	17
Infrequently	17
Frequency not determinable	22
Never	17
TOTAL	100

(N=23)

The table shows that 83% of the workers reported that they do receive instructions from their superiors that conflict with their own views, more or less frequently, whereas only 17% said that this has never happened. Several points should be noted here. First, the study does not specify the areas in which these conflict-producing orders are located. The researcher comments only that, in general, these conflicts pertain to the regulations for processing welfare grants. Second, the Orchard County welfare department is a public welfare agency under the jurisdictions of state and local governments. This fact is reflected in the major organizational goals and in the qualifications of the personnel. The major purpose of the agency is to provide services and economic assistance to clients, "but there has been a trend away from mere financial support and limited services."[37] The data show that the dominant organizational goal perceived as important by members is service to clients, with emphasis on the rehabilitation of welfare recipients. Third, of the twenty-three workers who make up the membership of the welfare office, only three have had graduate training in social work, and only the director holds a Master of Arts degree. Finally, it is of some interest to note that in comparison with a sample of school teachers in the same study, the social workers felt the pressure of conflict-producing instructions much more than did the teachers. Forty percent of the teachers studied reported that they never experienced such conflict, and of the 60% who reported having received orders from their superiors that were incompatible with their own views, no one said that this had occurred frequently.

The findings mentioned above indicate that even though the

agency under study was not highly professionalized (in terms of its main goal and its personnel), conflict produced by superiors' orders, as perceived by the workers, was frequent.

The study was not directly concerned with the effects of supervisor-worker conflict upon the relation of the worker with the client. However, when workers were asked what they did in response to such conflict-producing instructions, 82% of the respondents said they would comply with their superiors' orders although they did not agree with them, and only 18% said they would not carry them out and would react by evasion, modification, or open rejection.[38]

The finding of Peabody's study, that in most cases of conflict social workers, nevertheless, carry out the bureaucracy-oriented orders of their superiors, is confirmed by another study, conducted within a completely different setting, i.e. "among professionally trained social caseworkers in voluntary social casework agencies with high professional standards."[39] The study concerned two such agencies in Massachusetts: one, a child protective agency, specializing in the provision of family casework services on behalf of children who are neglected or abused by their parents, and who are referred to the agency by persons outside their families; the second, a family counseling agency, specializing in the provision of counseling services to families and adults who come to the agency voluntarily, seeking help with interpersonal problems. This study assumed that the social worker is involved, and must cope with conflicting expectations of four subsystems: client needs, professional standards, agency policies, and community expectations. The 110 respondents were asked how they thought these various conflicts should be resolved by the worker. It was found that workers in both agencies were primarily oriented to carrying out agency policies; next, adhering to professional standards; then meeting client needs; and last, living up to community expectations. The prevalence of bureaucratic orientations among workers is surprising in view of the fact that as compared, for example, with the Orchard County welfare agency mentioned above, the two agencies studied by Billingsley were much more professionalized, both in regard to their major functions, and the qualifications of their members. All forty-nine respondents in the family agency had Master's degrees in social work, and of the sixty-one workers in the protective agency, fifty had Master's degrees, and six others had at least one year of graduate education in social work.

The above finding was further reinforced by classifying the respondents according to their relatively strong commitment to the policies and procedures of the agency, which was considered a "bureaucratic orientation," and a relatively high commitment to the standards and values of the profession, which was termed a "professional orientation."

Percentage of Respondents Exhibiting Bureaucratic and Professional Orientations[40]

Agency	Number	Percentage Bureaucratic	Percentage Professional	Total
Family	49	61	39	100
Supervisors	10	80	20	100
Case Workers	39	56	44	100
Protective	61	62	38	100
Supervisors	20	60	40	100
Caseworkers	41	63	37	100

Billingsley claims that two major reasons account for the fact that social workers exhibit a different orientation pattern from other professional workers. First, social work education has a historical relationship to agencies, and second, that unlike some other professions, social casework is practiced primarily within agency settings. "Thus both the socialization processes and the mechanisms of social control available to the agencies are stronger than those available to the law office and the lawyer, or the hospital and the physician. Because social casework is tied to the agency, a bureaucratic orientation seems functional."[41]

However, the author does not consider another fact which is revealed by the data (see table above), that notwithstanding the fact that a large percentage of supervisors as well as case workers have a bureaucratic orientation, there still remains a great discrepancy between the workers' orientations and those of their supervisors. Supervisors in the Family Agency are more bureaucratically oriented (80%) than caseworkers (56%); or, in other words, caseworkers are more professionally oriented (44%) than supervisors (20%). This relationship between position and orientation does not hold in the Protective Agency in which the differences between supervisors and caseworkers, regarding each orientation, are very small (3%). One possible explanation of the divergence in the distribution of professional and bureaucratic orientations between supervisors and case workers in the two agencies is that the Protective Agency is by definition more bureaucratic, since it deals with law enforcement and with clients who do not apply voluntarily. By comparison, the discrepancy between the orientations of supervisors and caseworkers in the professionalized Family Agency is much greater.

The above cited studies have shown that orientations and evaluations of supervisors and practitioners, regarding role performance, are frequently incompatible. This fact, coupled with the workers' aspirations to autonomy, may engender feelings of insecurity, dissatisfaction, frustration, or even hostility on part of the worker. In turn, this tension in the supervisor-worker relationship may be reflected in the worker-client relationship in some way or other. Very little empirical data are available concerning the nature of the consequences of supervisor-worker conflict for the worker-client relationship. One study that bears on the problem is Blau's research conducted in a public welfare agency that explored the consequences of bureaucratic constraints for workers' orientations toward recipients of public assistance.[42]

Since bureaucratic pressures are, in large part, transmitted to workers through their supervisors, the study examined their impact by comparing the orientations of workers under supervisors who stressed strict adherence to official procedures, with those under supervisors who interpreted procedures more liberally. Workers were classified as being mainly oriented toward eligibility checking (bureaucratic orientation), or toward

providing some casework services (service orientation). Of the
workers under "liberal" supervisors, 61% exhibited a service
orientation, whereas only 24% of the workers under procedure-
oriented supervisors were so oriented. In other words, workers
under strict bureaucratic supervision tended to be more rigid
and "ritualistic"[43] in their dealings with clients, and defined
their role responsibilities more narrowly.

In another study on two welfare agencies, Blau and Scott
found that

> "Authoritarian practices by the supervisor adversely affected work
> satisfaction, the willingness to assume responsibility, and the
> tendency to extend casework service to clients. But in contrast to
> the findings obtained in other types of organizations, authoritarian
> supervision did not lower productivity in the two welfare
> agencies."[44]

It seems that close supervision impinges mainly upon the
ability and readiness of the social worker to adapt, in a flexible
manner, his knowledge and resources in terms of the special
problems posed by each case. Initiative and flexibility are
particularly important in the human-relations, helping professions, in which categorization of clients according to prede-
fined, bureaucratic rules interferes with effective service. In the
study on supervision carried out by the Western New York
Chapter of NASW,[45] the one aspect of supervision that was
most frequently mentioned by respondents as objectionable was
"limitations on initiative." One executive, when asked to
comment on the existing supervisory system, said,

> "This tight supervision concept spawns weaklings and produces more
> insecure, unhappy, dependent, and consequently ineffective social
> workers. . . . This kind of system enhances mediocrity and our
> leaders will probably come from other professions where full,
> imaginative thinking is not stifled in this threatened and threatening
> relationship called supervision."[46]

To conclude, studies on supervision in social work show that
in spite of the fact that social workers tend to adhere to
organizational rules more than most full-fledged professionals,

their perceptions of their tasks and their orientations toward clients, and those of their supervisors—representing the bureaucratic structure and its demands—are often incongruent.

An autocratic disposition on part of the supervisor may be "transferred" by the worker into his relationship with the client. On the other hand, a more collegial and democratic style of supervision will result in a more flexible and understanding orientation toward clients.[47] In any case, close, personal supervision, of the kind exercised in social work, is liable to create feelings of insecurity and inadequacy on the part of the worker which are not conducive to the types of attitude and activity necessary for producing motivational and behavioral change in clients.

The Nature of the Clientele

Finally, we want to deal with another factor which impinges upon the client-worker relationship, and consequently upon the ability of the worker to produce change in the client, namely, the special characteristics of the clientele of social work. As compared to the knowledge-base, the ethics, the prestige, and the degree of autonomy of the professional, the nature of the clientele is not one of the inherent properties of the profession. However, professions in general, and the helping-professions in particular, deal with people who are in trouble—the deviant, the poor, the disabled—and, to quote Merton,

> "clients are normally in a state of anxiety when they do seek out a professional. Concerned with troubles important to them, clients cannot easily remain emotionally detached, for involvement in a contingent situation where the outcome matters is an excellent generator of anxiety. This condition has important consequences for the emergence of ambivalence toward a profession. . . . Affective involvement with the problem and uncertainty about its outcome thus help to account both for the disproportionate esteem sometimes accorded the professions and for the sometimes disproportionate distrust and hostility."[48]

Merton emphasizes that his analysis is restricted to structural sources of ambivalence that are common to the professions as a whole. He suggests, however, that ambivalence toward a profession will differ according to the degree to which it is prophylactic or preventive, preparatory, remedial, or therapeutic.[49] Although he does not say so, it can be speculated that the ambivalence, distrust, and hostility of the client will be most intense in cases of the remedial-therapeutic professions, i.e those who attempt to help people with their troubles after they have arisen, of which social work is a notable example.

The welfare client shares with clients of other professions the basic situation of being in trouble and in need of help. However, his situation is distinguished from theirs in certain important aspects. A person who is unable to support himself and his family, is regarded by the public as responsible for his situation. Hence, to be dependent on public assistance imputes stigma, and is damaging to the moral and social identity of the individual. It is true that in certain more liberal circles of our society, and especially among professional groups, the welfare client, the mentally ill, or even certain types of delinquents are not held wholly responsible for their "deviance." Their situation and activities are explained by, and assigned to social conditions, and are not viewed as the deliberate choice of the individual himself. Professionals, in particular, are not supposed to impute stigma in any case. However, "the man-in-the-street" still views the situation of "the poor" as being basically the consequence of their own inadequacies and motivations. This attitude is an expression of the deep-rooted tradition of the Protestant Ethic, in its later development, with strong emphasis on individual responsibility and achievement.

If we compare the sick person with the welfare client, it is obvious that the patient is usually viewed as the victim of objective contingencies, such as inheritance or accidents, and is not blamed for his situation. His deviance is tolerated by others, though only so long as he is a "good patient" who tries, with the help of the doctor, to return to normal.[50] By comparison, the welfare client is implicitly, or partially, blamed for his deviation. This is reflected, for example, in the fact that many more people are legally eligible for public welfare than those who are actually receiving it.[51] This is often due to ignorance on the part of potential recipients, but also to the fact that people are ashamed to ask for welfare even if they know that they are formally eligible.

In an interesting article, Freidson claims that the assumption of a deviant role or career by an individual is frequently reinforced by a process of public labeling, imputation of stigma, and visible segregation from the community; "the process may be said to be deviance-producing in that, by labeling the individual, it may organize the responses of the community toward him as a stereotyped deviant."[52] In addition, the demand on the individual to accept special treatment by special control agencies and institutions such as mental hospitals, prisons, and clinics for the handicapped

> "stimulates the community to organize its response to the individual, to a degree segregating him by those special responses and encouraging him to behave the way the community has come to expect him to behave—to accept the role of the blind man, the village idiot, or the cripple. In this, the 'treatment' process may be said to create organized or stereotypical behavior, [and] ... to organize and stabilize deviant behavior into special roles, rather than eradicate it."[53]

Though Freidson refers mainly to deviance that is more immediately visible, such as mental illness, blindness, and other physical handicaps, his analysis applies to welfare clients as well. The welfare client is labeled by the community and by the agencies with which he is in contact; he is stigmatized to a greater or lesser degree by various groups in society, and he is segregated from the rest of the community by living in certain residential areas.

Comparing the prevailing attitudes in socializing organizations (such as schools), with those of treatment organizations in general, Meyer writes,

> "the clientele of treatment organizations are perceived as deviant or ill, as not moving along normal developmental gradients, and as insufficiently motivated to abandon socially disapproved roles and learn acceptable conventional ones. ... Public attitudes toward treatment organizations reflect this valuation, often producing adverse sentiments and fears accompanied by the demand for punitive and repressive controls. ... The belief that deviance is

intentional persists, and hence rehabilitative goals of treatment organizations are more precarious than custodial, punitive, and educational goals."[54]

Our main interest, in this context, is not the community orientation toward welfare clients per se, but the ways in which it is reflected in the social worker's attitude toward the client, and in the image the client holds of himself. We may assume that the worker's attitude toward the client is initially accepting and permissive, rather than condemning and punitive. However, this is the case only on condition that the client shows that he is motivated to change in the direction assigned by the worker. Clients are required to exhibit their "good intentions," to cooperate with the worker, and to comply with his directives. If a client does not comply, he is labeled as "difficult," "hard to reach," and the like. In such cases it seems likely that the worker's initial permissive attitude toward the client will change into a more authoritative, controlling orientation.

As for the client, the stigma attached to his position by the community, and the worker's demands to change his behavior in accordance with accepted patterns, affect his orientation toward the worker and the agency. The client usually views society and its institutions as the cause of his troubles, and the worker as representing these institutions. This again differentiates the welfare client from the patient, and makes the acceptance of the social worker's suggestions, advice, and prescriptions much more difficult. The client's trust in the professional is a very important factor in their relationship. Social workers do not directly "live off"[55] their particular clients' troubles, as many other professionals do, so that in this case the mistrust does not stem from suspecting the professional's "self-interest." Nevertheless, the very fact that most social workers are employees of public organizations undermines the client's confidence that the worker will subordinate all other interests to the welfare of the client. Thus, it is not uncommon that when a worker tells the client, "I want to help you," the client thinks or says, "You just want to get me off the rolls."

Of course, the degree of ambivalence, mistrust, or hostility varies among different types of clients, and within different organizational settings, but these feelings constitute a general problem generated by the objective position of the client, his social definition, and his almost complete dependency upon the social worker.

Vinter describes the client's situation, and the possible reactions to it, thus:

> "Permanency of lower status, exclusion from decision-making, and application of powerful sanctions are circumstances (stated in extreme form) usually regarded as unattractive in other areas of life. Customary responses to these conditions are alienation and disaffection, withdrawal, submissive dependency, or covert rebellion. None of these responses is considered desirable for the effective use of social services, yet all are evidenced in various degrees among agency clientele. Non-participation and drop-outs from the leisure-time services, non-returns to the family casework agencies, and 'prisonization' and covert hostility in the correctional setting, are familiar phenomena. Furthermore, it is well known that many persons and groups who may need the services most are often least willing to become clients."[56]

Our discussion indicates, again, that the combination of financial assistance and casework in public welfare is detrimental to the inducement of motivational and behavioral change in clients. The client comes to the agency with the "wrong" motivation; his expectations are, more or less, incompatible with those of the organization and the worker. Casework is cast upon him without his consent, and his ambivalence and suspicions are intensified by the demands made upon him by the worker to change his behavior, as an exchange for economic assistance which is his legal right. Thus, there seems to be a strong case for those advocating the segregation of income maintenance from casework services, and for implementing the first task in an impersonal, routine manner.

In this discussion we have also tried to point out the repercussions of the main properties of social work as a semi-profession upon the social worker's role performance and role relations with the client. The relatively low prestige accorded to social work, the nature of its knowledge-base, the type of organizational structure in which it is performed, its code of ethics, and the characteristics of its clientele explain the great difficulties of the profession, as it is structured at present, to function effectively as a mechanism of social control.

Concluding Remarks

In this part we have presented the main theoretical arguments supporting our proposition that the worker-client dyadic relationship is inadequate as a change-inducing mechanism for welfare clients. The power that the worker commands in relation to this client has been classified into four types: coercive, instrumental, social, and normative. It was suggested that the functioning of mechanisms through which social and normative power are generally exerted, i.e. identification and internalization, are inhibited in the welfare client-social worker encounter. It was also noted that the combination of types of power in the worker's role and their activation in the interaction with the same client may produce superficial change without lasting effects. Research data indicate that social workers tend to exercise influence upon clients through mechanisms related to social power. However, no empirical evidence is available concerning the consequences of this process.

Finally, we linked the semi-professional attributes of social work discussed in earlier chapters with the ability of the worker to effect change in clients. The analysis suggested that the present nature and characteristics of social work lessen the capacity of the worker to induce change through the casework relationship.

Notes

1. "Influence" is one type of control. It will be used mainly in relation to social and normative power, whereas "control" will be used in relation to instrumental and coercive power. It is sometimes not possible to make a complete distinction between the two as for example in the case of influence based on prestige, for prestige may in turn be associated with other sources of control, such as, instrumental power.

2. See, for example, Solomon E. Asch, "Studies in the Principles of Judgements and Attitudes: II. Determination of Judgements by Groups and by Ego-Standards," Journal of Social Psychology 12 (1940): 433-465; Ronald Lippitt, Norman Polansky, Fritz Redl, and Sidney Rosen, "The Dynamics of Power," and Alvin F. Zander, J. I. Hurwitz, and B. Hymovitch, "Some Effects of Power on the Relation Among Group Members," both in Dorwin Cartwright and Alvin F. Zander, eds., *Group Dynamics: Research and Theory* (Evanston, Ill.: Row, Peterson and Company, 1953), pp. 462-482, 483-492; Kurt W. Back, "The Exertion of Influence through Social Communication," Journal of Abnormal and Social Psychology 46 (1951): 9-23; George C. Homans, *Social Behavior,* ch. 5.

3. National Opinion Research Center, "Jobs and Occupations: A Popular Evaluation," in Reinhard Bendix and Seymour M. Lipset, eds., *Class, Status and Power* (New York: Free Press, 1953), pp. 411-426. See also Albert J. Reiss, Jr. et al., Occupations and Social Status (New York: Free Press, 1961), pp. 59-82.

4. R. Clyde White, "Prestige of the Social Worker," Social Work Journal 36 (January 1955): 21.

5. Emma Y. Meyerson, "The Social Work Image and Self-Image," Social Work 4 (July 1959): 70.

6. Norman Polansky, "Social Workers in Society: Results of a Sampling Study," Social Work Journal 34 (April 1953): 74-80. See also R. Clyde White, "Social Workers in Society: Some Further Evidence," Social Work Journal 34 (October 1953): 161-164.

7. Polansky, "Social Workers in Society," p. 77.

8. Alfred Kadushin, "Prestige of Social Work—Facts and Factors," p. 40. Italics added.

9. Babcock, "Social Work as Work," p. 416.

10. A. Kadushin, "Prestige of Social Work," p. 41.

11. Ibid., p. 42.

12. Ibid., p. 43.

13. Elliot Freidson, "Dilemmas in the Doctor-Patient Relationship," in Arnold M. Rose, ed., *Human Behavior and Social Processes* (Boston: Houghton Mifflin Company, 1962), p. 219.

14. For a survey and critique of this type of studies see, Katz and Lazarsfeld, *Personal Influence,* pp. 66-72.

15. Charles Kadushin, "Social Distance Between Client and Professional," American Journal of Sociology 67 (March 1962): 517.

16. See Part III, Chapter 7.

17. See, for example, Charles F. Gosser, "Local Residents as Mediators Between Middle-Class Professional Workers and Low-Class Clients," Social Service Review 40 (March 1966): 56-63; Perry Levinson and Jeffrey Schiller, "Role Analysis of the Indigenous Nonprofessional," Social Work 11 (July 1966): 95-101; Williard C. Richman, "A Theoretical Scheme for Determining Roles of Professional and Non-Professional Personnel," Social Work 6 (October 1961): 25-30. For an overview of recruiting and employing local nonprofessional workers in various disciplines, see Robert Reiff and Frank Riessman, The Indigenous Non-Professional, Report 3 (New York: National Institute for Labor Education), pp. 44-48.

18. See Hans O. Mauksch, "The Organizational Context of Nursing Practice," in Fred Davis, ed., *The Nursing Professions: Five Sociological Essay* (New York: John Wiley and Sons, 1966), pp. 109-137.

19. Talcott Parsons, *The Social System,* p. 441.

20. It seems that length of education, by itself, does not account for the amount of prestige granted to an occupation by the public. The study by White, conducted on a sample of social workers with graduate education, found that they think that the prestige of engineers, pilots, and ministers is higher than theirs, and that of school teachers and accountants is equal to theirs, in spite of the fact that not many teachers and engineers go beyond the bachelor's degree, and pilots and accountants have no graduate education at all. He comments, "The kind of learning which social workers acquire seems not yet to have great prestige in itself." See White, "Prestige of the Social Worker," p. 22.

21. Coleman, for example, notes that psychiatrists tend to exploit the preseige value of their medical sanctions. See Jules V. Coleman, Distinguishing Between Psychotherapy and Casework," Journal of Social Casework 30 (June 1949): 244-251.

22. Alfred Kadushin, "Prestige of Social Work," p. 42.

23. Carl R. Rogers, "The Characteristics of a Helping Relationship," in Warren G. Bennis, Edgar H. Schein, David E. Berlew, and Fred J. Steele, eds., *Interpersonal Dynamics* (Chicago: Dorsey Press, 1964), p. 319.

24. Manford H. Kuhn, "The Interview and the Professional Relationship," p. 203.

25. "Code of Ethics," adopted by the Delegate Assembly of the

National Association of Social Workers, October 13, 1960, *Encyclopedia of Social Work* (1966), p. 1027.

26. Bylaws of the National Association of Social Workers, adopted by membership referendum, June 1, 1963, p. 7.

27. See Parsons' critical analysis of "self-interest" versus "disinterestedness" as a distinguishing property between the professions and other occupations, "The Professions and Social Structures."

28. Piliavin, "Restructuring Social Services," p. 35. To solve this problem Piliavin suggests substituting the present organization of service for the private entrepreneurial model.

29. Wilensky and Lebeaux, *Industrial Society and Social Welfare,* pp. 233-235.

30. "Working Definition of Social Work Practice," Social Work 3 (April 1958): 85.

31. See Part I, Chapters 2 and 3.

32. Scott Briar, "The Casework Predicament," p. 10.

33. See the discussion of this factor in Chapter 3.

34. For example, Sample Index for a Welfare Advocates Manual, The Birth of the Movement: June 30, 1966, and Round-Up of June 30th Welfare Demonstrations (Washington, D.C.: Poverty/Rights Action Center).

35. Robert L. Peabody, *Organizational Authority.*

36. Ibid., p. 105.

37. Ibid., p. 66.

38. Ibid., Table 7, p. 107.

39. Andrew Billingsley, "Bureaucratic and Professional Orientation Patterns in Social Casework," Social Service Review 38 (December 1964): 401.

40. Ibid., p. 403.

41. Ibid., p. 404.

42. Blau, "Orientations Toward Clients."

43. Merton, "Bureaucratic Structure and Personality."

44. Blau and Scott, *Formal Organizations,* p. 163. For studies analyzing the effects of different styles of supervision in industry, see, for example, Michael Argyle, Godfrey Gardner, and Frank Cioffi, "Supervisory Methods Related to Productivity, Absenteeism, and Labor Turnover," Human Relations 11 (February 1958): 23-40; Robert L. Kahn and Daniel Katz, "Leadership Practices in Relation to Productivity and Morale," in Dorwin Cartwright and Alvin Zander, eds., *Group Dynamics,* pp. 612-628. The general effects of leadership types on group members are examined by Malcolm G. Preston and Roy K. Heintz, "Effects of Participatory Vs. Supervisory Leadership on Group Judgement," and Ralph White and Ronald Lippitt, "Leadership Behavior and Member

Reaction in Three Social Climates," both in Cartwright and Zander, eds., *Group Dynamics,* pp. 573-584, 585-611.

45. "Opinions on Supervision: A Chapter Study," p. 21.

46. Ibid., p. 25.

47. See Blau, "Orientations Toward Clients."

48. Robert K. Merton and Elinor Barber, "Sociological Ambivalence," in Edward A. Tiryakian, ed., *Sociological Theory, Values, and Sociocultural Change* (New York: Harper and Row, 1967), p. 108.

49. Ibid., p. 106.

50. Parsons, *The Social System,* pp. 297-321.

51. For example, see Cloward and Piven, "A Strategy to End Poverty." They report that in New York City in 1959, the average monthly total of residents receiving assistance was 325,771, but according to the 1960 census, 716,000 persons lived on income at, or below the prevailing eligibility levels.

52. Elliot Freidson, "Disability as Social Deviance," in Marvin B. Sussman, ed., *Sociology and Rehabilitation* (American Sociological Association, 1966), p. 85. Concerning the problem of labeling, see also Edwin M. Lemert, *Human Deviance, Social Problems, and Social Control* (Englewood Cliffs, N.J.: Prentice-Hall, 1967); Ohlin and Lawrence, "Social Interaction Among Clients," p. 11; and Stanton Wheeler and Leonard S. Cottrell, Jr., *Juvenile Delinquency: Its Prevention and Control* (New York: Russell Sage Foundation, 1966), pp. 22-27.

53. Freidson, "Disability as Social Deviance," p. 87.

54. Henry J. Meyer, Eugene Litwak, Edwin J. Thomas, and Robert D. Vinter, "Social Work and Social Welfare," in Paul F. Lazarsfeld, William H. Sewell, and Harold L. Wilensky, eds., *The Uses of Sociology* (New York: Basic Books, 1967), p. 171.

55. Merton and Barber, "Sociological Ambivalence," p. 113.

56. Robert D. Vinter, "The Social Structure of Service," pp. 266-267.

It has been suggested at the beginning of this study to substitute working with groups of clients for the current predominant casework method in social work. This change of the basic structure of the worker-client relationship seems to us feasible, and also the most promising way through which social work's effectiveness in producing normative and behavioral change in clients can be enhanced.

This proposition is based on the fundamental sociological approach

> "that the behavior, attitudes, beliefs, and values of the individual are all firmly grounded in the groups to which he belongs. How aggressive or co-operative a person is, how much self-respect and self confidence he has, how energetic and how productive his work is, what he aspires to, what he believes to be true and good, whom he loves or hates, and what beliefs and prejudices he holds—all these characteristics are highly determined by the individual's group

Part III

INFLUENCE AND CHANGE

THROUGH SOCIAL GROUP WORK

memberships. In a real sense, they are properties of groups and of the relationships between people. Whether they change or resist change will, therefore, be greatly influenced by the nature of these groups. Attempts to change them must be concerned with the dynamics of groups."*

We shall first describe some of the prevalent approaches in group work, their origin and their bearing on practice. Subsequently, these problems will be critically examined in view of our approach to group work as a method through which the achievement of social work's main objectives can be enhanced. The following chapter will analyze the structure and dynamics of small groups and their relevance to the process of influence and its acceptance by group members.

*Dorwin Cartwright, "The Group as a Medium of Change," in Cartwright and Zander, eds., *Group Dynamics,* p. 387.

Chapter 6

SOME ISSUES IN SOCIAL GROUP WORK

The idea of treating clients not one-by-one but in groups is of course not new to the practice of social work. Group work practitioners are now serving in a wide range of agencies and programs, and the distinctive knowledge and skills needed for group work practice are part of the curricula of graduate schools of social work.

We shall briefly describe the evolution of group work as a method of social work practice, and the ways in which the historical development of this subfield, and its relation to casework, have shaped the contemporary approaches and practices of group work. Special attention will be devoted to current controversies and debates among group workers concerning the definition, purposes, and techniques of their role. These different trends and approaches in group work refer to such issues as therapy versus education, the enhancement of self-awareness versus learning; the emphasis on the individual in the group versus the group as a whole, the growth-oriented versus the task-oriented group, and so on.

From Movement to Profession

Historically, casework as a distinct discipline of social work first adopted Freudian psychoanalysis as its major scientific

161

knowledge base, while group work, which developed later, was influenced by a variety of behavioral sciences such as sociology, progressive education, group dynamics, and anthropology:

> "Group work as *a method of social work* is only a recent concept. Originally it was conceived of as a movement, a way of democratic action and a part of several fields of social services. Foremost among these were informal education, youth services, recreation, camping, the labor movement, settlement houses and community centers."[1]

In the 1930s, when the emphasis of casework shifted almost entirely to individual therapy, "The prospect of the 'normal' client was completely antipathic to the development of social work as a therapeutic profession."[2] So were other characteristics of group work, such as its basic informal approach to service, its emphasis on self-help and voluntary participation, its action-orientation, and its concern with environmental and social factors.[3]

However, after World War II, a process of rapprochement between group work and casework started to develop. At that period, as has been noted earlier, casework became more aware of the social environment and interpersonal group processes as factors affecting individual personality and behavior, and incorporated many concepts of the social sciences.[4] Group workers, on the other hand, were seeking to attain a more specific professional identity, or to quote Schwartz, were looking for a "reference group."

The turning point in the identification of group work with social work came in the mid 1940s, and has sometimes been linked with the name of Grace Longwell Coyle.[5] At the National Conference of Social Work in 1946, Coyle spoke for the American Association for the Study of Group Work (established in 1936); she said, "One baffling problem has plagued the development of professional consciousness among group workers over this decade. It is usually phrased in terms of alignment, and a dilemma is presented. We must, it seems, be either educators or social workers."[6] And she concluded,

> "Casework, group work, and community organization have this common factor, that they are all based on understanding human

relations. While the specific relations used in each are different, the underlying philosophy and approach are the same: a respect for personality and a belief in democracy. . . . It is for this reason that I believe group work as a method falls within the larger scope of social work as a method."[7]

This resolution was accepted by the American Association of Group Workers, but it took another decade until the AAGW formally became part of the National Association of Social Workers in 1956.

Group work had the potential of bringing the "social" back into social work, or to be more precise into social casework, and it did so to a certain degree. However, the exchange between the two fields of social work was not even; group work tended to disengage itself from its broader theoretical and professional connections, and to accept the original individualistic orientation of casework. This was an expression of the general trend toward professionalization, and of the aspiration of group workers to achieve professional status. Casework was then, and it is at present, the most professionalized and the most prestigious subfield in social work. In order to become a profession instead of a movement, populated mainly by volunteers, group workers had to define their function and techniques in a more formal, accurate, and specific fashion.[8] This they did at first, by adopting the existing philosophy and methodology of casework. Some objections were, nevertheless, raised against this trend in the development of group work:

"Social group work has found a comfortable professional family in social work . . . though who adopted whom is occasionally a question. . . . The younger member of the profession relied on social casework for many of its concepts. But the psychoanalytic view of the individual adapts poorly to the group, and its explanations by no means always consort with observed group facts."[9]

Although the glamor and superiority of casework, especially in its psychiatric connotation, overshadowed the younger conceptualization and humbler origins of group work, this field gained substantial support from the postwar increase of small group research, especially by social-psychologists such as Festinger, Lewin, Lippit, and Mayo. Kaiser, as well as other prominent and dedicated group workers, urged their colleagues to overcome their "inferiority complex" in relation to case-work, and to develop their own unique contribution to the profession as a whole: "Group workers often feel like 'poor relations' in the family of social work practitioners, but instead of feeling resentment toward our sibling, casework, let us emulate her where this will deepen our insights and skills and let us develop the special methods which pertain to the helping process through the medium of group interaction and participa-tion."[10]

The Controversy about the Primary Purpose of Social Group Work

Thus, accompanying the realization of the convergence of certain basic values and goals of the different subfields in social work, and the application of group work as a special method in various settings, a renewed tendency to define the distinct characteristics of group work has emerged. Group work, like any other professional discipline, was confronted with the problem of clarifying and defining its distinct functions and goals. On the conceptual level, group work attempted to integrate elements of the individual-psychological as well as the interpersonal-sociological orientations:

> "To understand human behavior fully, the knowledge acquired from the fields of psychology, psychiatry, and medicine must be integrated with interaction theories on relationship, group process, and the influences of cultural patterns of behavior. Group and intergroup theory formulations, for their part, rest on knowledge derived from social psychology, sociology, and anthropology . . . there is a beginning evidence of the gradual convergence of these two interests. . . . It also becomes apparent that to understand an individual fully, he must be viewed in his social interaction with others. Conversely, full understanding of group process requires depth understanding of the dynamics of the individual as well as the group as a whole."[11]

On a more pragmatic level, the purpose of group work was defined as a synthesis between therapy related to personality growth and adjustment, and the wider institutional goal of maintaining a democratic society. Defining group work in the context of the various professional fields that aim at the development of "social skills," Coyle writes:

> "Group work's special contribution lies perhaps in its focus on the individual within the group and its use of psychiatric concepts in the attempt to understand his behavior; and in its social frame of reference which sees as essential and complementary both the growth and fulfilment of individuals and the creation of social change toward a more democratic society."[12]

And, in 1949, a committee of the American Association of Group Workers published a report entitled "Definition of the Function of the Group Worker," which includes the following statements:

> "The objectives of the group worker include provision for personal growth according to individual capacity and need. . . . Through his experience he aims to produce those relations with other groups and the wider community which contribute to responsible citizenship, mutual understanding between cultural, religious, economic or special groupings in the community, and a participation in the constant improvement of our society toward democratic goals."[13]

There are many more similar definitions of social group work in the professional literature; let us quote just one more that expresses the combination of the psychological and the societal goals of group work. Sullivan defines group work as "a method by which the group worker enables various types of groups to function in such a way that both group interaction and program activities contribute to the growth of the individual and the achievement of desirable social goals."[14]

Many writers on group work theory and practice have realized that the formal broad definitions of social group work are too comprehensive and that further classifications of purposes, techniques, skills, and types of groups are needed. This has been underscored, for example, by Hollis and Taylor:

"The concept of group work as an educational process aiming at the development and social adjustment of individuals through voluntary group association is imperfectly understood even within the profession. Here there seems to be a need for greater classification of the distinction between group work as a therapeutic device closely related in objectives and criteria to casework, group work as a method of assisting people to work together and as such closely allied to community organization, and group work as a process having some separate and wider objectives and techniques of its own."[15]

The recognition of the varied nature of group work practice led Wilson to suggest a distinction between "social group work" and "work with groups":

"we propose that the distinction between work with groups and social group work may be made on the basis of the following assumption: the distinction is to be found in the difference between the nature of the task-oriented group as compared to that of the growth-oriented group. In the former the group enabler's primary responsibility is to support the group to accomplish its task; in the latter, the enabler's primary responsibility is to help members use the group experience to resolve problems which are interfering with their personal growth and social adjustment."[16]

It should be noticed that the above distinction is not widely accepted by group workers, mainly because it indicates that task-oriented groups do not fall within the province of social group work. Konopka for example, suggests another classification, that between therapy groups, i.e. growth-oriented groups, and social-action-oriented groups. Both types of groups are considered by her to be within the realm of social group work, though she notes that a more refined system of classifying groups served by social group workers is still lacking.[17]

A related controversial issue is the question whether the client of social group work is primarily the individual in the group, or the group as a whole. Some regard the group as a means through which the worker can achieve individual treatment goals.[18] Others, by contrast, view the group and its experience as the crucial focus for the worker, and the individual members as growing essentially through their group-oriented efforts to accomplish the group's purpose.[19]

However, these two approaches to the group and its use in social work are not mutually exclusive. In this respect Coffey's distinction between "psyche group process" and "socio group process" is relevant. The purpose of the psyche group is to satisfy the emotional needs of group members, whereas the socio group's objective is to reach the visualized goal of the group. He notes that these two types "do not represent a true dichotomy, but rather separate ends of a continuum of group process."[20]

The democratic-action orientation, expressed in the general definitions of the goals of group work, is another aspect which is not shared by all group workers to the same degree. This is partly related to the varied origins of practitioners in the field, and their different commitments. Thus, "Practitioners from the traditional field of informal education and recreation feared that the concern with mental hygiene and the focus on therapy would detract from the valuable use of the group work method to help citizen action and services to normal youth."[21]

On the other hand, younger and more professionally ambitious group workers tended to emphasize their contribution to the established goal of social casework, i.e. the promotion of personality growth and adjustment, albeit through guided group experiences, and to reduce the identification of group work with recreation and leisure-time programs. This reminds one of the debate about social reform versus casework that accompanied the development of social work since the 1920s.

The aspiration to attain a distinct identity was promoted not only by diverse ideological orientations. As a group of professionals, group workers faced the danger of getting lost among the "host agencies" in which they worked, and among other professional disciplines; group workers are not happy that "Today, caseworkers in ever increasing numbers are serving clients directly in groups. It seems probable that in a few years, if present trends continue, we will more often find client groups being served by caseworkers than by group workers."[22] And Konopka writes, "It is distressing to see the haphazard way in which caseworkers rush into using the group. . . . A caseworker who wants to work with groups should learn the group work method."[23]

The fear of encroachment by other subfields, particularly by casework, can be understood in view of group work's historical development described earlier, and its present position in the framework of social work. Group work suffers from a chronic shortage of professional manpower. By 1958, group work constituted from eight to nine percent of all social work students. This represented an increase of nine percent in the enrollment of group work students in graduate schools of social work over one year.[24] Nevertheless, (1) total enrollment in the graduate schools of social work now barely exceeds the level attained in 1950; (2) group work enrollment increased in the past few years (1954-1958) but not in proportion to total enrollment in graduate schools of social work—total enrollment increased by twenty-nine percent while group work enrollment advanced only fifteen percent; (3) the gap between demand for trained group workers and available personnel is increasing rather than decreasing.[25] In 1960, group work agencies and programs (excluding recreation) still accounted for only nine percent of the total field of social work.[26] Thus, group work still encounters great problems of recruiting social work students and trained personnel, and represents, to a certain extent, a "profession without professionals."[27]

The oscillation between a rapprochement, or convergence, between group work and other social work disciplines, and a tendency to maintain a distinct professional identity, may well represent a general pattern in the process of integration and differentiation of professions. At the initial stage, when a newer professional specialty attempts to join an older more established profession, it emphasizes those functions, methods, and skills that are common to both. Later, after the new subfield has been accepted as a member of the broader profession, it will attempt to underscore its unique contribution, and the distinct knowledge and skills needed to render its specific functions.[28] The "ideal" stage of development of adjacent professional disciplines would be one in which there is, at the same time, a division of labor among subfields according to knowledge and areas of competence, and a fruitful collaboration and exchange between them.

Different Techniques Employed in Group Work

The debate about the purposes of social group work is at present still unresolved, and its content reflects the two major theoretical orientations—the individual-focused psychological, and the interpersonal sociological—that influenced group work during its development.

The controversy is concerned with such questions as: Is the purpose of group work mainly therapeutic or educational? Should its primary emphasis be on curing individual pathology, or "aimed at those faculties of the ego which are undisturbed by conflict?"[29] Furthermore, is group work mainly concerned with social conditions and the socialization of individuals, or does it aim at the resolution of unconscious conflicts within the individual and the restructuring of personality?[30]

These questions have direct implications for the specific methods to be applied in group work, beyond the fact that the worker interacts with more than one client at a time, and for the type and range of its clientele. The therapeutic or clinical approach limits the clientele of social group work to those individuals who suffer from problems of maladjustment and personal conflicts, and for whom group treatment is recommended. The nonclinical approach, on the other hand, virtually encompasses an unlimited variety of groups, from play groups to youth organizations and camps, to neighborhood centers, clubs, and classes, which undertake a wide range of activities.

Concerning the selection of methods in group work, if therapy is emphasized, the techniques to be used are those of psychotherapy in general; the expression of feelings is encouraged, anxieties and fears are brought to the surface and dealt with in group discussions, and, hopefully, group members will gain more self-awareness and new insights of their problems, and will be able to cope with them more rationally.[31] This type of group work includes the well-known concepts of psychotherapeutic treatment processes, such as transference, counter-transference, intrapsychic conflict, resistance, interpretation, and insight. This, however, does not imply that group therapy and social group work are merely different labels for the same thing, only that there are different trends and emphases in social group work. It is perhaps significant to note that those who warn social group workers not to confuse what they are doing with psychotherapy, are practitioners from the medical professions, in particular psychiatrists. Scheidlinger defines the tasks of the group worker, distinguishing them from those of the psychotherapist, thus: "the group worker is a carrier of social values and in this area will actively promote democratic attitudes and behavior patterns. In his educational role he may function as a teacher of skills, a leader of program, a mediator, an adviser, a limiter, and a friendly counselor. These aspects are largely absent in psychotherapy."[32]

On the other hand, the educational or socializational approach in group work emphasizes learning of new behavior patterns or modification of old ones, a fuller perception of the individual's behavior in relation to the behavior of others, and the improvement of his functioning in interpersonal relationships. In this sense the goals and methods of group work are similar to those of Training-Groups. T-Group programs conducted, for example, by the National Training Laboratory for Group Development at Bethel, Maine are implemented in a wide range of settings, such as industry and government. These programs are mainly engaged in "sensitivity training," i.e. the increase of sensitivity of group members to their own behavior, the actions of others, and the nature of group development. Sensitivity training, however, is not basically therapeutic in the sense described above:

"While there are many obvious similarities between T-Groups and therapy groups—in part because any effective education has therapeutic overtones—the T-Group differs in a number of important ways. It tends to utilize data about present behavior and its consequences rather than delving into genetic causes. It tends to deal with conscious and preconscious behavior rather than with unconscious motivation. The T-Group makes the important assumption that persons participating are well rather than ill."[33]

Obviously, the individual-psychological and the interpersonal-sociological approaches in group work are not mutually exclusive, either in theory or in practice. T-Group experience may enhance self-insight of participants,[34] and therapy-oriented treatment may result in the learning of new activities and the assumption of social roles. Nevertheless, greater emphasis on one or the other of these objectives is possible.

The debate about the primacy of the different purposes of group work is not merely academic. Since it has been accepted as a special method for attaining social work goals, group work has been increasingly practiced in a variety of agencies. Its particular nature depends, among other things, upon the setting in which it is carried out. It is geared to training, recreation, informal education, and socialization, in community centers, settlement houses, and youth-serving organizations; in hospitals, psychiatric settings, child guidance clinics, and casework agencies, it is more therapeutic and individual-centered.[35]

We shall now attempt to evaluate the opposing trends in group work, particularly the therapeutic and the educational approaches, in light of some theoretical concepts advanced in the field of adult education, sociology, and laboratory training. We shall also draw upon some research evidence in these spheres, and indicate its implications for social group work.

Some Implications for Social Group Work from Sociological Theory and Research

Regarding the controversy between therapeutically oriented group work and action-oriented group work, and the related debate about individual needs contrasted with group needs, some important insights may be gained from Bales' empirical studies on small group process, and Parsons' theoretical formulation of the four "functional prerequisites" of social systems.[36]

In his studies of small problem-solving groups, Bales hypothesized, and empirically confirmed, that groups working toward the goal of a group decision on a full-fledged problem, "tend to move in their interaction from a relative emphasis upon problems of *orientation,* to problems of *evaluation,* and subsequently to problems of *control,* and that concurrent with this [sic] transitions, the relative frequencies of both *negative reactions* and *positive reactions* tend to increase."[37] Orientation, evaluation, and control compose the "task area"; positive and negative reactions are in the "social-emotional area." The authors emphasize that empirically, different directions of phase movement may take place depending on different types of conditions and problems with which groups are confronted.

No particular phase of interaction can serve simultaneously, with maximum effectiveness, all the functional needs of the group as a social system. Activities in the task-area, that is, efforts to solve problems of orientation, evaluation, and control, are concomitant with differentiation of roles, authority, and rewards within the group. These processes of differentiation tend to impair the basic solidarity of the group. To deal with these expressive and integrative problems the group concentrates its efforts upon tension release and integrative activities, to enhance group cohesion and solidarity. This in turn, removes the group from task accomplishment, and hence, after a period of time activities will again be focused on task achievement, and so on, until the task has been accomplished.[38]

It may be argued, as Bales and Strodtbeck themselves do, that this action cycle occurs only under specific conditions and in groups that are working on joint problem-solving, and that the phase-movement model is not relevant to other types of groups, such as social work groups and therapy groups.

Let us assume for the moment that therapy groups are not engaged in collective task accomplishment, and have no group goal. Is Bales' model applicable to this type of group?

It was probably the same question that led Parsons and Bales to attempt the application of the phase-movement model of task-oriented groups to psychotherapy and socialization as special cases of social control processes.

They write,

"We feel there is an important relationship between the phases, i.e., changes in pattern of action over time, of a task-oriented group, the phases of the psychotherapeutic [more generally, social control] process, and those of the process of socialization. The essential principle of the relationship is that both therapy and socialization involve the same basic phases as task-performance, but *in reverse order.*"[39]

Parsons has previously worked out a paradigm of social control with special reference to the psychotherapeutic relationship in which four components appear in broad sequential order.[40] The relationship begins with a "permissive" attitude on the part of the psychotherapist in which the patient is allowed to express his feelings freely, and to deviate to some extent from patterns of behavior which would "normally" be expected from him. The second element is "support" which gives the patient a feeling of security, and of being part in a basically solidary relationship. Permissiveness and support, however, have to be limited if control is to be accomplished. One form of such restriction is the third element, namely, "denial of reciprocity." The therapist (or more generally the agent of control) will refuse to reciprocate the patient's dependence, domination, hostility, and the like. The fourth component is that of "manipulation of rewards" in which rewards (particularly relational rewards) will be given or withheld in accordance with the patient's behavior and attitudes. These components of the mechanisms of control were found (after a certain amount of rearrangement and theoretical interpretation) to correspond in broad lines to the phase movement of task-oriented groups.[41]

The phase-movement model was later applied to an empirical study of the process of psychotherapy, in which the authors found that

"the patterning of therapist behavior over the life (or early life) of therapy was indeed similar to that of the participants in the problem-solving groups studied by Bales. . . . Therapist behavior characterized as orientation (asking for and giving information clarifications, and confirmations) decreases through the first fifty hours of therapy, while evaluative behavior (asking for and giving opinions, evaluations, analyses, and expression of feeling) increases and then appears to reach a plateau."[42]

The point is, that no matter which type of group social work is concerned with, whether a therapeutically oriented group (growth-oriented), or a more educational or action-oriented group (task-oriented), a certain equilibrium of adaptive-instrumental and integrative-expressive activities will have to be achieved. It is true, though, that concrete groups differ from each other in respect to the dominance that either sphere has over the other in the group's life.

Pertinent evidence, in relation to the instrumental and expressive functions of groups and the relationship between them is provided by Hopkins' evaluative study of a training program, The Encampment for Citizenship, in 1958.[43] The program's explicit aim was to promote democratic and liberal political attitudes of the campers during their six weeks' stay in camp. Each camper was assigned to several subgroups. For present purposes, we shall refer only to the findings concerning two types of such subgroups: the discussion group, and the dormitory group. The discussion groups were part of the organized educational activities of the encampment; interaction in these groups was in the form of "set events": "The groups met at regularly scheduled times for stated intervals of time and usually with everyone present; there was in each a single common activity and a single center of activity [the discussion leader]; and the interaction that occurred engaged most of the participants most of the time."[44]

The dormitory groups were part of the communal activities designed to enhance feelings of belonging, identification, and loyalty to the encampment as a whole. These groups were loosely organized as compared with the discussion groups; interaction within them was not in the form of set events; they were informal, and usually not all of the group members were present; conversations ranged over a wide array of topics, and did not take place at scheduled times.

The major finding concerning the effectiveness of these two types of groups is that the discussion groups contributed directly to the achievement of the program's intended goal, i.e. it changed campers' opinions in the direction of increased liberalism, whereas the dormitory groups produced no such effect.[45] This finding was the opposite of the predicted relationship that expected the informal-communal aspects of the program to be the principal source of change rather than the formal-educational ones.

One possible explanation, advanced by the author, ascribes

the high effectiveness of discussion groups to the predominance
of set events; these groups were clearly structured, the meetings
were attended by all group members, the discussions, following
a daily lecture, were guided in each group by a staff leader who
restrained members to "keep to the point"; to discuss the issues
presented at the lecture, and not others, was the explicit task of
the discussion group.

By comparison, the activities and discussions in the dormitory groups were not constrained in the same fashion. The
primary function of this type of group was to allow the
development of group solidarity, esprit de corps, and "it was to
be a place where tensions built up in the course of interacting in
other contexts could be lessened, where campers could recover
psychologically from the taxing pace and intensity of an
ordinary day at the encampment."[46] These groups then,
taken by themselves, were not effective in achieving the
encampment's main purpose, namely, increasing the liberal
attitudes of campers. This occurred because

"The development of a relaxing, congenial atmosphere within a
group, or of solidarity among its members, is usually, at a certain
point, incompatible with the development of increased conformity
to group-opinion, principally, because the kind of interaction which
facilitates the one has, after a while, a depressing effect on the
other."[47]

These findings and their interpretation, correspond to, and
support Bales' and Parsons' proposition about the differentiation between adaptive and integrative functions in social
systems. The activities of the discussion groups in the encampment were predominantly in the "task area"; the dormitory
groups were primarily engaged in the "social-emotional area."
Each camper was a member in both a discussion group and a
dormitory group (whose memberships did not overlap), so that
the adaptive and integrative needs, sometimes satisfied in one
and the same group, were in this case provided for by two
different groups that thus complement each other. One may
speculate that though the discussion groups were the most
important medium of opinion change toward more liberalism,

they would probably not be so effective if campers had no opportunity to "escape" from the pressure exerted on them, into the more informal, solidary dormitory groups.

To summarize the argument, different social work groups may be primarily task-oriented or primarily growth-oriented. In general, however, a group cannot function over a period of time if it is restricted to either goal-achievement or emotional-expressive activities alone. In the first instance the group will be disrupted by tensions and hostilities, and group members will leave it sooner or later; or in case the individual participant cannot leave the group for some reason, the process of goal-achievement itself will be impaired, as for example in work groups in industry or in combat groups of soldiers. In the second instance, in which activities in the social-emotional area alone will be encouraged, group members will drop out because of sheer frustration for not being able to accomplish any task. In this connection it should be noted that we assumed at the beginning, for the argument's sake, that therapy groups do not have goals. Nevertheless, therapy does have goals or tasks, as do other processes of social control, whether to cure the patient, prevent delinquency, or help a child progress from one stage of development to the next. It is true that these are mainly individual goals as distinguished from group goals, however the task of the group is to enable the achievement, and to work toward the accomplishment of these goals.

Learning Theory and Laboratory Training

Another body of knowledge from which social group work could benefit is learning theory, especially as developed in the Laboratory Training Movement (see above, sensitivity-training, T-Group method). It seems that social workers, including social group workers, have not been congenial to learning theory in general because they have associated it with such concepts as "behaviorism" and "manipulation." Behavior modification by way of conditioning techniques is perceived as being incompatible with the prevailing psychodynamic orientation of social work and its focus on intrapsychic processes and motives.

Hans Eysenck created a storm in psychoanalytic circles when he suggested in 1952,[48] and later in 1965,[49] on the basis of experimental research carried out by himself and by others, that the effects of psychotherapy in curing neurotic disorders are very small indeed, and "that neurotic disorders tend to be self-limiting, that psychoanalysis is no more successful than any other method, and that in fact all methods of psychotherapy fail to improve on the recovery rate obtained through ordinary life experiences and non-specific treatment."[50]

Moreover, he argued that the data strongly support his conclusion that methods of treatment based on the learning theory model are significantly more successful in treating neurotics than psychotherapy of the psychoanalytic type. The learning theory model, to which he refers, views neurotic disorders as conditioned responses, or learned behavior, that is nonadaptive, but becomes persistent because it is constantly reinforced, and,

"Like all other habits they are subject to extinction according to rules elaborated by modern learning theory and sufficiently well understood to make possible deductions which can be tested experimentally. . . . It would appear advisable, therefore, to discard the psychoanalytic model, . . . and to adopt, provisionally at least, the learning theory model which, to date, appears to be much more promising theoretically and also with regard to application."[51]

Closely related to this model of learning, stimulus-response techniques, positive and negative reinforcements, and so forth, is the concept of manipulation that seems to be in direct opposition to social work's moral commitments and basic values—"respect for human beings and the right of self-determination."[52] These principles are violated,

"if enablers to groups are trained in use of techniques without understanding the principles and basic concepts from which they are drawn. Such training raises the floodgates for streams of 'manipulation' rather than 'enabling' people to participate in decision-making processes which safeguard their rights of self-determination."[53]

However, the behaviorists' view of the learning process, their refusal to acknowledge the importance of such "hypothetical constructs" as personality structure, and congnitive and emotional internal dynamics, and the use of conditioning techniques, constitute only one approach to learning and behavior modification.[54]

Here, we would like to mention another theory of learning which seems relevant to social group work. This approach does not reject the importance of intrapsychic processes, and should not evoke the ethical problems connected with the behavioristic learning model. We refer to the theory of learning developed in the Laboratory Training Movement.

Following Kurt Lewin, Schein and Bennis developed a model of the learning process that involves at one and the same time cognitive, emotional, and behavioral elements.[55] Defined in very general terms, "laboratory training is an educational strategy which is based primarily on the experiences generated in various social encounters *by the learners themselves,* and which aims to influence attitudes and develop competencies toward learning about human interactions."[56]

The goals of laboratory training are:

(1) increased awareness about oneself, and about interpersonal and intergroup relationships;
(2) change of underlying attitudes;
(3) improved competence of role performance and social relationships.

These goals correspond to the three components or levels of the learning process, i.e. the cognitive (increased awareness), the emotional (changed attitudes), and the behavioral (changed interpersonal competence). The assumption is that these elements evolve in the form of a cycle or a sequence of partially overlapping steps. The process begins with some disconfirming information about the person's self and his interrelationships with others (unfreezing); this situation is followed by attitude change (change), followed by new behavior (refreezing), which, in turn, releases new information and sets a new cycle into motion.

This model of learning, again, may seem to be "manipulative" and to jeopardize the individual's freedom and independence. However, laboratory training is guided by certain values or meta-goals, e.g. democracy and self-determination, that restrict this possibility. A spirit of collaboration is prevalent in the training process—the preparation, involvement, and self-control of trainees are encouraged; the traditional authoritarian educational relationship (teacher-student) is curtailed; and the interdependence of the trainer and trainee is emphasized. In more concrete terms, the staff creates a setting which imposes the value of learning and the norms of how to learn ("deutero-learning")[57] but not of what to learn. The first step of the training process is designed to change the trainee's attitude toward learning itself, but from that point on, the contents of the learning process are determined by mutual effort on the part of the trainer and the group. Generally, a group framework is, by definition, more democratic than a professional-client setting in which the asymmetry of positions is more pronounced. Thus it seems that group work, as compared to casework, is better able to adhere to the value of "self-determination" that is emphasized by the code of ethics of social work.

Examination of the specific conditions of laboratory training that enable learning of social roles and interpersonal skills, is directly germane to the questions concerning the impact of the group's structure and the degree of its isolation, on producing desired change in clients.

Laboratory training is a learning process which is experienced on a "cultural island," physically and socially removed from day-to-day living. Laboratory training theory is aware of the problems entailed in relating the focus of the training period on the "here-and-now," to the delegate's (trainee's) "back-home" environment. Linking these two systems in a meaningful and constructive manner is of utmost importance because the very purpose of laboratory training is to influence the delegate in terms of his social roles in the organization from which he has come and to which he is going to return. Establishing this connection is made more difficult, because for different steps in the process of attitude change, different degrees of isolation of the T-Group from the outside world are optimal. The first step in the process of attitude change, namely, the unfreezing of existing attitudes requires a climate of psychological safety which is best achieved by removing the trainee from real-life relationships and pressures. By contrast, the stability (refreezing) of new attitudes and patterns of behavior depends upon the degree to which they are reinforced and confirmed by significant others back home. For this purpose, a lower degree of isolation from the trainee's "organization of origin" is functional, by avoiding too great discrepancies between current organizational attitudes and patterns of behavior, and those learned in the laboratory. If refreezing does not occur, the person must "(1) give up the new responses, producing the well known fadeout effect, or (2) seek new significant others, which may mean leaving the organization, or (3) attempt to change the organization."[58]

All this highlights the problems involved in stabilizing and perpetuating attitude and behavior change adopted outside the usual social milieu of the individual. The problems exist, though to varying degrees, even when change is produced in a group setting, and even if methods different from psychotherapy are employed. There are no easy resolutions to the problem of integrating personal change achieved in therapy, task-oriented, or learning groups, into the ongoing relationships of the client. It seems, however, that recognition of the problem is a precondition to any constructive suggestion.

A follow-up study designed to evaluate the outcomes of the application of laboratory training, as compared to traditional therapy, for two groups of psychiatric patients, showed some interesting differences in outcome.[59] The samples were drawn from two groups of patients in the Houston VA Hospital. One group participated in the Patient Training Laboratory program emphasizing learning and human relations training, the other program was conducted according to usual group therapy methods. There was no difference between the groups regarding isolation from everyday life and relationships—both were part of the hospital population—though the Patient Training Laboratory sessions were for a four-week period, whereas the group therapy treatment usually lasted longer.

The follow-up was carried out during the tenth month after

the patients' discharge.[60] By means of a mailed question-naire, information was obtained on rehospitalization, employ-ment, psychological well-being, physical well-being, social participation, and estimated benefit derived from hospital treatment.

Rehospitalization percentages were 16.2 for the Patient Training Laboratory and 26.1 for the group therapy program.

Of the training laboratory group, 65.8% were employed nine months after leaving the program, as compared to 50% of the group therapy patients. The measures of psychological status (anxiety, depression, tiredness, insomnia) yielded very similar results for both groups. The Patient Training Laboratory veterans reported more physical distress on the Somatic Symptom Scale than did the group therapy participants. No differences appeared in the reports of Patient Training Labora-tory or group therapy patients in regard to their social and interpersonal adjustment, e.g. on the feelings of community alienation scale, or in their marital relationships. Of the Patient Training Laboratory veterans, 66.7%, and of the group therapy patients, 61.5%, felt they had changed as a result of the hospital programs. However, a significantly higher proportion of Patient Training Laboratory veterans stressed interpersonal gains—24.6%, as compared to 10.5% of the group therapy veterans.[61]

These findings suggest that the main advantage of Patient Training Laboratory over group therapy is in the area of improving social effectiveness of clients. Patients of the training laboratory were hospitalized for a shorter period of time, less of them were rehospitalized, more of them were employed, and for longer periods of time, and more felt that they improved their interpersonal relationships.

The relevance of these findings for social group work is limited by the fact that the subjects studied were psychiatric patients. Similar experiments with social work clients, and their evaluation, could provide more direct and accurate knowledge about the relative effectiveness of different methods in social group work. Nevertheless, the study indicates that if the purpose of treatment is to improve social functioning of clients, laboratory training may have some distinct advantages over traditional group therapy so heavily relied on in social group work. Moreover, it should be noted again that in addition to better social adjustment, the felt psychological improvement of the training laboratory patients was not less than that of group therapy patients.

At this point we would like to raise a question that goes beyond the findings of the above study, and to which the answer can only be speculative. What would the findings of later follow-ups of the two patient groups reveal about their psychological and social well-being? Or in other words, what are the possible long-range effects of the two different methods—laboratory training as compared with group therapy—in terms of desirable psychological and social change of clients?

It is conceivable that the greater improvement in the objective situation of the Patient Training Laboratory veterans, e.g. being employed, will have a feedback effect ameliorating their psychological problems. To some extent this assumption is supported by the lower percentage of rehospitalization of laboratory veterans as compared with group therapy patients (see above). On the theoretical level the problem concerns the direction of the causal relationship between attitude and behavioral change, and the modification of the external situation. The practical implications for social work, and for other modes of intervention, seem to be that it is possible to concentrate first on helping the client achieve certain goals and improvement of his interpersonal relationships, that this improvement in the objective or relational situation would then have beneficial repercussions upon the client's intrapsychic problems, and make him more receptive to attitude and behavior change.[62] This mode of intervention may prove to be more effective, at least in some cases, than helping the client gain more self-awareness or insight into his motivations.

Notes

1. Gisela Konopka, *Social Group Work: A Helping Process* (Englewood Cliffs, N.J.: Prentice-Hall, 1963), p. 2. Italics added.

2. William Schwartz, "Group Work and the Social Scene," in Alfred J. Kahn, ed., *Issues in American Social Work*, p. 124.

3. A relatively early analysis of the similarities and differences between casework and group work is found in Gertrude Wilson, *Group Work and Casework–Their Relationship and Practice* (New York: Family Welfare Association of America, 1941).

4. One of the most frequent sociological concepts applied in social work writings and research is that of "role," for it provides a link between the system of personality and the social system. See, for example, Paul H. Glasser, "Social Role, Personality and Group Work Practice," in *Social Work Practice* (New York: Columbia University Press, 1962), pp. 60-74; Helen Harris Perlman, "Intake and Some Role Considerations," Social Casework 41 (April 1960): 171-176; Herbert S. Strean, "Role Theory, Role Models, and Casework: Review of the Literature and Practice Applications," Social Work 12 (January 1967): 77-88; and Barbara K. Varley, "The Use of Role Theory in the Treatment of Disturbed Adolescents," Social Casework 49 (June 1968): 362-368.

5. See, Konopka, *Social Group Work*, p. 11.

6. Grace L. Coyle, "On Becoming Professional," in Harleigh B. Trecker, ed., *Group Work Foundations and Frontiers* (New York: Whiteside, 1955), p. 328.

7. Ibid., p. 338

8. For a lively description of the conversion from movement to profession, see William Schwartz, "Small Group Science and Group Work Practice," Social Work 8 (October 1963): 39-76.

9. Frank J. Bruno and Louis Towley, *Trends in Social Work, 1877-1956* (New York: Columbia University Press, 1955), p. 49.

10. Clara Kaiser, "Characteristics of Social Group Work," in *The Social Welfare Forum, 1957*, pp. 168-169.

11. Florence Ray, "Introduction," in *Social Work With Groups* (1958), p. 6.

12. Grace Longwell Coyle, "Social Group Work: An Aspect of Social Work Practice," Journal of Social Issues 8 (1952): 33.

13. Harleigh B. Trecker, *Social Group Work: Principles and Practices* (New York: Whiteside, 1955), p. 4.

14. Dorothea Sullivan, *Readings in Group Work* (New York: Association Press, 1952), p. 420.

15. E. V. Hollis, and A. L. Taylor, *Social Work Education in the United States* (New York: Columbia University Press, 1951), p. 14.

16. Gertrude Wilson, "Social Group Work Theory and Practice," in *The Social Welfare Forum* (1956), p. 157.

17. Konopka, *Social Group Work*, ch. VI.

18. See, for example, Robert D. Vinter, "Small-Group Theory and Research: Implications for Group Work Practice Theory and Research," in Leonard S. Kogan, ed., *Social Science Theory and Social Work Research* (New York: National Association of Social Workers, 1960), pp. 123-134.

19. William Schwartz, "The Social Worker in the Group," *New Perspectives on Services to Groups: Theory, Organization, and Practice* (New York: Association of Social Workers, 1961), pp. 7-17. See also Cartwright's distinction between the group as a "medium of change" and as a "target of change," Cartwright, "The Group as a Medium of Change."

20. Hubert S. Coffey, "Socio and Psyche Group Process: Integrative Concepts," Journal of Social Issues 8 (1952): 69.

21. Konopka, *Social Group Work*, p. 10.

22. Robert D. Vinter, "Group Work: Perspectives and Prospects," in *Social Work with Groups* (1959), p. 133.

23. Gisela Konopka, "Social Group Work: A Social Work Method," Social Work 4 (October 1960): 61.

24. *Statistics on Social Work Education* (New York: Council on Social Work Education, 1958), p. 1.

25. See Vinter, "Group Work: Perspectives and Prospects."

26. Salaries and Working Conditions of Social Welfare Manpower in 1960, U.S. Department of Labor Statistics (New York: National Social Welfare Assembly), p. 7.

27. William Schwartz, "Group Work and the Social Scene," p. 130.

28. Kelman and Lerner, for example, outline the harmful consequences of disregarding both the similarities and the differences among group therapy, social group work, and adult education. See, H. C. Kelman and H. H. Lerner, "Group Therapy, Group Work and Adult Education: The Need for Classification," Journal of Social Issues 8 (1952): 3-10.

29. See, Peter B. Neubauer, "The Technique of Parent Group Education; Some Basic Concepts," in *Parent Group Education and Leadership Training* (New York: Child Study Association of America, 1952), p. 12.

30. For the classification of the distinction between group work and group therapy, see, for example, Gisela Konopka, "Similarities and Differences between Group Work and Group Therapy," in *Selected Papers*

of the National Conference of Social Welfare (1951), pp. 51-60, and Kelman and Lerner, "Group Therapy, Group Work and Adult Education."

31. This type of group work has sometimes been called group-casework. See, for example, Sanford N. Sherman, "Utilization of Casework Methods and Skill in Group Counseling," in *Social Work With Groups* (New York: National Association of Social Workers, 1958), pp. 106-118, and, "The Choice of Group Therapy for Casework Clients," *Social Work Practice* (New York: National Conference on Social Welfare, Columbia University Press, 1962), pp. 174-186; Saul Scheidlinger, "Patterns of Casework Services in Group Work Agencies," and W. T. Lindeman, "An Experiment in Casework-Group Work Co-operation," The Group 8 (November 1945): 1-7; 11-13.

32. Saul Scheidlinger, "The Concepts of Social Group Work and of Group Psychotherapy," Social Casework 34 (July 1953): 294. For an examination of the differences between psychotherapy and casework, see, for example, Coleman, "Distinguishing Between Psychotherapy and Casework." It must, however, be noted that group therapy is by no means a profession with a uniform theoretical basis and practice. The divisions and differences among group therapists concerning aims and methods are described, for example, by Louis A. Frey and Ralph L. Kolodny, "Illusions and Realities in Current Social Work with Groups," Social Work 9 (April 1964): 80-89.

33. Leland P. Bradford, Jack R. Gibb, and Kenneth D. Benne, eds., *T-Group Theory and Laboratory Methods* (New York: John Wiley and Sons, 1964), p. 2. See also Edgar H. Schein and Warren G. Bennis, eds., *Personal and Organizational Change Through Group Methods: The Laboratory Approach* (New York: John Wiley and Sons, 1965); Terence K. Hopkins with the assistance of Sanci Michael, *Group Structure and Opinion Change: An Analysis of an Effective Training Program* (New York: Bureau of Applied Social Research, Columbia University, 1963). The potential relation and contribution of the T-Group movement to social group work theory and practice is discussed by C. G. Gifford, "Sensitivity Training and Social Work," Social Work 13 (April 1968): 78-86.

34. See Warren G. Bennis, "Goals and Meta-Goals of Laboratory Training," in Warren G. Bennis, Edgar Schein, David E. Berlew, and Fred J. Steele, eds., *Interpersonal Dynamics: Essays and Readings in Human Interaction* (Chicago: Dorsey Press, 1964), pp. 692-698, and C. G. Gifford, "Sensitivity Training and Social Work," pp. 78-86.

35. For a survey of several studies on the relation between different patterns of intervention and type of agency see Henry S. Maas, "Group Influences on Client-Worker Interaction."

36. See Talcott Parsons, Robert F. Bales, and Edward Shils, *Working*

Papers in the Theory of Action (New York: Free Press, 1953), pp. 183-186.

37. Robert F. Bales and Fred L. Strodtbeck, "Phases in Group Problem Solving," in Cartwright and Zander, eds., *Group Dynamics,* p. 625. Italics added.

38. See Robert F. Bales, "Adaptive and Integrative Changes as Sources of Strain in Social Systems," in Paul A. Hare, Edgar F. Borgatta, and Robert F. Bales, eds., *Small Groups* (New York: Alfred A. Knopf, 1955). Also see Homans' distinction between the "external" and the "internal" systems of the group, in Homans, *The Human Group,* chs. IV and VI.

39. Talcott Parsons and Robert F. Bales, *Family, Socialization and Interaction Process,* p. 38. Italics added.

40. Parsons, *The Social System,* ch. VII.

41. See Parsons and Bales, *Family, Socialization and Interaction Process,* Figure 1, p. 39.

42. Henry L. Lennard and Arnold Bernstein, *The Anatomy of Psychotherapy: Systems of Communication and Expectation* (New York: Columbia University Press, 1960), p. 65; see the chart on same page which depicts the distribution of 101 psychotherapeutic sessions, and 9,282 therapists' propositions between "orientation" and "evaluation."

43. Hopkins and Michael, *Group Structure and Opinion Change,* pp. 118-150; also Hopkins, *The Exercise of Influence.*

44. Ibid., p. 142.

45. See Hopkins and Michael, *Group Structure and Opinion Change,* Tables, 5.11, 5.8, 5.9, p. 101, 103.

46. Ibid., p. 157.

47. Ibid., p. 161.

48. Hans J. Eysenck, "The Effects of Psychotherapy: An Evaluation," Journal of Consulting Psychology 16 (October 1952): 319-324.

49. Hans J. Eysenck, "The Effects of Psychotherapy," International Journal of Psychiatry 14 (January 1965): 125-138.

50. Ibid., 1965, p. 137.

51. Ibid., p. 137. See also Hans J. Eysenck and Stanley Rachman, *The Causes and Cures of Neurosis* (San Diego: Robert R. Knapp, 1965), pp. 3-10; Joseph Wolpe, "The Comparative Clinical Status of Conditioning Therapies and Psychoanalysis," in Joseph Wolpe, Andrew Slater, and L. J. Reyna, eds., *The Conditioning Therapies* (New York: Holt, Rinehart and Winston, 1965).

52. Wilson, "Social Group Work Theory and Practice," p. 150.

53. Ibid., p. 150.

54. See, for example, John Dollard and Neal E. Miller, *Personality and Psychotherapy* (New York: McGraw-Hill, 1950); Donald H. Ford and Hugh B. Urban, *Systems of Psychotherapy: A Comparative Study* (New

York: John Wiley and Sons, 1965); and Louis Breger and James L. McGaugh, "Critique and Reformulation of 'Learning Theory' Approaches to Psychotherapy and Neurosis," *Psychological Bulletin* 63 (May 1965): 342-357.

55. Kurt Lewin, *Field Theory in Social Science,* especially pp. 60-86, and Schein and Bennis, eds., *Personal and Organizational Change,* ch. 14; see also, L. P. Bradford, J. R. Gibb, and K. D. Benne, eds., *T-Group Theory and Laboratory Method,* and Kurt Lewin, "Group Decision and Social Change," in Guy E. Swanson, Theodore M. Newcomb, and Eugene L. Hartley, *Readings in Social Psychology* (New York: Henry Holt and Company, 1952), pp. 459-473.

56. Schein and Bennis, eds., *Personal and Organizational Change,* p. 4. Italics added.

57. This concept was coined by Bateson and applied to the process of psychotherapy in Lennard and Bernstein, *The Anatomy of Psychotherapy,* pp. 27-30.

58. Ibid., p. 319.

59. D. L. Johnson, P. G. Hanson, P. Rothans, R. B. Morton, F. A. Lyle, and R. Moyer, "Follow-up Evaluation of Human Relations Training for Psychiatric Patients," in Schein and Bennis, eds., *Personal and Organizational Change,* pp. 152-168.

60. Here we consider only the results obtained by the mailed questionnaire sent to former patients, and not those of the field interview conducted nine months after discharge.

61. Ibid., Tables 7-12, pp. 162-163.

62. A similar approach has been presented in Chapter 4 in the discussion of the application of different types of power.

Chapter 7

THE EXERCISE OF NORMATIVE AND
SOCIAL POWER IN GROUP WORK

In the following chapter we will attempt to show how the group setting provides for conditions that increase the likelihood of group members, i.e., clients, to accept influence exerted within the group. The discussion will be focused, in particular, on those group properties and processes that distinguish the group context from the one-to-one situation characteristic of the casework relationship. We shall first discuss the general implication of the group framework for social workers and for clients, their respective role-definitions, and their interrelation.

The process of influence exertion in groups will be compared to those processes in dyadic relationships, with special reference to the mechanisms that facilitate the acceptance, by group members, of changes that are mediated through the group.

Another advantage of the group as a change-inducing medium is suggested by the group's greater proximity to the real-life situations and relationships, as compared with the casework dyad. Thus, attitudes and social skills acquired in groups are more easily transmitted from the treatment situation to the clients' broader interpersonal relations in their original social milieux.

Throughout we shall draw upon research evidence from small-group studies, laboratory training, and evaluations of social work intervention programs, to support the main argument that, other things being equal, welfare clients are more susceptible to accept influence exerted within a group framework than in the person-to-person encounter with a social worker.

The Group Setting and its Effects on Clients and Professionals

For dealing with the problem of creating change in individuals through social group work, it is first necessary to examine the relevant generic characteristics of groups. For this purpose, we shall ignore, for the time being, the diverse goals of group work, and the variety of settings in which it is being practiced.

The universal elements of groups that impinge upon social group work, and set it apart from other methods of social work, particularly from casework, are group structure and group process. The most elementary feature of a group is related to a quantitative factor, i.e. the group is composed of a number of individuals (more than two), and each member interacts with more than one other individual.[1]

In sociological and psychological literature, small groups are sometimes defined as consisting of two individuals or more; for example, a small group is "an aggregate of people, from two up to an unspecified but not too large number,"[2] and Freud referred to the psychiatrist-patient unit as "a group of two."[3] On the other hand, Hopkins following Merton writes,

"we can say that *a number of people* constitute a group if they (1) interact with one another in accord with established patterns, (2) define themselves as 'members,' i.e., . . . have patterned expectations of forms of interaction which are morally binding on them and on other 'members' but not on those regarded as 'outside' the group, and (3) are defined by others as belonging to the group."[4]

And to quote Homans, "We mean by a group *a number of persons* who communicate with one another often over a span of time, and who are few enough so that each person is able to communicate with all the others, . . . face-to-face."[5]

This basic numerical characteristic of group structure is usually taken for granted in small-group research as part of the definition of groups, and attention is focused on other variables, such as group climate, group norms, patterns of interaction, leadership, and hierarchy.

If, however, an attempt is made to compare the problems of control and influence in casework (dyads) with those in group work (groups), the mere fact that a group includes "a number of people" as contrasted with "a pair of people" is significant. This factor, namely, the number of group members and its impact upon "forms of sociation" is part of Simmel's Formal Sociology. He observed, for example, that the dynamics of dyads differ from those of triads in certain important respects.[6]

The second basic attribute of the group is group process. This denotes, essentially, those emergent properties of groups that evolve in the course of interaction among group members: the development of group standards, esprit de corps and group cohesion, role differentiation, subgrouping and divergence of interests, scapegoating, and so on. These and other group phenomena are sometimes classified as a sequence of phases through time.[7]

Group structure, denoting a number of participants and the patterns of interrelations among them, and group processes have significant consequences both for group members and the social group worker. Referring to the individual group member, Lifton writes,

"The growth that comes about by identifying with another person who is working out a similar problem, the attempt to redefine reality by testing how many peers need to see something the same way for it to be real, and the learning involved in assuming a leadership role are all samples of phenomena that are based on group life. No equivalent experience can be presented in the individual therapy session."[8]

The client, within a group setting, is involved in two types of relationships: those with the social worker and those with other group members. Concerning the first, the client shares the worker with other clients; he cannot monopolize the worker's time or attention. This may interfere with the purpose of group work, either therapy or learning, to the degree that the client reacts to the need to share the worker with others with anxiety, agression, or withdrawal. On the other hand, the presence of others may have beneficial consequences by diluting such common emotional responses as hostility, dependence, and transference that are concentrated, and therefore, intensified in the dyadic relationship of social casework.

From a psychiatrist's point of view, the different effects of psychotherapy and group-therapy upon the patient are described by Ackerman who suggests that individual treatment "reawakens the infantile experience of symbiotic, omnipotent unity with the parent, whereas the group epitomizes in large measure the realities of social relations."[9]

The need to interact and relate to other people in the group presents a challenge as well as an opportunity both for the client and the social worker. The individual group member is brought into contact with other individuals who are his equals within the group framework and who are confronted with similar problems outside the group, as is the case in groups of unwed mothers, of adolescent school drop-outs, or of old people. The sharing of similar problems has often proved to be conducive to the free expression of opinions, attitudes, and emotions in group sessions, and,

> "it often turns out that group members learn that others in the group have similar feelings . . . and learning this in live confrontation with one's peers is a most powerful change-inducing experience. In fact one of the key virtues of the group method is that people are indeed readier to take help from one another than from a worker."[10]

On the other hand, group members are not professionally trained and represent different personality types. Thus, their reactions to any one group member cannot be completely regulated and predicted. The social group worker is therefore constrained by the presence of more than one client, and is unable to manipulate the basic mechanisms of therapeutic

treatment, namely, acceptance, permissiveness, support, reciprocity, and rewards,[11] as freely as in a dyadic relationship. As
Kelman and Parloff, referring to group psychotherapy, say,
"One cannot assume that the patients will always be accepting
and supporting of one another."[12]

Again, this phenomenon may have "antitherapeutic"
effects,[13] such as when a client exposes himself prematurely,
that is, before the group is ready to understand and support
him. However, it must be remembered that social group work
does not, or at least, ought not, to deal with mentally or
emotionally sick persons, but with people who are burdened by
economic and social problems. If this idea is accepted, then the
less permissive atmosphere of the client group, and the more
varied responses and relationships within it, as compared to the
casework relationship, may indeed have a decided advantage
over the rational and professionally guided responses of a
caseworker toward a single client.

Working with groups provides the social worker with the
opportunity to observe each client in his interaction with others,
and to direct his efforts to the modification of interpersonal
relationships. Of course, the group situation also presents
certain problems for the worker which he may not encounter in
relation with a single client.

Referring to the role of the group therapist as distinguished
from that of the psychoanalyst, Ackerman writes,

"His social identity is revealed. His emotions and counter-emotions
are more exposed. He is therefore a more real person, a less magical
figure; less omnipotent, less immune. He cannot be so exclusively
the stimulus and object of the patient's irrational projections, nor
can he be the exclusive catalyzing agent for the processes of
reorientation to the meaning of interpersonal experience."[14]

Group members may unite and reinforce each other's
resistance or hostility toward the worker, certain group norms
may develop that are incompatible with the worker's value
system and plans,[15] and his authority may be challenged by
an indigeneous leader. All these problems have direct implications for the ability of the worker to influence and control each
member and the group as a whole. His professional authority

has less weight here than in the dyadic situation, and he is at best regarded as *primus inter pares.* The group therapist sometimes has the experience of being excluded from the ongoing interaction, and he "must pay attention to the area of power and influence and realize that, no matter how sensitive or skillful he is, he cannot have the same degree of influence on the interpersonal situation that he would in a two-person relationship."[16]

The structure and processes that distinguish the group experience from the dyad do not assure success; efforts to change people by taking them away from their "natural" groups and giving them special training in contrived groups "so often have disappointing results."[17] The business manager who participated in a training program with a human-relation emphasis, and who returns to an organization in which rigid hierarchical divisions and formal procedures are the norm, or the boy who spent the summer in a camp where equality, achievement, and democracy were encouraged, and goes back to a social environment that does not adhere to these principles, may find themselves on the margins of their former groups whose members did not take part in their experiences.[18] The effectiveness of group work, as compared to casework, in producing personal change is a matter of degree. We propose that, other things being equal, attitudes and social skills that have been acquired in a group setting, and have been reinforced by other group members for a certain period of time, are more enduring and more transferable to real-life situations than those acquired in a clinical dyadic relationship. To quote Festinger, "The group is frequently the anchorage for attitudes and behavior patterns and the changes produced will be greater and more lasting if a group anchorage for the new attitudes and the new behavior patterns is provided."[19]

The argument that personal change which is supported by a group is more enduring, has to be supplemented by an analysis of the operation of the process of influence in groups, attempting to show that individuals are indeed more susceptible to various types of power wielded within groups, as compared with dyadic relationships.

To do so, we have to relate the present discussion to the

previous, general analysis of types of power and their mechanisms of exertion and acceptance.[20] A distinction was made among three types of power—normative, instrumental, and coercive. Normative power was then classified into two subcategories—"pure" normative power which is exerted through activation of value orientations, and social power which is mediated through interpersonal relationships. We shall concentrate, again, on the processes accompanying the exercise and acceptance of normative power (pure and social) in groups, called in general, influence. This limitation is made not only in order to simplify the analysis, but mainly because relational and normative rewards are the prevailing mechanisms of power operating in social work groups.

As noted earlier, there are certain conditions under which these processes work: social power takes effect when the recipient of influence values his relationship with the source of influence (individual or group), and wants to maintain it. It depends, therefore, on the degree of attraction this relationship has for the individual; normative power operates when the contents of influence is relevant in terms of the influencee's own value commitments, and is related to the degree of perceived credibility of the source of influence. It should be noted that the relations among the various factors, as here presented, are ideal-types abstracted from concrete, more diversified configurations.

In respect to the attributes of the sources of normative and social power (credibility and attractiveness), we have pointed out that the social worker may, to a greater or lesser extent, lack these characteristics from the point of view of his client. In addition, certain structural properties of the situation, in particular of the one-to-one casework encounter, have been considered to impair the acceptance of influence by the client. These were mainly the insulation of the casework relationship from an "immediate audience" and its support, and the inability of the worker to observe the actual consequences of his influence attempts.

The Process of Influence in Small Groups

The crucial questions are now: How does the process of influence function in small, face-to-face groups? What particular impact does the structure of the group have on this process? And, are there any additional factors that enhance the induction of change within groups that do not obtain in the social worker-client relationship?

There exists an extensive literature dealing with the process of influence in small, face-to-face groups. Here we shall refer, specifically, to a study by Festinger, Schachter, and Back on housing projects, in which they advanced a theory of this process.[21]

Their underlying assumption is that social groups occupy a strategic position as determinants of the behavior and attitudes of their members in accordance with group standards. The concepts by which this process is defined are

The "cohesiveness" of the group—the forces acting on the member of a group to remain a member.

The "attractiveness" of the group—the extent to which a group is a goal in and of itself and has positive valence. The positive valence of an informal group is usually affected by the extent to which one has satisfactory relationships with other members of the group.

The "means control" of the group—the extent to which it mediates goals which are important for the members.

The "internal power" of the group—the magnitude of the change it can induce in its members.

The "power field" of the group—the range of activities over which the group has power.[22]

The hypotheses in respect to the strength of group standards are as follows: The greater the attractiveness of a group and the greater the importance of the goals accessible in and through the group, the more cohesive the group will be. The greater the cohesiveness of a group, the stronger will its internal power be, and the wider its potential power-field. These hypotheses were confirmed in the study of housing projects mentioned above. People living in the more cohesive courst of the projects were most likely to conform with regard to activities of the community council.[23]

It can be readily seen that the concepts of "attractiveness" and "importance" parallel those of "salience of relationship" and "relevance of issue" that have been used earlier.[24] The question to be raised now is whether these two variables have greater positive value for the individual client within social work groups than in the casework situation. It is realized that these groups differ from small informal groups, among other reasons, because of the presence of the group worker, and the temporary and sometimes involuntary nature of the group.

It should also be remembered that we only attempt to compare the operation of social and normative power in group work and casework. It is necessary to exclude the type of worker-client relationship in which the worker commands direct remunerative power, i.e. the authority to decide if the client is eligible for financial relief and other benefits, and to consider only casework proper. In the first instance, the forces operating on the client to maintain his relationship with the social worker would be very strong, but would tell us very little about the attractiveness or the significance of this relationship for him.

Cohesion and Credibility in Group Work and Casework

There exists an abundance of research evidence to the effect that influence and change operate through various group processes.[25] However, not many studies have directly compared the effectiveness of change induction upon single individuals with influence exerted in small face-to-face groups, with the exception of the pioneering studies of Lewin.[26] He writes, "experience in leadership training, in changing of food habits, work production, criminality, alcoholism, prejudices—all seem to indicate that it is usually easier to change individuals formed into a group than to change any one of them separately."[27]

A possible source of evidence in respect to the degree of "cohesion" of the caseworker-client relationship is furnished by "continuance studies" in social casework (although these studies were originally used for measuring treatment effectiveness).[28] Continuers are defined as clients who continue beyond an arbitrary fixed number of interviews, ranging from one in some studies to four in others.

One such study, on psychiatric clinics for children, reported that of the 1,500 cases that made up the research population, 59% did not continue treatment beyond intake.[29] Other studies have reported somewhat lower percentages of "dropouts" depending, among other things—on the definition of continuance and the type of clientele.

It seems to us, that rates of discontinuance in casework can serve at least as a partial indicator of the magnitude of the forces acting upon the client to maintain the relationship with the worker, or, in other words, as a criterion of the degree of valence of this relationship and the significance of the goals to be attained through it, as perceived by the client. Unfortunately, there are no adequate data available concerning clients' discontinuance of participation in group work in small face-to-face groups that would permit a systematic comparison of attrition in casework and in group work of this type.

Research findings are available about the processes of recruitment and drop-out of members (clients), especially in social group programs directed with large groups of preadolescents and adolescents, such as Boy and Girl Scouts, Camp Fire Girls, and Boys' Clubs of America. These various studies report similar findings, that (a) the membership in these organizations is drawn more from the higher than the lower socioeconomic groups in the community, and (b) that lower-income children tend to drop out sooner than higher-income children.[30]

These studies are not directly relevant to our purpose as regards rates of discontinuance because of the special type of program and type of population they deal with. The general point that apparently applies to both casework and group work of various kinds is that a client is apt to come to the agency and continue treatment or participation, the more congruent the worker's and client's definitions of the germane needs and interests of the client. The degree of such congruence depends among other factors on the class distance between worker and client.[31]

The one-to-one casework relationship is, by definition, characterized by a greater or lesser degree of sociocultural difference between worker and client, and hence, "the normal gap between teacher and student, doctor and patient, social worker and public, can be a real obstacle to acceptance of the advocated conduct."[32]

In group work, beside his relationship with the worker, each client interacts with other members who are roughly from the same socioeconomic background, and who share similar problems and interests. Therefore, it is argued that the group is a more favorable setting for the development of credibility, which is one of the major factors contributing to the induction of attitude and behavior change.

The recognition by an individual that the group is engaged in discussing, learning, or performing things that are significant and relevant is likely to increase the attractiveness of the group for him, namely, to enhance his "sense of belonging" or "degree of identification,"[33] his valuation of group membership, and his desire to maintain this membership.

Thus, it is suggested that in social work groups, the relation between the factors that make up the "internal power" of the group may, initially, develop in a different direction than in informal friendship groups. As has been mentioned before, available evidence indicates that the more highly a person values his membership in a group the more he will be influenced by communications from other group members.[34] Furthermore, a positive correlation has been found between the degree of attraction the group has for a member, and the extent of credibility which he will attribute to communications from other group members. Individuals with high liking for other group members as compared with individuals with lower liking for the others "(a) judge the opinions expressed by others in the group as being more likely to be correct, and (b) show greater conformity to these opinions."[35]

In client groups in social work, a reverse process seems to operate—relevance and credibility of intragroup communications will lead to stronger feelings of belongingness, liking, and attraction to the group. It should be noted, however, that in later stages of group development, the relationship between credibility and attractiveness is circular, and the two factors tend to reinforce each other.

Credibility is a compound variable; it is commonly subdivided into "(1) the extent to which a communicator is perceived to be a source of valid assertions [his 'expertness'], and (2) the degree of confidence in the communicator's intent to communicate the assertions he considers most valid [his 'trustworthiness']."[36]

Above, we have used the term primarily in this second connotation, and the question may be raised whether the first element of credibility, namely, the degree of the communicator's perceived expertness would not be greater in relation to the social worker than that attributed to a fellow client.

First, it must be noted that, in general, social workers' expert knowledge is estimated as relatively low by clients, as compared with other professionals. This problems was mentioned earlier when we discussed the "nonesoteric" knowledge of the human-relations professionals in general. It seems that a further distinction is needed between two types of expert knowledge. The first is based on special training and proficiency that the professional commands, and the client does not, the classic examples being again the cases of the physician and the lawyer. The second type of "expertness" is based on resemblance and likeness between influencer and influencee. This would usually not be called expert knowledge but rather, understanding, empathy, and the like; nevertheless, it may, under certain conditions, be an important element in the process of change induction. To illustrate the point—a social worker, working with a group of welfare mothers reported that she was continuously asked by her clients if she too had children (which she did not). This problem seemed, at least at the beginning of the relationship, to impede the willingness of the clients to accept the worker's suggestions and directives.

This is not to deny that the worker does possess expert knowledge in the usual sense of the term, which other members in the group do not. This is not only objectively true but is also recognized by clients. In short, the worker's credibility as perceived by the client may be greater in certain specific aspects than that of other group members.

This notion is confirmed, to a certain degree, by the so-called Motivation, Capacity, and Opportunity (MCO) studies that constitute one type of the "continuance studies" in casework mentioned earlier.[37] It is assumed that the client's motivation concerning treatment, his capacity (intellectual and emotional), and his opportunity (provided by his environment and by service) are the major discriminating factors determining continuance in contrast with discontinuance in casework.

Ripple and Alexander developed a typology in relation to continuance[38] that classifies clients into two groups according to their main problems: (1) external problems and (2) psychological problems. It was found that clients in the category of external problems had a higher rate of continuance (55%) than clients in the psychological problems category (33%).[39] These findings indicate that the relationship with the caseworker is perceived by the client as more relevant and helpful when the client's main problems are located in his external environment than when his problems are mainly of a psychological nature.

In a subsequent analysis these findings were related to the factors of motivation, capacity, and opportunity. This analysis indicated that continuance is unrelated to the type of problem per se, and that the difference between continuance rates are due to the presence or absence of a set of "negative factors." Negative factors were attributed to cases in which the client was judged to have negative motivation, or the worker was rated as not encouraging, or the environment was judged to be unmodifiable, (or various combinations of these three).[40] When the presence of negative factors was held constant, the relationship between type of problem and continuance disappeared.

Percentages of Presence and Absence of Negative Factors in Each Type of Problem (Numbers given in brackets)[41]

Problem	Psychological	External	Total
Negative Factor Present	76(150)	24(48)	100(198)
Negative Factor Absent	46(71)	54(82)	100(153)

The Table shows that in the psychological problem category negative factors are more often present (76%) than absent

(46%). One possible explanation is that the workers expertness is greater in solving external, situational problems of the client than his expertness in psychological matters, in which worker and client are more likely to differ in their definitions and attitudes because of sociocultural distance.

Obviously, external and intrapersonal problems are closely related. However, the interpretation of the research evidence suggests a possible division of labor between group worker and group members in regard to spheres of influence. The worker can be most effective in inducing change in those areas in which his credibility is acknowledged by the clients; fellow-clients will be more influential in those areas in which credibility is based on "trustworthiness" derived from a feeling of affinity and identification.

The Contagion of Change

An additional characteristic of influence in groups, which distinguishes it from influence exercised in the professional-client dyad, is the process contagion. Polansky, Lippit, and Redl distinguish, within the general area of social influence, between a "direct attempt at influencing" which is "defined as an event where the actor deliberately and openly tries to evoke a particular response in the recipient," and between "contagion" in which "the initiator does not envince an intent to be imitated."[42] Behavioral contagion is "an event in which a recipient's behavior has changed to become 'more like' that of the actor or initiator. This change has occurred in a social interaction in which the actor has not communicated intent to evoke such a change."[43]

When this distinction is applied to the process of influence in social group work, we can say that, in general, influence exerted by the social worker upon the client or group is of the type called direct influence attempts. Among group members, in addition to direct influence attempts that may be communicated from one client to another, a "spreading" of attitudes and behavior patterns, i.e. contagion, will take place.

A social worker may, of course, influence a client's behavior or attitudes, by a word, a gesture, or an act, without direct intent. In principal, however, the process of intervention should be a rational, conscious, and planned attempt at influence. Even those workers who hold to the idea that the client should "think and decide for himself" attempt to accomplish this goal by intentionally influencing the client to achieve maximum "self-direction."[44]

Thus, without referring specifically to the contents of the transmitted behavior, it seems that contagion presents an additional dimension in the process of influence among members of social work groups that is lacking in the professional-client interaction.

The study by Polansky, Lippitt, and Redl mentioned above explored the process of contagion in eight boys' groups and eight girls' groups, both in a summer camp setting, specializing in work with children referred by community agencies, for study, for treatment, or because they were considered unable to adjust to the more usual kinds of camps. A particularly interesting finding of the study was that one of the major variables affecting the amount of contagion in the group was the leadership style of the group's counselor. In groups in which a high volume of contagion was observed, the counselor was a warm accepting type of leader, usually called a "nondirective" leader. In the low-volume groups the leader was of the "directive" type, exhibiting a controlling leadership style.[45] This finding has important implications for the types of leadership most suitable for different purposes of social group work. Very generally, if group work aims at psychotherapy, a more directive leadership might be appropriate; if, however, it is geared to learning and change by "self-determination," a more democratic type of leadership will be more functional.

Another factor that promotes contagion among group members is the feeling of security of an individual within the group. In contrast to the two former factors (professional orientation and style of leadership) which are characteristics of the worker or leader role, security is an attribute of the group member. The study, mentioned above, found that the more an individual was secure within the group, and felt that he could act freely in it, the more susceptible he was to behavioral contagion.[46] In applying this relationship to social work, we assume that an individual surrounded by others who are his equals, as in the event of group work, will usually feel more free and secure than a client who confronts the professional singly.[47]

In conclusion of this discussion of certain features and mechanisms that distinguish influence in social work groups from influence in casework, several qualifications should be pointed out. First, the discussion was necessarily general, that is, we did not attempt to examine the possible variations of the group's power, its cohesiveness, or the contents of influence, in different types of social work groups. Second, various features of groups that impinge upon the process of influence have not been discussed, such as the frequency of interaction among members, the level of visibility, group size, role and status differentiation, and so forth.[48] Third, and this is a more serious problem, the theories and research on which our discussion is based are all built on the assumption, or empirical evidence, that small face-to-face groups develop group standards, and that pressure is exerted on members to change their attitude and behavior to conform more closely to these group standards. In the course of time such group norms will also develop in client groups in social work. These norms may not be those that the group worker adheres to; they may sometimes even be in contradiction to the norms he thinks are right and proper, and to which he would like the clients to conform. Discussing the problems involved in re-education of groups that hold standards which are contrary to those of society at large, as in the case of delinquency, minority prejudices, alcoholism— and we may add, lower-class culture—Lewin and Grabbe write,

"the feeling of group belongingness seems to be greatly heightened if the members feel free to express openly the very sentiments which are to be dislodged through re-education. . . . Expression of prejudices against minorities or the breaking of rules of parliamentary procedures may in themselves be contrary to the desired goals. Yet a feeling of complete freedom and a heightened group identification are frequently more important at a particular stage of re-education than learning not to break specific rules."[49]

It is precisely because of the probability that the group norms may be incongruent with the norms of the worker or the agency that the group worker should be aware of such phenomena—group cohesion, the need of an individual to be accepted and approved of by the group, the feeling of belongingness derived from having shared the same experiences and problems, the involvement in a group engaged in relevant issues—and recognize them as powerful incentives for attitude and behavior change.

The Proximity of the Group to Real Life

Earlier, we attributed the relative ineffectiveness of casework mainly to the isolation of the one-to-one relationship from other significant and lasting relationships in the client's role-set.[50] So far, the same questions that have been raised in regard to the effectiveness of casework in producing behavioral change and better social functioning pertain to the group work method as well. Does the client apply the new insights he has gained in the course of group treatment to his interpersonal relations outside the group in the frameworks of family, neighborhood, and work? Does he transfer newly learned patterns of behavior to wider, external social settings? And if so, are these patterns supported and hence reinforced by the people he encounters outside the treatment group, or are they rejected and eventually unlearned?

Concerning these problems, it should be noted at the outset that, in general, group experience is nearer to real-life situations than the interaction with one professional worker who

> "in having 'separate' patients, who do not form a collectivity, is able to exclude the world from a dyad in which communication is privileged. Often he has nothing to do with other people who affect the patient's life. He can give individual support and help to sustain the [necessary] fiction that he is exclusively available to his patient."[51]

The group situation, by the mere multiplicity of individuals, implies that opinions, attitudes, and behavior will be of a varied nature, and may to a greater or lesser extent represent the real social environment of different clients. Thus, the attitudes and patterns of behavior learned in a group setting, may have more relevance to the external world than those acquired in the professional-client dyad.

Different types of groups may be isolated from real-life situations to varying degrees. This depends, to a large extent, upon the particular theoretical orientation of various professional fields that use the group medium for achieving specific purposes, such as group psychotherapy, social group work, adult education, sensitivity training, and the relatively new field of "social psychiatry" or "community psychiatry."[52]

In the concluding article of the issue of the Journal of Social Issues dedicated to the analysis of the convergence of group psychotherapy, social work, and adult education, Kelman suggests conceptualizing the differences between fields of group work "in terms of the degree of isolation of the group situation, and the relative emphasis on practice and action."[53]

Comparing the degree of group isolation in social group work, adult education and group therapy, he writes,

> "In group work and adult education groups, the degree of isolation is, ideally, low, . . . The trend in both fields has been towards making the group experience an integral part of community life and of the member's on-going problem-solving activities. . . . Quite different is the orientation in the therapy group. Here the emphasis is on separating the group experience from real life. . . . The therapy group situation *as such* . . . is a thing apart. It is clearly distinguished from the rest of the individual's life as a situation which is permissive and experimental and in which he is not 'playing for keeps'."[54]

In Kelman's view, this apparent contradiction between the assumptions of group therapy and those of social group work and adult education, concerning the degree of isolation of the group experience from real life, is resolved when it is realized that behavior change involves a phase of practice and a phase of action:

> "In adult education and group work the phase of practice is represented by the period of preliminary discussion which precedes

action, and which involves problem-setting, fact finding, and planning. . . .The phase of action, of course, is represented by member's participation in group activities and social action projects. . . . In group therapy, the phase of practice is represented by the therapy situation. The phase of action occurs outside of therapy, in real life."[55]

He proposes that the greater isolation of the therapy group is related to the emphasis that group psychotherapy puts on the practice phase. To maximize the effectiveness of this phase, it is important to separate it from action. By comparison, the integration of the group in the community and real-life is associated with the emphasis that group work and adult education place on the action phase.

In turn, these different emphases on practice and action are related to the nature of the group members' problems and to the purposes of professional intervention. An individual is assigned to a therapy group because he has certain interpersonal problems stemming from intrapsychic conflicts and inappropriate emotional responses. In order for him to express his feelings freely and try out new responses, the group should be removed from real-life pressures and persons with whom the individual shares a history of strained relationships.

On the other hand, individuals participating in groups of adult education, social work groups, and T-groups do not usually suffer from personality disturbances, but from lack of opportunities and training to develop satisfying and effective interpersonal relationships. In this type of group, concern with the individual's psychic problems is, at least theoretically, not as deep as in group therapy. The group provides the individual with a social environment in which he can acquire new information and experience in problem-solving, interpersonal relations, and group processes.

We have quoted Kelman's analysis of the different structures and processes of groups in different settings, in detail, because he relates them primarily to the degree of group isolation from the everyday social milieu of its members. This factor has, in our opinion, important repercussions for the effectiveness of different social work methods in producing enduring behavioral change. It is interesting to note that in the growing criticism launched at casework by social workers, this variable of the remoteness or nearness of the social worker-client interaction to the everyday life of the client has only rarely been taken into account. One exception, for example, is Tropp's opinion of how social group work should be practiced in order to fulfill its central role of helping people cope more effectively with their interpersonal relations. He writes,

> "If one would help people in their social functioning, what better way to do it than to give them the opportunity *to make it happen,* not after they leave the agency, but while they are enjoying its hospitality, with the worker as part of the common enterprise, in groups in which they share with others some common concern."[56]

We have already suggested earlier that group experience is in general more similar to the individual's real-life social relationships than the encounter with the caseworker, and that groups are more or less isolated from the everyday environment depending on the ideology and general orientation of the human-relations profession that employs group methods. Moreover, within social group work itself, different approaches are adhered to, particularly because of the great variety of settings in which it is practiced, and the varying commitments of workers to different theoretical trends in social group work.

Natural and Artificial Groups

At this point, let us depart from the description of the generic properties of small groups, relevant to social group work, and introduce the distinction between "natural" and "artificial" groups. Though social group work is applied to both types of groups, the practical implications of their structural differences for the mode of intervention, and for the achievement of specific purposes, have been largely overlooked.

Natural groups are part of the structures of family, work, and community in which the individual lives his everyday life. If the group worker works with a family or a gang of boys, he is dealing with a natural group. Artificial groups are created by the worker or the agency for a specific purpose, whether for therapy, training, discussion, task-accomplishment, or the like.

The degree of isolation from real-life and the broader community is an important distinguishing factor between natural and artificial groups. The natural group is integrated with the client's real life situation; it has a past and a future beyond the social group work experience. On the other hand, the artificial group which is constructed by plan, exists only for the duration of the treatment or program. It is composed of individuals who are strangers and have had no former relations with each other, and probably will not continue to interact after the group has been disolved by the worker. The contrived group is, as such, more detached from the everyday life of its members than the natural group which is part of it.

This distinction is, of course, a matter of degree. The artificial group is not totally cut off from real life if only by virtue of the fact that each group member is, at the same time, the incumbent of an array of roles in other social groups, outside the social work or therapy group (perhaps with the exception of group members in "total institutions"). By the same token, the natural group is not completely "natural" because of the presence of the worker, and also because members usually meet in the agency, clinic, or club, and not at their place of residence or work.

Natural groups are usually more heterogeneous than artificial groups, particularly in terms of role and status differentiation, and in case of the family, also in terms of age and sex. By contrast, members of artificial groups are chosen to participate in the group on the basis of their similarity, especially in respect to age, sex, and their personal and social needs.

Another distinguishing characteristic between the two types of groups is that artificial treatment groups are initially unstructured; there are no established role relationships among members, no hierarchy, no division of labor, and no group norms. Later, in the course of interaction, these properties will develop. However, the role the individual plays, and the position he holds within the group do not necessarily correspond to those he has in the outside world which is invisible to other group members.

By contrast, the natural group, especially the family which is now increasingly treated as a social unit in social work,[57] comes to the agency with its well established patterns of role relationships and sentiments. One aspect of this structure which is of particular significance is that the natural group brings into the situation an organized power distribution among its members. The natural group usually has some kind of leadership, whether the father or mother in the family, or the informal leaders of gangs, work groups, and groups of people in closed institutions.[58] The group worker has to take this fact into account in his attempt to produce change in interpersonal relations among members. The worker should not ignore the group's indigeneous leadership, for this will arouse hostility and resistance, yet he cannot wholly accept it, especially if it proves to inhibit the group's development in the desired direction. What the worker might have to do, under certain circumstances, is to influence the group leader first, and use him as a communicator of new norms and patterns of behavior, thus establishing a "two-step flow" of influence.[59]

It seems, that other things being equal, artificial groups of the type described above, are more likely to develop deviant norms and behavior, than natural groups. The individual's role within the artificial group is detached, to a greater or lesser degree, from his other social roles, and the group as a whole is removed from other social frameworks that usually exert control on attitudes and behavior. The natural group, by comparison, is influenced and constrained by its members' ties and responsibilities in the wider community. This hypothesis is proposed with caution, and it is realized that more research is needed to specify the conditions under which deviation will develop in contrived social work groups.

Each of these types, the natural and the artificial group, has its advantages and disadvantages in relation to the different purposes for which group work is employed. When psychotherapy is the main purpose of group work (which in our opinion is not the task of social group workers but that of psychotherapists), the insulation of the group from the "natural" environment has important functions. In these groups the expression and interpretation of feelings are the main therapeutic means. This can be best accomplished in a permissive and supportive atmosphere. Though we noted earlier that permissiveness and support cannot be regulated in therapy groups to the same extent as in the therapist-patient dyad, an artificial group setting is more adequate than a natural one if psychotherapy is the aim. The individual in the artificial group is not burdened by a history of problematic interpersonal relationships with other group members. It is easier to ventilate one's feelings and express opinions in the presence of strangers, particularly if they share similar personal problems. Moreover, as compared with casework, the presence of a peer group may lessen distrust, resentment, and resistance, often exhibited by individual's who fear exposing themselves to an "authority figure" for fear of being judged and criticized.

Working with natural groups is more adequate when the main purpose is education, socialization to role performance, and interpersonal relationships. In these cases the main instruments for producing behavior change are joint planning, experimental learning, problem solving, task achievement, and so on. Intrapsychic conflicts are not probed, and the group experience is more geared to decision-making and action than to the expression of emotions.

The anchorage of the group to the everyday milieu and personal relationships lends value to what happens within the group. It has been found although the evidence comes from studies of experimental groups, that the feeling that the group was engaged in something that was real and meaningful for its members was more effective in inducing change than the verbalization of emotions and the acquisition of insights. In a study of disturbed adolescents, Varely found that the boy who "cannot easily tolerate probing into his developmental history can be positively involved in a therapeutic process that is focused on current realities."[60]

Mann and Mann investigated the relative effectiveness of task-oriented and role-playing activities in six groups of students from a graduate course in Education. The task-oriented study groups were engaged in drawing up a plan for the course's curriculum. "An analysis of group member ratings obtained at the third and tenth session indicated that study group member ratings changed significantly more than role-playing group members on the variables of 'desirability as a friend', 'leadership initiative', 'cooperativeness', and 'general adjustment'."[61]

The different emphases on task-achievement, problem-solving, and activity, as against verbalization, free expression, and interpretation, correspond roughly to the general distinction between group psychotherapy and social group work.[62] In addition, within each field, diverse views as to the purpose of group work are held.[63]

A Comparison between the Consequences of Casework and Group Work

Much has been written about the techniques, problems, and the need for more evaluative research in social work.[64] However, systematic description, interpretation, and measurement of the outcomes of social work intervention, and their evaluation against a set of desired goals, is still quite scarce. Most of the so-called evaluations of deliberate social work intervention are in the form of case studies, or to be more precise case stories; for example, Jerome made dramatic progress in three short weeks; he showed great improvement in self-control; or, good will developed in the group, and members have come to reveal personal materials and problems never shared previously with individual caseworkers.[65] In this type of studies, individuals or groups are observed only after they have been exposed to the program being evaluated. The changes that are assumed to have taken place cannot be compared with a base-line ("before") measurement, or with an unexposed control group. Hence, there is really no way of telling whether the observed effects have been caused by the treatment program.

More systematic research on the effectiveness of casework is usually of the type called Movement Studies, measuring the improvement of a client according to a standardized Movement Scale.[66] Evaluative studies of group work have been largely concerned with the impact of various programs upon delinquency rates,[67] and some addressed themselves to the problem of studying individual change and growth in the group context.[68] Usually, the effects of social intervention are studied by comparing the relevant aspects (e.g. rate of delinquency) in the experimental group after a period of treatment, and in the control group which has not been exposed to treatment. We do not know of any studies that explicitly compare the effectiveness of casework and group work for matched populations of clients. One study that does provide data concerning this problem is *Girls at Vocational High,*[69] although this was not its proclaimed purpose. The main purpose of the study was to examine "the consequences of providing social work services to high school girls whose record of earlier performance and behavior at school revealed them to be potentially deviant."[70] In passing, it should be mentioned that many professional social workers and the spokesmen of their association regarded the conclusions of this study as a wholesale attack on the profession, and felt that "the researchers point a dagger at the heart of social work."[71] In part, this reaction was generated by the publicity given to the findings in the press, stating that the study demonstrates the ineffectiveness of social casework in preventing delinquency to any significant degree.[72] The researchers' own conclusion is more restrained, however; they state, "We must conclude that, with respect to all of the measures we have used to examine effects of the treatment program, only a minimal effect can be found."[73]

In the present context, the interesting finding of the study is that "The use of group approaches to treatment emerged clearly as the method of choice in this instance."[74] The caseworkers in the agency that was involved in the research[75] considered the group work program conducted with the girls as more successful than the individual casework treatment.

Here are two examples of workers' ratings:

Social Workers' Ratings on the Question, "How Involved Did This Client Become in a Treatment Relationship?" (Percentage)[76]

Rating Category	Individual Treatment	Group Treatment	All Cases
Very much or quite a bit	27	40	36
Some or a little	26	41	37
Hardly or not at all	47	19	27
TOTAL	100	100	100
Number of cases	47	127	174

This table indicates that according to the workers' assessment, girls participating in the group program became more involved in the treatment than those in individual casework. Almost half (47%) of the girls in the casework program were judged by workers to be "hardly or not at all" involved in the treatment relationship, whereas only 19% of the girls in group treatment were so rated. (Still, only about a third of all girls were judged to have become "very much or quite a bit" involved.)

The following table shows the workers' assessment of how much change they perceived had been produced in their cases in the course of treatment:

Social Workers' Rating on the Question, "How Much Change Do You Feel the Casework or Group Experience Produced in This Client?" (Percentage) [77]

Rating Category	Individual Treatment	Group Treatment	All Cases
Very great deal or quite a bit	10	19	17
Some or little	30	49	44
Hardly any or not at all	60	32	39
TOTAL	100	100	100
Number of cases	47	126	173

Substantially more of the girls in individual treatment (60%) than those in group treatment (32%) were judged to have changed "hardly or not at all." (Again, only 17% of the total number of subjects were rated to have undergone a "very great deal or quite a bit" of change.)

These findings, and others,[78] indicate that social workers rated the group approach as more appropriate and more successful with the kind of clients served in this project. The study, however, does not demonstrate that group work was in fact more effective in preventing deviant careers of girls singled out as potentially deviant. This could have been done by comparing two samples of girls each participating in one of the two different programs. But apparently, the workers' conviction that group work was a more adequate method of treatment than casework was an "unanticipated finding." The objective consequences of treatment (e.g. rate of drop-outs, rate of out-of-wedlock pregnancies), therefore, were compared only for the experimental group of girls participating in group work and/or casework programs, and the control group of potential problem cases who did not receive any services in the agency. We may, nevertheless, view the findings of the subjective criteria, namely, the perceived greater effectiveness by workers of group methods as compared with individual treatment, as reflecting the actual better results achieved by group work in this project.

Concluding Remarks

It is by now evident that we have been suggesting a number of alternatives to the current dominant approaches and practices in welfare and social services. Our arguments have been mainly based on theoretical considerations and on research findings of social work studies as well as on relevant sociological research of small groups, clinical studies of psychotherapy, and evidence gained from the experience of Training-Group programs.

In this last part we concentrated mainly on the proposal that working with small groups of clients, instead of with a single client at a time, would prove more effective in producing changes in clients, such as developing their abilities, modifying perspectives and attitudes, and inculcating new patterns of behavior.

It should be emphasized again that working with groups of people is not suggested as an "omnipotent" technique for the solution of personal and social problems. Like any other method that attempts to produce attitude and behavior change, it can be applied effectively only under specific conditions, and to a specific range of problems. Thus, different types of groups—therapy groups, discussion groups, learning groups, and task-oriented groups—are not the only devices through which change can be attained, and do not furnish a general substitute for casework, community organization, and other forms of professional intervention. In some instances, group work may only provide a useful supplement to these other methods.

Finally, the group approach is not suggested as a substitute or even as a necessary precondition for a new allocation of educational, economic, political, and social resources. As noted above, in some cases, the improvement of a person's position in respect to one or all of these aspects may precede socialization and readjustment. We consider, however, that the potentialities of group work have not been sufficiently explored, and hence underestimated. To a large extent, this has been due to the discrepancies in the background and the process of professionalization between casework and group work.

Notes

1. The discussion will be confined to small, face-to-face groups and will not deal with group work related to larger aggregates of people such as recreational and leisure-time programs.

2. Bernard Berelson and Gary A. Steiner, *Human Behavior: An Inventory of Scientific Findings* (New York: Harcourt, Brace and World, 1964), p. 325.

3. See E. James Anthony, "The Generic Elements in Dyadic and in Group Psychotherapy," International Journal of Group Psychotherapy 17 (January 1967): 58.

4. Hopkins, *The Exercise of Influence in Small Groups,* pp. 10-11. Italics added.

5. Homans, *The Human Group,* p. 1. Italics added.

6. Georg Simmel, "Quantitative Aspects of the Group," in Kurt H. Wolff, trans and ed., *The Sociology of Georg Simmel* (New York: Free Press, 1965), pp. 87-174, and Theodore M. Mills, "Some Hypotheses on Small Groups from Simmel," The American Journal of Sociology 64 (May 1958): 642-650.

7. See Robert F. Bales, *Interaction Process Analysis,* and "Adaptive and Integrative Changes as Sources of Strain in Social Systems," in Hare, Borgatta, and Bales, eds., *Small Groups,* pp. 127-131.

8. Walter M. Lifton, *Working with Groups: Group Process and Individual Growth* (New York: John Wiley and Sons, 1966).

9. Nathan W. Ackerman, *Psychodynamics of Family Life* (New York: Basic Books, 1958), p. 283.

10. Emanuel Tropp, "The Group: In Life and in Social Work," Social Casework 49 (May 1968): 270.

11. See, for example, Talcott Parsons, *The Social System,* pp. 299-301; Jerome D. Frank, "Group Methods in Psychotherapy," The Journal of Social Issues 3 (1952): 35-44; and Kaspar D. Naegele, "Clergymen, Teachers, and Psychiatrists: A Study in Roles and Socialization," Canadian Journal of Economics and Political Science 22 (February 1956): 46-62.

12. Herbert C. Kelman and M. B. Parloff, "Interaction Among Three Criteria of Improvement in Group Therapy: Comfort, Effectiveness, and Self-Awareness," Journal of Abnormal and Social Psychology 54 (May 1957): 287.

13. Ibid., p. 288. See also Morton A. Lieberman, "The Implications of Total Group Phenomenon Analysis for Patients and Therapists," International Journal of Group Psychotherapy 17 (January 1967): 71-81. He

claims that a patient never feels as "safe" to reveal feelings in a therapy group as in a one-to-one relationship. It must be noted, however, that he refers to a special type of client, namely, the neurotic patient. On the other hand, activity-oriented group work has been found to be more advantageous than psychodynamically oriented individual treatment in the treatment of psychotic patients; see Martin R. Towey et al., "Group Activities with Psychiatric Inpatients," Social Work 11 (January 1966): 50-56.

14. Ackerman, *Psychodynamics of Family Life,* p. 282.

15. See, for example, Ohlin and Lawrence, "Social Interaction Among Clients."

16. Lieberman, "The Implications of Total Group Phenomena Analysis," p. 78.

17. Cartwright, "The Group as a Medium of Change," p. 389.

18. The degree of convergence of different types of groups with broader social environments will be discussed in detail later.

19. Leon Festinger, Stanley Schachter, and Kurt Back, *Social Pressures in Informal Groups: A Study of Human Factors in Housing* (Standford, Calif.: Stanford University Press, 1967), p. 6.

20. See the discussion of types of power in Part II, ch. 4.

21. Festinger, Schachter, and Back, *Social Pressures in Informal Groups.* See also Festinger, Schachter, and Back, "The Operation of Group Standards," in Cartwright and Zander, eds., *Group Dynamics,* pp. 204-222; Festinger, "An Analysis of Compliant Behavior"; Solomon Asch, "Effects of Group Pressure Upon the Modification and Distortion of Judgements"; Kurt Back, "The Exertion of Influence"; Festinger and John Thibaut "Inter-Personal Communication in Small Groups," Journal of Abnormal and Social Psychology 46 (1951): 92-99; Herbert C. Kelman, "Processes of Opinion Change," Public Opinion Quarterly (Spring 1961); Leonard Berkowitz, "Liking for the Group and the Perceived Merit of the Group's Behavior," Journal of Abnormal and Social Psychology 54 (May 1957): 353-356; and Hopkins, *The Exercise of Influence in Small Groups.* For a summary of research findings on relations in small groups see Berelson and Steiner, *Human Behavior,* ch. VIII.

22. Festinger, Schachter, and Back, *Social Pressures in Informal Groups,* pp. 163-177.

23. Ibid., Table 16, p. 92.

24. See the above discussion of public and private conformity in Chapter 4.

25. In addition to the books and articles referred to earlier, several others, including theoretical formulations and empirical investigations of group processes, are relevant; for example, A. Paul Hare, Edgar F. Borgatta, and Robert F. Bales, eds., *Small Groups: Studies in Social*

Interaction (New York: Alfred A. Knopf, 1955); A. Paul Hare, *Handbook of Small Group Research* (New York: Free Press, 1962); John W. Thibaut and Harold H. Kelly, *The Social Psychology of Groups* (New York: John Wiley and Sons, 1959); Barry E. Collins and Harold Guetzkow, *A Social Psychology of Group Processes for Decision-Making* (New York: John Wiley and Sons, 1964); Bennis, Schein, Berlew, and Steele, *Interpersonal Dynamics;* Warren G. Bennis, Kenneth D. Benne, and Robert Chin, *The Planning of Change* (New York: Holt, Rinehart and Winston, 1961); Theodore M. Mills, *The Sociology of Small Groups* (Englewood Cliffs, N.J.: Prentice-Hall, 1967); and Marie Jahoda and Neil Warren, eds., *Attitudes* (Baltimore: Penguin Books, 1966).

    26. See, for example, Kurt Lewin, *Resolving Social Conflicts* (New York: Harper and Brothers, 1948), ch. 4.

    27. Lewin, *Field Theory,* p. 228.

    28. See, for example, George Levinger, "Continuance in Casework and Other Helping Relationships: A Review of Current Research," Social Work 5 (July 1960): 40-51; Ann W. Shyne, "What Research Tells Us about Short-Term Cases in Family Agencies," Social Casework 38 (May 1957): 223-231; Leonard S. Kogan, "The Short-Term Case in a Family Agency," Parts I, II, III, Social Casework 38 (May 1957): 231-238, 296-302, 366-374; Eugene E. Levitt, "A Comparative Judgemental Study of 'Defection' from Treatment at a Child Guidance Clinic," Journal of Clinical Psychology 14 (1958): 429-432.

    29. Jacob Tuckman and Martha Lavell, "Attrition in Psychiatric Clinics for Children," Public Health Reports 74 (1959): 309-315.

    30. See especially, Survey Research Center, Institute for Social Research, University of Michigan, *A Study of Boy Scouts and Their Scoutmasters* (Ann Arbor, 1960), and Survey Research Center, Institute for Social Research, University of Michigan, *The Program of the Girl Scouts of America* (Ann Arbor: Survey Research Center for the Girl Scouts of America, 1958).

    31. See, for example, Martha Lake and George Levinger, "Continuance Beyond Application Interviews at a Child Guidance Clinic," Social Casework 41 (June 1960): 303-309; Jona M. Rosenfeld, "Strangeness Between Helper and Client: A Possible Explanation of Non-Use of Available Professional Help," Social Service Review 38 (March 1964): 17-25; David Fanshel, "A Study of Caseworkers' Perception of Their Clients," Social Casework 39 (December 1958): 543-551; Scott Briar, "Use of Theory in Studying Effects of Client Social Class on Students' Judgements," Social Work 6 (July 1961); Margaret Blenkner, "Predictive Factors in the Initial Interviews in Family Casework," Social Service Review 28 (March 1954): 65-73; and also Jerome D. Frank, "Why Patients Leave Psychotherapy," Archives of Neurology and Psychiatry 77 (March 1957): 283-299.

32. Kurt Lewin and Paul Grabbe, "Conduct, Knowledge, and Acceptance of New Values," Journal of Social Issues 1 (August 1945): 59.

33. Hopkins, *The Exercise of Influence,* p. 71.

34. For a summary of research findings on the correlation between the degree of attractiveness of the group for an individual and his tendency to be influenced by its members, see Hovland, Janis, and Kelley, *Communication and Persuasion,* pp. 139-149.

35. Leonard Berkowitz, "Liking for the Group and the Perceived Merit of the Group's Behavior," Journal of Abnormal and Social Psychology 54 (May 1957): 353; see also Festinger, et al.

36. Hovland, Janis, and Kelley, *Communication and Persuasion,* p. 21.

37. See, for example, Lilian Ripple and Ernestina Alexander, "Motivation, Capacity, and Opportunity as Related to the Use of Casework Service: Nature of Client's Problem," Social Service Review 30 (March 1956): pp. 38-54; and Beatrice Werble, "Motivation, Capacity, and Opportunity in Services to Adolescent Clients: Major Findings," Social Work 3 (October 1959): 22-30.

38. Clients were defined as continuers if they continued beyond the fourth interview.

39. Ripple and Alexander, "Motivation Capacity."

40. Lilian Ripple, "Factors Associated with Continuance in Casework Service," Social Work 2 (January 1957): 87-94.

41. These percentages are compounded from data presented in Ripple, ibid., Tables 1 and 2, pp. 92 and 94.

42. Norman Polansky, Ronald Lippitt, and Fritz Redl, "An Investigation of Behavioral Contagion in Groups," Human Relations 3 (1950): 320.

43. Ibid., p. 322.

44. See, Hollis, *Casework,* pp. 89-96.

45. See, Polansky, Lippitt, and Redl, "An Investigation of Behavioral Contagion," p. 342.

46. Ibid., p. 337.

47. This may vary according to the extent of prestige and power attributed by a client to different professionals. For example, everybody is familiar with the insecurity and awe one sometimes feels in the encounter with a doctor.

48. These variables and their relation to influence within groups have been systematically analyzed by Hopkins, *The Exercise of Influence,* pp. 10-26.

49. Lewin and Grabbe, "Conduct, Knowledge, and Acceptance," p. 62.

50. See the discussion of this problem in Chapter 4.

51. Naegele, "Clergymen, Teachers, and Psychiatrists," pp. 57-58.

52. Papers presented at the Conference on Community Psychiatry and Social Work, 1965, sponsored by the University of Chicago, have been

published in the Social Service Review 40 (September 1966): 246-282. The Introductory Statement to the series notes that "Of special interest is the fact that all the discussion groups pointed out the importance of the use of groups in providing services in social agencies. While skilled casework is in no sense outmoded, the caseworker also needs to be able to work with groups," p. 245.

53. Herbert C. Kelman, "Two Phases of Behavior Change," Journal of Social Issues 8 (1952): 88.

54. Ibid., p. 85. Italics added.

55. Ibid., p. 86.

56. Tropp, "The Group," p. 267-268. Italics added.

57. See, for example, Frances, H. Scherz, "Multiple-Client Interviewing: Treatment Implications," and Emily C. Faucett, "Multiple-Client Interviewing: A Means of Assessing Family Processes," Social Casework 43 (March 1962): 120-124, 114-119.

58. Groups of prisoners or mental patients are considered as natural groups even though they are not part of the wider community. However, they have a life of their own which extends beyond the professional intervention.

59. The term "two-step flow of communication" was coined by Katz and Lazarsfeld in connection with the effects of mass media upon voting decisions, in their *Personal Influence*, p. 32.

60. Varely, "The Use of Role Theory," p. 365.

61. John H. Mann and Carola H. Mann, "The Relative Effectiveness of Role Playing and Task Oriented Group Experiences in Producing Personality and Behavior Change," Journal of Social Psychology 51 (1956): 317. Bach compared the quality, quantity, and verbal interaction of members of psychotherapy groups engaged in duscussion versus play-drama; see George R. Bach, "Dramatic Play Therapy with Adult Groups," Journal of Psychology 29 (April 1950): 225-246.

62. See, for example, Frank, "Group Methods in Psychotherapy"; and Wilson's distinction between growth-oriented groups and task-oriented groups discussed earlier.

63. For a critical appraisal of the conflicting orientations, goals, and procedures within group psychotherapy and social group work, see, for example, Frey and Kolodny, "Illusions and Realities."

64. See, for example, Martin Wolins, "Measuring the Effects of Social Work Intervention," in Norman A. Polansky, ed., *Social Work Research* (Chicago: University of Chicago Press, 1960), pp. 247-272; Elizabeth Herzog, *Some Guide Lines for Evaluative Research* (Washington, D.C.: U.S. Department of Health, Education and Welfare, Social Security Administration, Children's Bureau, 1959); and Herzog, "One Type of Evaluative Research," Social Service Review 30 (September 1956):

322-331; Ann W. Shyne, "Evaluation of Results in Social Work, *Social Work* 8 (October 1963): 26-35; Harry L. Kitano, "The Concept of 'Precipitant' in Evaluative Research," *Social Work* 4 (October 1963): 34-38; Edward A. Suchman, *Evaluative Research: Principles and Practice in Public Service and Social Action Programs* (New York: Russell Sage Foundation, 1968); and Suchman, "Action for What? A Methodological Critique of Evaluation Studies," read at the 63rd. Annual Meeting of the American Sociological Association (August 1968); Ann W. Shyne, "Casework Research: Past and Present," *Social Casework* 43 (November 1962): 467-473.

65. For a collection of this type of studies see, for example, Norman Fenton and Kermit T. Wiltse, eds., *Group Methods in the Public Welfare Program* (Palo Alto, Calif.: Pacific Book, 1963).

66. Hunt and Kogan, *Measuring Results in Social Casework*; J. McV. Hunt, L. S. Kogan, and Phyllis Bartelme, *A Follow-Up Study of the Results of Social Casework* (New York: Family Service Association of America, 1953; and Ann W. Shyne and L. S. Kogan, "A Study of Components of Movement," *Social Casework* 39 (June 1958): 333-341.

67. For example, Powers and Witmer, *An Experiment*; Walter B. Miller, "The Impact of a 'Total Community' Delinquency Control Project," *Social Problems* 10 (Fall 1962): pp. 168-176; and Ellery F. Reed, "Families Served by Group Work Agencies in a Deteriorated Area Compared with the General Population of that Area," *Social Service Review* 28 (December 1954): 412-423.

68. Helen Northen, "Evaluating Movement of Individuals in Social Group Work," *Group Work Papers, 1957*, pp. 28-37; Henry S. Maas, "Evaluating the Individual Member in the Group," *Group Work and Communicty Organization, 1953-1954*, pp. 36-44. For a review of research in social group work, including evaluative research, see William Schwartz, "Neighborhood Centers," in Henry S. Maas, ed., *Five Fields of Social Service: Reviews of Research* (New York: National Association of Social Workers, 1966), pp. 144-184.

69. Meyer, Borgatta, and Jones, *Girls at Vocational High.*

70. Ibid., p. 15.

71. Alvin L. Schorr, "Mirror, Mirror on the Wall . . .," *Social Work* 10 (July 1965): 112. See also a detailed critique of the study and its methodology by Mary E. McDonald, "Reunion at Vocational High," *Social Service Review* 40 (June 1966): 175-189.

72. Articles by Earl Ubell, science editor of the New York Herald Tribune, and by Alfred Friendly of the Washington Post, March 17, 1966.

73. Meyer, Borgatta, and Jones, *Girls at Vocational High,* p. 204. The various measures to detect the impact of the treatment program were (1) objective measures: completion of school by the girls in the sample,

academic performance, school-related behavior, and out-of-school behavior; and (2) self-reports and responses: attitude responses, personality tests, and sociometric data.

74. Ibid., p. 205.

75. The Youth Consultation Service, a nonsectarian, voluntary social agency engaged mainly in casework services for adolescent girls.

76. Ibid., p. 149.

77. Ibid., p. 151.

78. Workers' ratings of client change in other aspects are presented in Tables 15 and 16, Ibid., p. 153 and 154.

SUMMARY AND CONCLUSION

In this study we have joined those who have claimed, lately, that "something is wrong with social work." Criticism has been launched at two main targets, one pertains to the present public-assistance system and the war on poverty programs in general. This includes the problem of the magnitude of allowances for "minimum income," and the procedures through which eligibility is determined and welfare payments allocated.

The second area with which dissatisfaction has become increasingly pronounced is the treatment aspect of social work practice. In this respect the attack has been directed mainly at the casework method whose effectiveness and adequacy are now being questioned by many social work practitioners, and others outside the profession.

We have focused attention on this second point, and referred to the broader problems of welfare policy only insofar as they impinge upon the effectiveness of the provision of professional services to welfare clients. Moreover, we have not dealt specifically with the issue of social workers' involvement in social reform and political action. These problems, have been referred to only in their conjunction with, and implications for the operation of social work, i.e., casework in welfare agencies.

Our analysis of this felt incompatibility has been guided by a sociological-theoretical perspective. We have traced the tensions created by the combination of financial-aid and professional treatment, and their manifestations in various spheres: in the profession-organization relation, particularly as demonstrated in the supervisor-worker relationship; in the conflict created in the role-definition of the social worker, and its repercussions on role-performance; and in the interaction between worker and client, exhibited mainly in the problems involved in exertion and acceptance of different types of power and influence.

The examination of each of these aspects supported the conclusion that the task of income-maintenance should be separated from the function of bringing about change in client perceptions, self-images, attitudes, normative commitments, and patterns of behavior.

On the basis of a comparison of social work with the established professions, such as medicine and law, along the principal dimensions of professionalism, social work has been classified as a semi-profession, signifying a relatively undeveloped knowledge base on which practice is built, no distinct monopoly of unique skills and competence, and relatively little professional autonomy within formal organizations. It was noted that one of the core attributes of the professions, namely, their code of ethics, is strongly emphasized in social work; however, it was suggested that a highly developed service orientation, when not combined with esoteric knowledge and competence, does not endow the profession with an established, prestigeful position. The implications of semi-professionalism have been scrutinized in the social worker-bureaucracy relation, and in particular, in the interaction between the worker and his client. Regarding the worker-client relationship, it was suggested that the pattern of casework and its dyadic structure are the main sources of the limited results achieved by this method. It was argued that the attractiveness and salience of the casework relationship for clients cannot be manipulated as bases for influence exertion, because their significance for and impact upon the client are relatively low. We, therefore, proposed to shift much of the operation of social work, now conducted in dyads, to small group settings, in order to enhance its effectiveness. This contention was based on the assumption, and on available research evidence, that people are more disposed to change their orientations and activities if influence in this direction is exercised in small groups than in isolated professional-client pairs. This is particularly so when the professional's authority is restricted by lack of exclusive knowledge, and by subjection to bureaucratic controls.

In respect to the diverse approaches toward the purposes and techniques of group work, it was argued that group work can be more effective if it will disengage itself from the psychotherapeutic tradition of casework. We think that people who suffer from deep-rooted intrapersonal disturbances should not be included in the clientele of social group work, nor for that matter, should they be treated by caseworkers. The essential purpose of group work, as we see it, is to help clients acquire new interpersonal skills, and perform their social roles in a more constructive and rewarding manner.

EPILOGUE

The idea of needed change and innovation in social work is, of course, not new, nor is it original. Its most enthusiastic advocates, and the most severe critics of the established, present patterns of practice, are to be found within the profession itself.

Those who suggest far-reaching changes in the purpose and practice of social work will surely encounter strong resistance. The professional ideology and the patterns of training and performance are by now established; so are the formal organization, "vested interests," and positions of power. The fact that social work is a semi-profession, and is still striving to move up on the professional hierarchy may intensify resistance to relinquish hard-gained achievements of professional status. It is well known that in our society the theoretically oriented scientist is accorded higher esteem as compared with the action-oriented professional within the same discipline. This situation, however, may change if present trends continue to develop, and the contribution of social workers and other human relations professionals in dealing with pressing social problems becomes more manifest.

Another factor related to semi-professionalism, and which makes the struggle for change even harder, is the bureaucratic organizational context in which virtually all social work is being practiced, and the consequent relative low degree of professional autonomy of social workers.[1] Innovation and experimentation are inhibited by agency structure and policy in public as well as voluntary agencies. If a social worker ventures to get involved in social action such as performing the role of advocate for his clients, or stating his opinion on highly controversial issues, he will usually be reprimanded, and in some agencies, the consequences could be even more severe. The Hatch Act prohibits political activity by employees of the federal government and by employees of state programs financed by federal funds. In voluntary agencies political activity may also adversely affect the fund raising capacity of the agency to which its governing board is naturally very sensitive.

The state of the body of knowledge upon which social work practice is based furnishes another obstacle to constructive change. As has been mentioned earlier, "practice theory"[2] in social work has been developed mainly in a trial-and-error manner. It has not developed through systematic research directed by a body of theory, and later converted into practice principles. Therefore, in the process of professionalization, social work turned to the behavioral sciences, first to psychiatry and later to the social sciences, in an attempt to utilize their theories and findings. At this point the problem of defining the specific pattern of collaboration of social work with the social sciences emerged, and has since been a recurrent theme in social work literature.[3]

The fundamental difficulty for cooperation stems from the diverse approaches of social science and social work to knowledge. The social scientist's approach is basically theoretical, and his aim is the production of knowledge for its own sake; the practitioner's orientation is basically pragmatic, he is mainly concerned with the applicability of knowledge and its effectiveness in solving the problems with which he is confronted. This engenders barriers for communication and mutual trust; social scientists accuse social workers of not being research minded, and social workers argue that social science formulations are too abstract to be directly applicable to practice. Moreover, social workers claim that until now the social sciences have been of little help in supplying new, more effective alternatives to the methods employed in social work because they lack the interest as well as adequate knowledge about change and particularly about the induction of change.[4]

Thus, we see that the characteristic features of semi-professionalism may impede the needed change and reconstruction of social work's orientation and practice. This rigidity has caused critics to describe the present situation as "disengagement from the poor," as "turning a deaf ear to the real needs of clients," and as being "out of touch" with current social developments. However, the one professional attribute that has not been mentioned as hindering change, namely, the code of ethics—the dedication to serve the client—may in fact play a major role in future modifications of conceptions and activities. Concern for the client's well-being has always guided the profession, and although this goal is sometimes pushed into the background in social work, as well as in other professions, it becomes prominent in times of crisis and change. At present, the professional ethic, and different interpretations of its "real" meaning are at the source of the criticism and debate about the desired goals to be aimed at, and the effective mehtod for achieving them in social work practice.

Notes

1. This and other attributes of semi-professionalism have been discussed in more detail in Part I.

2. "Practice theory" is defined by Greenwood as the collection of principles, that is, the description of diagnostic and treatment typologies which guide the practitioner; see Greenwood, "Social Science and Social Work," p. 26.

3. For an early discussion of this problem see, for example, Werner W. Boehm, "Social Work and the Social Sciences: A Theoretical Note," Journal of Psychiatric Social Work 21 (September 1951): 4-8. See also William Schwartz, "Small Group Science and Group Work Practice," pp. 39-46, and Martin Bloom, "Connecting Formal Behavioral Science Theory to Individual Social Work Practice," Social Service Review 39 (March 1965): 11-22; Edwin J. Thomas, ed., *Behavioral Science for Social Workers* (New York: Free Press, 1967), especially Part I.

4. See, for example, Briar, "The Casework Predicament."

BIBLIOGRAPHY

"A Study of Boy Scouts and Their Scoutsmasters." Ann Arbor: Survey Research Center, Institute for Social Research, University of Michigan, 1960.

Ackerman, Nathan W. *Psychodynamics of Family Life.* New York: Basic Books, 1958.

Anthony, James E. "The Generic Elements in Dyadic and Group Psychotherapy." International Journal of Group Psychotherapy 17 (January 1967).

Argyle, Michael, Godfrey Gardner, and Frank Cioffi. "Supervisory Methods Related to Productivity, Absenteeism, and Labor Turnover." Human Relations 11 (February 1958).

Asch, Solomon E. *Social Psychology.* New York: Prentice-Hall, 1952.

——"Effects of Group Pressure upon the Modification and Distortion of Judgements," in Guy E. Swanson, Theodore M. Newcomb, and Eugene L. Hartley, eds., *Readings in Social Psychology.* New York: Holt and Company, 1952.

——"Studies in the Principles of Judgements by Groups and by Ego-Standards." Journal of Social Psychology 12 (1940).

Austin, Lucille N. "An Evaluation of Supervision." Social Casework 37 (October 1952).

——"The Changing Role of the Supervisor." Smith College Studies in Social Work 31 (June 1961).

——"Supervision in Social Work," in Russell H. Kurtz, ed., Social Work Yearbook. New York: National Association of Social Workers, 1960.

Babcock, Charlotte. "Social Work as Work." Social Casework 34 (December 1953).

Bach, George R. "Dramatic Play Therapy With Adult Groups." Journal of Psychology 29 (April 1950).

Back, Kurt W. "The Exertion of Influence through Social Communication." Journal of Abnormal and Social Psychology 46 (1951).

233

Bales, Robert F. "Adaptive and Integrative Changes as Sources of Strain in Social Systems," in Paul A. Hare, Edgar F. Borgatta, and Robert F. Bales, eds., *Small Groups*. New York: Alfred A. Knopf, 1955.

——*Interaction Process Analysis*. Cambridge, Mass.: Addison-Wesley, 1950.

——and Fred L. Strodtbeck. "Phases in Group Problem Solving," in Dorwin Cartwright and Alvin Zander, eds., *Group Dynamics: Research and Theory*. New York: Row, Peterson and Company, 1953.

Ballard, Robert G. and Emily H. Mudd "Some Sources of Difference Between Client and Agency Evaluation of Effectiveness of Counseling." Social Casework 39 (January 1958).

——"Some Theoretical and Practical Problems in Evaluating Effectiveness of Counseling." Social Casework 38 (October 1957).

Becker, Howard S. "Personal Change in Adult Life." Sociometry 27 (March 1964).

——"The Nature of a Profession," in Nelson B. Henry, ed., *The Sixty-first Yearbook of the National Society for the Study of Education*. Chicago: University of Chicago Press, 1962.

Ben-David, Joseph. "The Professional Role of the Physician in Bureaucratized Medicine: A Study in Role Conflict." Human Relations 11 (1958).

Bennis, Warren G., Kenneth D. Benne, and Robert Chin. *The Planning of Change*. New York: Holt, Rinehart and Winston, 1961.

Bennis, Warren G., N. Berkowitz, M. Affinito, and M. Malone. "Authority, Power and the Ability to Influence," Human Relations, 11 (1958).

Bennis, Warren G., Edgar Schein, David E. Berlew, and Fred J. Steele, eds. *Interpersonal Dynamics: Essays and Readings in Human Interaction*. Chicago: Dorsey Press, 1964.

Berkowitz, Leonard. "Liking for the Group and the Perceived Merit of the Group's Behavior." Journal of Abnormal and Social Psychology 54 (May 1957).

Berelson, Bernard and Gary A. Steiner. *Human Behavior: An Inventory of Scientific Findings*. New York: Harcourt, Brace and World, 1964.

Biestek, Felix P. "An Analysis of the Casework Relationship." Social Casework 35 (February 1954).

Billingsley, Andrew. "Bureaucratic and Professional Orientation Patterns in Social Casework." Social Service Review 38 (December 1964).

Bisno, Herbert. "How Social Will Social Work Be?" Social Work 1 (April 1956).

Blau, Peter M. *Exchange and Power in Social Life*. New York: John Wiley and Sons, 1964.

——"Orientations Toward Clients in a Public Welfare Agency." Administrative Science Quarterly 5 (December 1960).

——and W. Richard Scott. *Formal Organizations: A Comparative Approach.* London: Routledge and Kegan Paul, 1963.

——, Wolf V. Heydebrand, and Robert E. Stauffer. "The Structure of Small Bureaucracies." American Sociological Review 31 (April 1966).

Bleckner, Margaret. "Predicative Factors in the Initial Interview in Family Casework." Social Service Review 28 (March 1954).

Bloom, Martin. "Connecting Formal Behavioral Science Theory to Individual Social Work Practice." Social Service Review 39 (March 1965).

Boehm, Werner W. "Relationship of Social Work to Other Professions," in Harry L. Lurie, ed., *Encyclopedia of Social Work.* New York: National Association of Social Workers, 1965.

——"The Nature of Social Work." Social Work 3 (April 1958).

——"Social Work and the Social Sciences: A Theoretical Note." Journal of Psychiatric Social Work 21 (September 1951).

Bradford, Leland P., Jack R. Gibb, and Kenneth D. Benne, eds. *T-Group Theory and Laboratory Method.* New York: John Wiley and Sons, 1964.

Breger, Louis and James L. McGaugh. "Critique and Reformulation of 'Learning Theory' Approaches to Psychotherapy and Neurosis." Psychological Bulletin 63 (May 1965).

Briar, Scott. "The Casework Predicament." Social Work 13 (January 1968).

——"The Current Crisis in Casework." *Social Work Practice, 1967.* New York: Columbia University Press, 1967.

——"Family Services," in Henry S. Maas, ed., *Five Fields of Social Service: Reviews of Research.* New York: National Association of Social Workers, 1966.

——"Use of Theory in Studying Effects of Class on Students' Judgements." Social Work 6 (July 1961).

Brennen, Earl C. "The Casework Relationship: Exerpts from a Heretic's Notebook." New Perspectives: The Berkeley Journal of Social Welfare 1 (Spring 1967).

Bruno, Frank J. and Louis Towley. *Trends in Social Work, 1877-1956.* New York: Columbia University Press, 1955.

Bucher, Rue and Anselm Strauss. "Professions in Process." American Journal of Sociology 66 (January 1961).

Burns, Mary E. "Supervision in Social Work," in *Encyclopedia of Social Work.* New York: National Association of Social Workers, 1965.

——"What's Wrong with Public Welfare?" Social Service Review 30 (June 1962).

Bylaws of the National Association of Social Workers. Adopted by Membership Referendum, June 1, 1963.

Carr-Saunders, Alexander M. "Metropolitan Conditions and Traditional Professional Relationship," in Robert M. Fisher, ed., *The Metropolis in Modern Life.* Garden City, N.Y.: Doubleday and Company, 1955.

——and P. A. Wilson. *The Professions.* Oxford: Clarendon Press, 1933.

Cartwright, Dorwin. "The Group as a Medium of Change," in Dorwin Cartwright and Alvin Zander, eds., *Group Dynamics: Research and Theory.* New York: Row, Peterson and Company, 1953.

Cloward, Richard A. and Irwin Epstein. "Private Social Welfare's Disengagement from the Poor: The Case of Family Adjustment Agencies," in Mayer N. Zald, ed., *Social Welfare Institutions.* New York: John Wiley and Sons, 1965.

Cloward, Richard A. and Lloyd Ohlin. *Delinquency and Opportunity: A Theory of Delinquent Gangs.* New York: Free Press, 1960.

Cloward, Richard A. and Frances F. Piven. "A Strategy to End Poverty." The Nation 202 (May 2, 1966).

"Code of Ethics," Adopted by the Delegate Assembly of the National Association of Social Workers, October 13, 1960, in Harry L. Lurie, ed., *Encyclopedia of Social Work.* New York: National Association of Social Workers, 1966.

Coffey, Hubert S. "Socio and Psyche Group Process: Integrative Concepts." Journal of Social Issues 8 (1952).

Cohen, Albert K. *Delinquent Boys: The Culture of the Gang.* New York: Free Press, 1955.

Cohen, Nathan E. "Social Work as a Profession," in Russell H. Kurtz, ed., *Social Work Yearbook.* National Association of Social Workers, 1957.

Coleman, Jules V. "Distinguishing Between Psychotherapy and Casework." Journal of Social Casework 30 (June 1949).

Collins, Barry E. and Harold Guetzkow. *A Social Psychology of Group Processes for Decision-Making.* New York: John Wiley and Sons, 1964.

Cooper, Shirley. "The Swing to Community Mental Health." Social Casework 49 (May 1968).

Coser, Lewis. *The Functions of Social Conflict.* New York: Free Press, 1956.

Coser, Rose Laub. "Insulation from Observability and Types of Social Conformity." American Sociological Review 26 (February 1961).

Coyle, Grace Longwell. "On Becoming Professional," in Harleigh B. Trecker, ed., *Group Work Foundations and Frontiers.* New York: Whiteside, 1955.

——"Social Group Work: An Aspect of Social Work Practice." Journal of Social Issues 8 (1952).

Dahlström, Edmund. "Exchange, Inlfuence and Power." Acta Sociologica 9 (1966).

Devis, Donald A. "Teaching and Administrative Functions in Supervision." Social Work 10 (April 1965).

Dollard, Charles. Proceedings of the First Annual Trustees Reception of the New York School of Social Work. Bulletin of the New York School of Social Work, Columbia University (September 1952).

Dollard, John and Neal E. Miller. *Personality and Psychotherapy.* New York: McGraw-Hill, 1950.

Eisenstadt, S. N. "Bureaucracy, Bureaucratization, and Debureaucratization." Administrative Science Quarterly 4 (December 1959).

Emerson, Richard M. "Power-Dependence Relations." American Sociological Review 27 (February 1962).

Etzioni, Amitai. *The Active Society.* New York: Free Press, 1968.

— — *Modern Organizations.* New Jersey: Prentice-Hall, 1967.

— — *A Comparative Analsyis of Complex Organizations.* New York: Free Press, 1961.

Eysenck, Hans J. "The Effects of Psychotherapy." International Journal of Psychiatry 14 (January 1965).

— —"The Effects of Psychotherapy: An Evaluation." Journal of Consulting Psychology 16 (October 1952).

— —and Stanley Rachman. *The Causes and Cures of Neurosis.* San Diego: Robert R. Knapp, 1965.

Fanshel, David. "A Study of Caseworkers' Perception of their Clients." Social Casework 39 (December 1958).

Faucet, Emily. "Multiple-Client Interviewing: A Means of Assessing Family Processes." Social Casework 43 (March 1962).

Fenton, Norman and Kermit T. Wiltse, eds. *Group Methods in the Public Welfare Program.* Palo Alto, Calif.: Pacific Books, 1963.

Festinger, Leon. *A Theory of Cognitive Dissonance.* Evanston, Ill.: Row, Peterson and Company, 1957.

— —"An Analsyis of Compliant Behavior," in Muzafer Sherif and M. O. Wilson, eds., *Group Relations at the Crossroads.* New York: Harper Bros., 1953.

— —, Stanley Schachter, and Kurt Back. *Social Pressures in Informal Groups: A Study of Human Factors in Housing.* Stanford, Calif.: Stanford University Press, 1967.

— —"The Operation of Group Standards," in Dorwin Cartwright and Alvin Zander, eds., *Group Dynamics: Research and Theory.* New York: Row, Peterson and Company, 1953.

— —and John Thibaut. "Interpersonal Communication in Small Groups." Journal of Abnormal and Social Psychology 46 (January 1951).

— —, Leon, K. Bach, S. Schacter, H. H. Kelley, and J. Thibaut. "Theory and Experiment in Social Communication." Ann Arbor: Research Center for Group Dynamics, Institute for Social Research 1950.

Fine, Reva. "Some Theoretical Considerations Basic to Supervising Technique." Social Work 1 (January 1956).

Fizdale, Ruth. "Peer Group Supervision." Social Casework 39 (October 1958).

Flexner, Abraham. "Is Social Work a Profession?" Proceedings of the National Conference of Charities and Corrections. Chicago, 1915.

Ford, Donald H. and Hugh B. Urban. Systems of Psychotherapy: A Comparative Study. New York: John Wiley and Sons, 1965.

Frank, Jerome D. Persuasion and Healing. New York: Schocken Books, 1963.

— —"Why Patients Leave Psychotherapy." Archives of Neurology and Psychiatry 77 (March 1957).

— —"Group Methods in Psychotherapy." Journal of Social Issues 8 (1952).

Freidson, Elliot. "Disability as Social Deviance," in Marvin B. Sussman, ed., Sociology and Rehabilitation. American Sociological Association, 1966.

— —"Dilemmas in the Doctor-Patient Relationship," in Arnold M. Rose, ed., Human Behavior and Sociological Association, 1966.

Freilich, Morris. "The Natural Triad in Kinship and Complex Systems." American Sociological Review 29 (August 1967).

French, D. G. Statistics of Social Work Education. New York: Council on Social Work Education, 1957.

French, John R. P., Jr. and Bertram Raven. "The Bases of Social Power," in Dorwin Cartwright, ed., Studies in Social Power Ann Arbor: University of Michigan, 1959.

— —"Organized and Unorganized Groups under Fear and Frustration," in Studies in Topological and Vector Psychology, III. Iowa City: University of Iowa, 1944.

Freud, Sigmund. The Complete Introductory Lectures on Psychoanalysis. James Strachey, trans. and ed. New York: W. W. Norton, 1966.

Frey, Louise A. and Ralph L. Kolodny. "Illusions and Realities in Current Social Work with Groups." Social Work 9 (April 1964).

Friedman, Milton. Capitalism and Freedom. Chicago: University of Chicago Press, 1962.

Fromm, Erich. Escape from Freedom. New York: Farrar and Rinehart, 1941.

Gifford, C. G. "Sensitivity Training and Social Work." Social Work 13 (April 1968).

Glasser, Paul H. "Social Role, Personality and Group Work Practice," in Social Work Practice, 1962. New York: Columbia University Press, 1962.

Goldner, Fred H. and R. R. Ritti. "Professionalization as Career Immobility." American Journal of Sociology 27 (March 1967).

Goode, William J. "Encroachment, Charlatanism, and the Emerging Professions: Psychology, Sociology and Medicine." American Sociological Review 25 (December 1960).

——"Illegitimacy in the Carribean Social Structure." American Sociological Review 25 (February 1960).

——"Community within a Community: The Professions." American Sociological Review 22 (April 1957).

Goss, Mary E. "Influence and Authority among Physicians in an Out-Patient Clinic." American Sociological Review 26 (February 1961).

Gosser, Charles F. "Local Residents as Mediators Between Middle-Class Professional Workers and Low-Class Clients." Social Service Review 40 (March 1966).

Gouldner, Alvin W. "Cosmopolitans and Locals: Toward an Analysis of Latent Social Roles,"—I, II. Administrative Science Quarterly 2 (December 1957, March 1958).

Greenwood, Ernest. "Attributes of a Profession." Social Work 2 (July 1957).

——"Social Science and Social Work: A Theory of their Relationship." Social Service Review 29 (March 1955).

Gross, Edward. "When Occupations Meet: Professions in Trouble." Hospital Administration 12 (Summer 1967).

Grosser, Charles. "Community Development Programs Serving the Urban Poor." Social Work 10 (July 1965).

Hare, Paul A. Handbook of Small Group Research. New York: Free Press, 1962.

——Edgar F. Borgatta, and Robert F. Bales, eds. Small Groups: Studies in Social Interaction. New York: Alfred A. Knopf, 1955.

Harris George. "Do We Owe People a Living?" Look 32 (April 30, 1968).

Hellerbrand, Shirley C. "Client Value Orientations: Implications for Diagnosis and Treatment." Social Casework 42 (April 1961).

Herzog, Elizabeth. "One Type of Evaluative Research." Social Service Review 30 (September 1956).

Hollis, E. V. and A. L. Taylor. Social Work Education in the United States. New York: Columbia University Press, 1951.

Homans, George C. The Human Group. London: Routledge and Kegan Paul, 1962.

——Social Behavior: Its Elementary Forms. New York: Harcourt, Brace and World, 1961.

Hopkins, Terence K. The Exercise of Influence in Small Groups. New Jersey: Bedminister Press, 1964.

——and Sanci Michael. Group Structure and Opinion Change: An Analysis of an Effective Training Program. New York: Bureau of Applied Social Research, Columbia University, 1963.

Hovland, Carl I., Irving L. Janis, and Harold H. Kelley. *Communication and Persuasion.* New Haven: Yale University Press, 1953.

Hughes, Everett C. *Men and their Work.* New York: Free Press, 1958.

Hunt, McVicker J. and Leonard S. Kogan. *Measuring Results in Social Casework: A Manual on Judging Movement.* New York: Family Service Association of America, 1950.

——and Phyllis Bartelme. *A Follow-Up Study of the Results of Social Casework.* New York: Family Service Association of America, 1953.

Hyman, Herbert H. "The Psychology of Status." Archives of Psychology 269 (1942).

Jahoda, Marie. "Conformity and Independence: A Psychological Analysis." Human Relations 12 (May 1959).

——"Psychological Issues in Civil Liberties." The American Psychologist 11 (May 1956).

——"and Neil Warren, eds. *Attitudes.* Baltimore: Penguin Books, 1966.

"Jobs and Occupations: A Popular Evaluation." National Opinion Research Center. In Reinhard Bendix and Seymour M. Lipset, eds., *Class, Status and Power.* New York: Free Press, 1953.

Johnson, D. L., P. G. Hanson, P. Rothans, Robert B. Morton, F. A. Lyle, and R. Moyer. "A Follow-Up Evaluation of Human Relations Training for Psychiatric Patients," in Edgar H. Schein and Warren G. Bennis, eds., *Personal and Organizational Change through Group Methods: The Laboratory Approach.* New York: John Wiley and Sons, 1965.

Judson, Jerome. "The System Really Isn't Working." Life (November 1, 1968).

Kadushin, Alfred. "The Knowledge Base of Social Work," in Alfred J. Kahn, ed., *Issues in American Social Work.* New York: Columbia University Press, 1959.

——"Prestige of Social Work—Facts and Factors." Social Work 3 (April 1958).

Kadushin, Charles. "Social Distance Between Client and Professional." American Journal of Sociology 67 (March 1962).

Kahn, Alfred J. "The Nature of Social Work Knowledge," in Cora Kasius, ed., *New Directions in Social Work.* New York: Harper, 1954.

Kahn, Robert L. and Daniel Katz. "Social Work and Organizational Change." *The Social Welfare Forum,* Proceedings of the National Conference on Social Welfare. New York: Columbia University Press, 1966.

——"Leadership Practices in Relation to Productivity Morale," in Dorwin Cartwright and Alvin F. Zander, eds., *Group Dynamics: Research and Theory.* Evanston, Ill.: Row, Peterson and Company, 1953.

Kaiser, Clara. "Characteristics of Social Group Work." *The Social Welfare*

Forum, 1957. Proceedings of the National Conference on Social Welfare. New York: Columbia University Press, 1960.

——"Social Group Work: A Social Work Method." Social Work 4 (October 1960).

Kallen, David J., Dorothy Miller, and Arlene Daniels. "Sociology, Social Work, and Social Problems." The American Sociologist 3 (August 1968).

Katz, Elihu and Brenda Danet. "Petitions and Persuasive Appeals: A Study of Official-Client Relations." American Sociological Review 31 (December 1966).

Katz, Elihu and S. N. Eisenstadt. "Some Sociological Observations on the Response of Israeli Organizations to New Immmigrants." Administrative Science Quarterly 5 (June 1960).

Katz, Elihu and Paul F. Lazarsfeld. *Personal Influence.* New York: Free Press.

Kelley, Harold H. and Christine L. Woodruff. "Members' Reaction to Apparent Group Approval of a Counternorm Communication." Journal of Abnormal and Social Psychology 52 (January 1956).

——and Edmund H. Volkart. "The Resistance to Change of Group-Anchored Attitudes." American Sociological Review 17 (August 1952).

Kelman, Herbert C. "Processes of Opinion Change." Public Opinion Quarterly (Spring 1961).

——"Compliance, Identification and Internalization: Three Processes of Attitude Change." Journal of Conflict Resolution 2 (March 1958).

——"Two Phases of Behavior Change." Journal of Social Issues 8 (1952).

——and M. B. Parloff. "Interaction Among Three Criteria of Improvement in Group Therapy: Comfort, Effectiveness, and Self-Awareness." Journal of Abnormal and Social Psychology 54 (May 1957).

——and Harry H. Lerner. "Group Therapy, Group Work and Adult Education: The Need for Classification." Journal of Social Issues 8 (1952).

Kidneigh, John C. "Social Work as a Profession," in Russell H. Kurtz, ed., *Social Work Yearbook.* New York: National Association of Social Workers, 1960.

Kitano, Harry L. "The Concept of 'Precipitant' in Evaluative Research." Social Work 4 (October 1963).

Kogan, Leonard S. "The Short-Term Case in a Family Agency." Social Casework 38 (May 1957).

Konopka, Gisela. *Social Group Work: A Helping Process.* Englewood Cliffs, N.J.: Prentice-Hall, 1963.

——"Social Group Work: A Social Work Method." Social Work 4 (October 1960).

——"Similarities and Differences between Group Work and Group Therapy." Social Work With Groups, 1951. New York: National Association of Social Workers, 1951.

Kornhauser, William. *Scientists in Industry: Conflict and Accommodation.* Berkeley: University of California Press, 1962.

Kuhn, Manford H. "The Interview and the Professional Relationship," in Arnold M. Rose, ed., *Human Behavior and Social Processes.* Boston: Houghton-Mifflin Company, 1962.

Lake, Martha and George Levinger. "Continuance Beyond Application Interviews at a Child Guidance Clinic." Social Casework 41 (June 1960).

Leader, Arthur L. "New Directions in Supervision." Social Casework 38 (November 1957).

Lemert, Edwin M. *Human Deviance, Social Problems, and Social Control.* Englewood Cliffs, N.J.: Prentice-Hall, 1967.

Lennard, Henry L. and Arnold Bernstein. *The Anatomy of Psychotherapy: Systems of Communication and Expectation.* New York: Columbia University Press, 1960.

Leonard, Peter. "Social Control, Class Values and Social Practice." Social Work 4 (January 1959).

Levinger, George. "Continuance in Casework and Other Helping Relationships: A Review of Current Research." Social Work 5 (July 1960).

Levinson, Perry and Jeffrey Schiller. "Role Analysis of the Indigenous Nonprofessional." Social Work 11 (July 1966).

Levitt, Eugene. "A Comparative Judgemental Study of 'Defection' from Treatment at a Child Guidance Clinic." Journal of Clinical Psychology 14 (1958).

Lewin, Kurt. *Field Theory in Social Science.* Dorwin Cartwright, ed., New York: Harper and Row, 1964.

——"Group Decision and Social Change," in Guy E. Swanson, Theodore M. Newcombe, and Eugene L. Hartley, eds., *Readings in Social Psychology.* New York: Henry Holt and Company, 1952.

——*Resolving Social Conflicts.* New York: Harper and Bros., 1948.

——and Paul Grabbe. "Conduct, Knowledge, and Acceptance of New Values." Journal of Social Issues 1 (August 1945).

Lieberman, Morton A. "The Implications of Total Group Phenomena Analysis for Patient and Therapist." International Journal of Group Psychotherapy 17 (January 1967).

Lifton, Walter M. *Working with Groups: Group Process and Individual Growth.* New York: John Wiley and Sons, 1966.

Lindeman, W. T. "An Experiment in Casework-Group Work Co-operation." The Group 8 (November 1945).

Lindenberg, Ruth E. "Changing Traditional Patterns of Supervision." Social Work 2 (April 1957).

Lippitt, Ronald, Norman Polansky, Fritz Redl, and Sidney Rosen. "The Dynamics of Power," in Dorwin Cartwright and Alvin F. Zander, eds., *Group Dynamics: Research and Theory.* Evanston, Ill.: Row, Peterson and Co., 1953.

Lockwood, David. "Some Remarks on 'The Social System'." British Journal of Sociology 7 (June 1956).

Lotrie, Dan C. "The Balance of Control and Autonomy in Elementary School Teaching," in Amitai Etzioni, ed., *The Semi-Professions and Their Organization.* New York: The Free Press, 1969.

Lurie, Harry L. "The Responsibilities of a Socially Oriented Profession," in Cora Kasius, ed., *New Directions in Social Work.* New York: Harper, 1954.

Lynn, Kenneth S. and the Editors of Daedalus, eds. *The Professions in America.* Boston: Beacon Press, 1967.

Maas, Henry S. "Group Influences on Client-Worker Interaction." Social Work 9 (April 1964).

——"Evaluating the Individual Member in the Group." *Group Work and Community Organization, 1953-1954.* Papers presented at the National Conference of Social Work. New York: Columbia University Press, 1954.

Mann, John H. and Carola H. Mann. "The Relative Effectiveness of Role Playing and Task Oriented Group Experiences in Producing Personality and Behavior Change." Journal of Social Psychology 51 (May 1960).

Mauksch, Hans O. "The Organizational Context of Nursing Practice," in Fred Davis, ed., *The Nursing Professions: Five Sociological Essays.* New York: John Wiley and Sons, 1966.

McCormick, Charles G. "Group Dynamics and Hemeophatic Treatment." International Journal of Group Psychotherapy 7 (January 1957).

McCormick, Mary J. "Professional Responsibility and the Professional Image." Social Casework 47 (December 1966).

——"The Role of Values in the Helping Process." Social Casework 47 (December 1966).

McDonald, Mary. "Reunion at Vocational High." Social Service Review 40 (June 1966).

McEntrie, Davis and Joanne Hayworth. "The Two Functions of Public Welfare: Income Maintenance and Social Services." Social Work 12 (January 1967).

McIsaac, Hugh and Harold Wilkinson. "Clients Talk About Their Caseworkers." Public Welfare 23 (July 1965).

McRae, Robert H. "Social Work and Social Action." Social Service Review 40 (March 1966).

Merton, Robert K. *Mass Persuasion: The Social Psychology of a War Bond Drive.* New York: Harper and Row, 1946.

––*Social Theory and Social Structure.* New York: Free Press, 1957.

––"The Role-Set: Problems in Sociological Theory." British Journal of Sociology 8 (June 1957).

––George Reader, and Patricia L. Kendall, eds. *The Student Physician.* Cambridge, Mass.: Harvard University Press, 1957.

––and Elinor Barber. "Sociological Ambivalence," in Edward A. Tiryakin, ed., *Sociological Theory, Values and Sociocultural Change.* New York: Harper and Row, 1967.

Meyer, Henry J. "Professionalization and Social Work," in Alfred Kahn, ed., *Issues in American Social Work.* New York: Columbia University Press, 1959.

––Eugene Litwak, Edwin J. Thomas, and Robert D. Vinter. "Social Work and Social Welfare," in Paul F. Lazarsfeld, William H. Sewell, and Harold L. Wilensky, eds., *The Uses of Sociology.* New York: Basic Books, 1967.

––, Edgar F. Borgatta, and Wyatt C. Jones. *Girls at Vocational High: An Experiment in Social Work Intervention.* New York: Russell Sage Foundation, 1965.

Meyerson, Emma T. "The Social Work Image and Self-Image." Social Work 4 (July 1959).

Miller, Henry. "Value Dilemmas in Social Casework." Social Work 13 (January 1968).

Miller, Irving. "Distinctive Characteristics of Supervision in Group Work." Social Work 5 (January 1960).

Miller, Walter B. "The Impact of a 'Total Community' Delinquency Control Project." Social Problems 10 (Fall 1962).

Mills, Theodore M. *The Sociology of Small Groups.* Englewood Cliffs, N.J.: Prentice-Hall, 1967.

––"Some Hypotheses on Small Groups from Simmel." American Journal of Sociology 64 (May 1958).

Mogulof, Melvin B. "A Developmental Approach to the Community Action Program Idea." Social Work 12 (April 1967).

Moynihan, Daniel P. *Maximum Feasible Misunderstanding.* New York: Free Press, 1970.

Naegele, Kaspar D. "Clergymen, Teachers, and Psychiatrists: A Study in Roles and Socialization." Canadian Journal of Economics and Political Science 22 (February 1966).

National Association of Social Workers Committee on Social Work Practice. "Opinions on Supervision: A Chapter Study." Social Work 3 (January 1958).

Neubauer, Peter B. "The Technique of Parent Group Education: Some Basic Concepts," in *Parent Group Education and Leadership Training.* New York: Child Study Association of America, 1952.

Northern, Helen. "Evaluation Movement of Individuals in Social Group Work," in *Group Work Papers, 1957.* New York: National Association of Social Workers, 1958.

Ohlin, Lloyd E. "Conformity in American Society Today." Social Work 3 (April 1958).

——and William C. Lawrence. "Social Interaction Among Clients as a Treatment Problem." Social Work 4 (April 1959).

Parsons, Talcott. "On the Concept of Influence." Public Opinion Quarterly 27 (Spring, 1963).

——"The Professions and Social Structure," in *Essays in Sociological Theory.* New York: Free Press, 1957.

——*The Social System.* New York: Free Press, 1951.

——and Robert F. Bales. *Family, Socialization and Interaction Process.* New York: Free Press, 1955.

——and Edward Shils. *Working Papers in the Theory of Action.* New York: Free Press, 1953.

Paull, Joseph E. "Recipients Aroused: The New Welfare Rights Movement." Social Work 12 (January 1967).

Peabody, Robert L. *Organizational Authority.* New York: Atherton Press, 1964.

Perlman, Helen H. "Casework is Dead." Social Casework 48 (January 1967).

——"Social Casework," in Harry L. Lurie, ed., *Encyclopedia of Social Work.* New York: National Association of Social Workers, 1965.

——"Intake and Some Role Considerations." Social Casework 41 (April 1960).

——*Social Casework: A Problem Solving Process.* Chicago: University of Chicago Press, 1957.

Piliavin, Irving. "Restructuring Social Services." Social Work 13 (January 1968).

Piven, Frances. "Participation of Residents in Neighborhood Community Action Programs." Social Work 11 (January 1966).

Polansky, Norman. "Social Workers in Society: Results of A Sampling Study." Social Work Journal 34 (April 1953).

——, Ronald Lippitt, and Fritz Redl. "An Investigation of Behavioral Contagion." Human Relations 3 (November 1950).

Powers, Edwin and Helen L. Witmer. *An Experiment in the Prevention of Delinquency: The Cambridge-Somerville Youth Study.* New York: Columbia University Press, 1951.

Preston, Malcolm G. and Roy K. Heintz. "Effects of Participatory Versus Supervisory Leadership on Group Judgement," in Dorwin Cartwright and Alvin F. Zander, eds., *Group Dynamics: Research and Theory.* Evanston, Ill.: Row, Peterson and Company, 1953.

——, Emily Mudd, and Hazel B. Froscher. "Factors Affecting Movement in Casework." Social Casework 34 (March 1953).

Prins, Herschel A. "Authority and the Casework Relationship." Social Work (U.K.) 19 (April 1962).

Program of the Girl Scouts of America. Ann Arbor: Survey Research Center for the Girl Scouts of America, 1958.

Ray, Florence. "Introduction," in *Social Work with Groups.* New York: National Association of Social Workers, 1958.

Reed, Ellery F. "Families Served by Group Work Agencies in a Deteriorated Area Compared with the General Population of that Area." Social Service Review 28 (December 1954).

Reiff, Robert and Frank Riessman. "The Indigenous Nonprofessional." Report 3. New York: National Institute for Labor Education.

Reiss, Albert J., Jr., and Otis Dudley Duncan. *Occupations and Social Status.* New York: Free Press, 1961.

Reissman, Leonard. "A Study of Role Conception in Bureaucracy." Social Forces 3 (January 1958).

Richman, Williard C. "A Theoretical Scheme for Determining Roles of Professional and Nonprofessional Personnel." Social Work 6 (October 1961).

Riessman, Frank, Jerome Cohen, and Arthur Pearl, eds. *Mental Health of the Poor: New Treatment Approaches for Low Income People.* New York: Free Press, 1964.

Ripple, Lilian. "Factors Associated with Continuance in Casework Service." Social Work 2 (January 1957).

——and Ernestina Alexander. "Motivation, Capacity, and Opportunity as Related to the Use of Casework Service: Nature of Client's Problem." Social Service Review 30 (March 1956).

Rogers, Carl R. "The Characteristics of a Helping Relationship," in Warren G. Bennis, Edgar Schein, David E. Berlew, and Fred J. Steele, eds., *Inter-Personal Dynamics: Essays and Readings on Human Interaction.* Chicago: Dorsey Press, 1964.

Rose, Sheldon D. "Students View their Supervisors: A Chapter Study." Social Work 3 (January 1958).

Rosenberg, Morris and Leonard J. Pearlin. "Power Orientations in the Mental Hospital." Human Relations 15 (1962).

Rosenfeld, Jona M. "Strangeness Between Helper and Client: A Possible Explanation of Non-Use of Available Professional Help." Social Service Review 38 (March 1964).

Rosow, Irving. "Form and Functions of Adult Socialization." Social Forces 44 (September 1965).

Sample, William C. "First Findings from Midway: The Findings on Client Change." Social Service Review 41 (June 1967).

Scheidlinger, Saul. "The Concept of Social Group Work and of Group Psychotherapy." Social Casework 34 (July 1953).

——"Patterns of Casework Services in Group Work Agencies." The Group 8 (November 1945).

Schein, Edgar H. and Warren G. Bennis. *Personal and Organizational Change Through Group Methods: The Laboratory Approach.* New York: John Wiley and Sons, 1965.

Scherz, Frances M. "A Concept of Supervision Based on Definitions of Job Responsibility." Social Casework 39 (October 1958).

——"Multiple-Client Interviewing: Treatment Implications." Social Casework 43 (March 1962).

Schorr, Alvin L. "Mirror, Mirror on the Wall...." Social Work 10 (July 1965).

——"The Retreat to the Technician." Social Work 4 (January 1959).

Schour, Esther. "Helping Social Workers Handle Work Stresses." Social Casework 34 (December 1953).

Schwartz, Edward E. "A Way to End the Means Test." Social Work 9 (July 1964).

——"First Finding from Midway: The Field Experiment, Background, Plan, and Selected Findings." Social Service Review 41 (June 1961).

Schwartz, William. "Neighborhood Centers," in Henry Maas, ed., *Five Fields of Social Service: Reviews of Research.* New York: National Association of Social Workers, 1966.

——"Small Group Science and Group Work Practice." Social Work 8 (October 1963).

——"The Social Worker in the Group," in *New Perspectives on Services to Groups: Theory, Organization and Practice.* New York: Association of Social Workers, 1961.

——"Group Work and the Social Scene," in Alfred J. Kahn, ed., *Issues in American Social Work.* New York: Columbia University Press, 1959.

Scott, W. Richard. "Professionals in Bureaucracies—Areas of Conflict," in Howard M. Vollmer and Donald L. Mills, eds., *Professionalization.* Englewood Cliffs, N.J.: Prentice Hall, 1966.

——"Reactions to Supervision in a Heteronomous Professional Organization." Administrative Science Quarterly 10 (June 1965).

Sherif, Muzafer. *The Psychology of Social Norms.* New York: Harper and Row, 1936.

——and Carl I. Hovland. *Social Judgement: Assimilation and Contrast Effects in Communication and Attitude Change.* New Haven: Yale University Press, 1961.

Sherman, Sanford, N. "The Choice of Group Therapy for Casework Clients," *Social Work Practice, 1962,* National Conference on Social Welfare. New York: Columbia University Press, 1962.

——"Utilization of Casework Methods and Skill in Group Counseling," in *Social Work with Groups, 1958.* New York: National Association of Social Workers, 1958.

Shyne, Anne W. "Evaluation of Results in Social Work." Social Work 8 (October 1963).

——"Casework Research: Past and Present." Social Casework 43 (November 1962).

——"What Research Tells Us About Short-Term Cases in Family Agencies," Social Casework, 38 (May, 1957).

——and L. S. Kogan. "A Study of Components of Movement." Social Casework 39 (June 1958).

Simmel, Georg. "Quantitative Aspects of the Group," in Kurt H. Wolff, trans. and ed., *The Sociology of Georg Simmel.* New York: Free Press, 1965.

——"Conflict," in *Conflict and the Web of Group Affiliations.* Kurt H. Wolff, trans. New York: Free Press, 1955.

Simpson, Richard L. and J. H. Simpson. "Women and Bureaucracy in the Semi-Professions," in Amitai Etzioni, ed., *The Semi-Professions and Their Organization.* New York: Free Press, 1969.

Slavson, S. R. "Are There 'Group Dynamics' in Therapy Groups?" International Journal of Group Psychotherapy 7 (April 1957).

Social Workers in 1950. New York: American Association of Social Workers, 1952.

Specht, Harry. "Casework Practice and Social Policy Formulation." Social Work 13 (January 1968).

Spellman, Eileen, "Authority and Social Work." Case Conference (December 1954).

Statistics on Social Work Education, 1958. New York: Council on Social Work Education, 1958.

Stetson, D. "Welfare Workers, They Say They Can't Do Their Job." New York Times (June 25, 1967).

Strean, Herbert S. "Role Theory, Role Models, and Casework: Review of the Literature and Practice Applications." Social Work 12 (January 1967).

Studt, Elliott. "Worker-Client Authority Relationships in Social Work." Social Work 4 (January 1959).

——"An Outline for Study of Social Authority Factors in Casework." Social Casework 35 (June 1954).

Suchman, Edward A. *Evaluative Research: Principles and Practice in Public Service and Social Action Programs.* New York: Russell Sage Foundation, 1968.

Sullivan, Dorothea. *Readings in Group Work*. New York: Association Press, 1952.

Svarc, Irving. "Client Attitudes Toward Financial Assistance: A Cultural Variant." Social Service Review 30 (June 1956).

Taylor, Robert K. "The Social Control Function in Casework." Social Casework 1 (January 1958).

Terrell, Paul. "The Social Worker as Radical: Roles of Advocacy." New Perspectives: The Berkeley Journal of Social Welfare 1 (Spring 1967).

Theobald, Robert. *Free Men and Free Markets*. New York: Clarkson and Tatten, 1953.

"The Question of Relative Values," Editorial Notes. Social Casework 41 (November 1960).

Thibaut, John W. and Harold H. Kelley. *The Social Psychology of Groups*. New York: John Wiley and Sons, 1959.

Thomas, Edwin J., ed. *Behavioral Science for Social Workers*. New York: Free Press, 1967.

Thompson, Jane K. and Donald P. Riley. "Use of Professionals in Public Welfare: A Dilemma and a Proposal." Social Work 11 (January 1966).

Tittle, Charles R. and Drollene P. Tittle. "Structural Handicaps to Therapeutic Participation: A Case Study." Social Problems 13 (Summer 1965).

Towey, Martin R., S. Wade Sears, John A. Williams, Nathan Kaufman, and Murray K. Cunningham. "Group Activities with Psychiatric Inpatients." Social Work 11 (January 1966).

Towle, Charlotte. *Common Human Needs*. New York: National Association of Social Workers, 1965.

——"The Place of Help in Supervision." Social Service Review 3 (December 1963).

——*The Learner in Education for the Profession*. Chicago: University of Chicago Press, 1954.

Trecker, Harleigh B. *Social Group Work: Principles and Practices*. New York: Whiteside, 1955.

Tropp, Emanuel. "The Group: In Life and Social Work." Social Casework 49 (May 1968).

Tuckman, Jacob and Martha Lavell. "Attrition in Psychiatric Clinics for Children." Public Health Report 75 (1959).

Varley, Barbara K. "The Use of Role Theory in the Treatment of Disturbed Adolescents." Social Casework 49 (June 1968).

Vinter, Robert D. "Small Group Theory and Research," in Leonard S. Kogan, ed., *Social Science Theory and Social Work Research*. New York: National Association of Social Workers, 1960.

——"Group Work: Perspective and Prospects," in *Social Work with Groups, 1950*. New York: National Association of Social Workers, 1959.

––"The Social Structure of Service," in Alfred J. Kahn, ed., *Issues in American Social Work*. New York: Columbia University Press, 1959.

Vollmer, Howard M. and Donald L. Mills, eds. *Professionalization*. Englewood Cliffs, N.J.: Prentice-Hall, 1966.

Wax, John. "Time Limited Supervision." Social Work 8 (July 1963).

Weber, Max. *The Theory of Social and Economic Organization*. A. M. Henderson and Talcott Parsons, trans., and Talcott Parsons, ed. New York: Oxford University Press, 1941.

Weisman, Irving and Jacob Chwast. "Control and Values in Social Work Treatment." Social Casework 41 (November 1960).

Werble, Beatrice. "Motivation, Capacity, and Opportunity in Service to Adolescent Clients: Major Findings." Social Work 3 (October 1959).

Wheeler, Stanton. "The Structure of Formally Organized Socialization Settings," in Orville G. Brim and Stanton Wheeler, ed., *Socialization After Childhood*. New York: John Wiley and Sons, 1966.

––and Leonard S. Cottrell, Jr. *Juvenile Delinquency: Its Prevention and Control*. New York: John Wiley and Sons, 1966.

White, Clyde R. "Prestige of the Social Worker." Social Work Journal 36 (January 1955).

––"Social Workers in Society: Some Further Evidence." Social Work Journal 34 (October 1953).

White, Ralph and Ronald Lippitt. "Leadership Behavior and Member Reaction in Three Social Climates," in Dorwin Cartwright and Alvin F. Zander, eds., *Group Dynamics: Research and Theory*. Evanston, Ill.: Row, Peterson and Company, 1953.

Wilensky, Harold L. "The Professionalization of Everyone?" American Journal of Sociology 70 (September 1960).

––and Charles N. Lebeaux. *Industrial Society and Social Welfare*. New York: Free Press, 1965.

Williamson, Margaret. *Supervision–Principles and Methods*. New York: Women's Press, 1950.

Wilson, Gertrude. "Social Group Work Theory and Practice," in *The Social Welfare Forum, 1956*. Proceedings of the National Conference on Social Welfare. New York: Columbia University Press, 1956.

––*Group Work and Casework–Their Relationship and Practice*. New York: Family Welfare Association of America, 1941.

Wolins, Martin. "Measuring the Effects of Social Work Intervention," in Norman A. Polansky, ed., *Social Work Research*. Chicago: University of Chicago Press, 1960.

Wolpe, Joseph. "The Comparative Clinical Status of Conditioning Therapies and Psychoanalysis," in Joseph Wolpe, Andrew Salter, and L. J. Reyna, eds., *The Conditioning Therapies*. New York: Holt, Rinehart and Winston, 1965.

"Working Definition of Social Work Practice." Social Work 3 (April 1958).

Wrong, Dennis H. "Some Problems in Defining Social Power." American Journal of Sociology 73 (May 1968).

Zander, Alvin F., J. I. Hurwitz, and B. Hymovitch. "Some Effects of Power on the Relation Among Group Members," in Dorwin Cartwright and Alvin F. Zander, eds., *Group Dynamics: Research and Theory.* Evanston, Ill.: Row, Peterson and Company, 1953.

Zetterberg, Hans L. "Compliant Actions." Acta Sociologica 1 (1956).

Zlozower, Abraham. *Career Opportunities and the Growth of Scientific Discovery in 19th Century Germany.* Jerusalem: Hebrew University Press, 1966.

U.S. GOVERNMENT PUBLICATIONS

Having the Power We Have the Duty. Report to the Secretary of Health, Education and Welfare, by the Advisory Council on Public Welfare. Washington, D.C.: U.S. Department of Health, Education and Welfare, June 29, 1966.

Herzog, Elizabeth. Some Guide Lines for Evaluative Research. Washington, D.C.: U.S. Department of Health, Education and Welfare, Social Security Administration, Children's Bureau, 1959.

The National Symposium on Guaranteed Income. Washington, D.C.: Chamber of Commerce of the U.S., December 9, 1966.

Salaries and Working Conditions of Social Welfare Manpower in 1960. U.S. Department of Labor and Statistics. New York: National Social Welfare Assembly.

Witmer, Helen L. and Edith Tufts. The Effectiveness of Delinquency Prevention Programs. Washington, D.C.: U.S. Department of Health, Education and Welfare, Social Security Administration, Children's Bureau, 1954.

UNPUBLISHED MATERIAL

Birth of the Movement: June 30, 1966. Washington, D.C.: Poverty Rights Action Center.

Goode, William J., Mary Huntington, and Robert K. Merton. The Professions in Modern Society. New York: Columbia University (unpublished manuscript).

Lewis, Harold. "Implications of Evaluation." in Houskeeping—A Community Problem; Summary of Workshop. Philadelphia: Friends Neighborhood Guild, 1961 (mimeographed).

Mann, James. "Clarifying Concepts in Group Dynamics." Presented at The Massachusetts Conference of Social Work, December, 1952 (mimeographed).

Round-Up of June 30th Welfare Demonstrations. Washington, D.C.: Poverty Rights Action Center.

Sample Index for a Welfare Advocates Manual. Washington, D.C.: Poverty Rights Action Center.

Suchman, Edward A. "Action for What? A Methodological Critique of Evaluation Studies." Presented at The 63rd Annual Meeting of the American Sociological Association, August, 1968 (mimeographed).

AUTHOR INDEX

Ackerman, Nathan W., 192, 193
Alexander, Ernestina, 201
Anthony, James E., 217n
Argyle, Michael, 155n
Asch, Solomon E., 126n, 153n, 218n
Austin, Lucille N., 71, 73

Babcock, Charlotte, 74, 153n
Bach, George R., 221n
Back, Kurt W., 153n, 196
Bales, Robert F., 82n, 171, 172, 173, 175, 217n
Ballard, Robert G., 29n
Barber, Elinor, 156n
Bartelme, Phyllis, 29n, 222n
Becker, Howard S., 46n, 92
Ben-David, Joseph, 61n
Bennis, Warren G., 127n, 185n, 219n
Berelson, Bernard, 217n
Berkowitz, Leonard, 218n, 220n
Bernstein, Arnold, 186n
Biestek, Felix P., 94
Billingsley, Andrew, 143, 144
Bisno, Herbert, 47n
Blau, Peter M., 61n, 77, 100, 145, 146
Blenkner, Margaret, 219n
Bloom, Martin, 232n
Boehm, Werner B., 46n, 66, 232n
Borgatta, Edgar F., 29n, 218n, 222n
Bradford, Jack, 185n
Breger, Louis, 187n
Brennen, Earl C., 29n
Briar, Scott, 29n, 140, 219n, 232n
Bruno, Frank J., 183n

Bucher, Rue, 31n
Burns, Mary B., 32n, 82n

Carr-Saunders, Alexander M., 38
Cartwright, Dorwin, 184n, 218n
Chwast, Jacob, 125n
Cloward, Richard A., 29n, 30n, 128n, 156n
Coffey, Hubert S., 167
Cohen, Albert K., 123n
Cohen, Jerome, 29n
Cohen, Nathan E., 47n
Coleman, Jules V., 154n, 185n
Collins, Barry E., 219n
Cooper, Shirley, 30n
Coser, Laub R., 83n, 123n, 127n
Coser, Lewis, 62n
Cottrell, Leonard S., 156n
Coyle, Longwell G., 162, 165

Dahlstrom, Edmund, 125n
Danet, Brenda, 101
Daniels, Arlene, 30n
Devis, Donald A., 84n
Dollard, Charles, 47n
Dollard, John, 186n

Eisenstadt, S. N., 47n, 101
Emerson, Richard M., 99
Epstein, Irwin, 29n
Etzioni, Amitai, 32n, 61-62n, 100, 103
Eysenck, Hans J., 177

Fanshel, David, 219n
Faucett, Emily C., 221n
Fenton, Norman, 222n
Festinger, Leon, 110, 163-164, 194, 196
Fine, Reva, 84n
Fizdale, Ruth, 84n
Flexner, Abraham, 40
Ford, Donald H., 186n
Frank, Jerome D., 91, 217n, 219n
Freidson, Elliot, 133, 149
Freilich, Morris, 83n
French, D. G., 31n
French, John R. P., 125n, 127n
Freud, Sigmund, 83n, 190
Frey, Louis A., 185n, 221n
Friedman, Milton, 31n
Fromm, Erich, 96
Froscher, Hazel B., 29n

Gifford, C. G., 185
Glasser, Paul H., 183n
Goffman, Erving, 123n
Goldner, Fred H., 61n
Goode, William G., 46n, 61n, 82n, 123n
Goss, Mary E. W., 79
Gosser, Charles F., 154n
Gouldner, Alvin W., 61n, 78
Grabbe, Paul, 204
Greenwood, Ernest, 39, 97, 232n
Gross, Edward, 51, 58, 72n
Grosser, Charles, 30n

Hare, Paul A., 218n
Haworth, Joanne, 32n
Heintz, Roy K., 155n
Hellerbrand, Shirley C., 125n
Herzog, Elizabeth, 221n
Heydebrand, Wolf V., 61n
Hollis, E. V., 184n
Hollis, Florence, 93
Homans, George C., 83n, 100, 153n,
    186n, 217n
Hopkins, Terence K., 126n, 174, 185n,
    190, 220n
Horland, Carl J., 123n, 126n, 220n
Hughes, Everett C., 46n
Hunt, McVicker J., 29n, 222n
Huntington, Mary J., 46n
Hyman, Herbert H., 123n

Jahoda, Marie, 111, 219n

Janis, Irving L., 123n
Johnson, D. L., 187n
Jones, Wyatt C., 29n, 222n

Kadushin, Alfred, 31n, 46n, 62n, 131,
    133, 136
Kadushin, Charles, 133
Kahn, Robert L., 91, 155n
Kaiser, Clara, 164
Kallen, David J., 30n
Katz, Daniel, 91, 155n
Katz, Elihu, 47n, 101, 123n, 154n, 221n
Kelley, Harold H., 123n, 126n, 219n
Kelman, Herbert C., 110, 184n, 193,
    206
Kidneigh, John C., 46n
Kitano, Harry L., 222n
Kogan, Leonard S., 29n, 219n
Kolodny, Ralph L., 185n, 221n
Konopka, Gisela, 166
Kornhauser, William, 58
Kuhn, Manford H., 137

Lake, Martha, 219n
Lawrence, Williams C., 93, 156n, 218n
Lazarsfeld, Paul F., 123n, 154n, 221n
Leader, Arthur L., 83n
Lebeaux, Charles N., 22, 59, 73, 139,
    155n
Lemert, Edwin M., 156n
Lennard, Henry L., 186n
Leonard, Peter, 97
Lerner, H. H., 184n
Levinger, George, 219n
Levinson, Perry, 154n
Levitt, Eugene E., 219n
Lewin, Kurt, 91, 164, 197, 204
Lewis, Harold, 127n
Lieberman, Morton A., 217n
Lifton, Walter M., 191
Lindennberg, Ruth E., 84n
Lippitt, Ronald, 153n, 155n, 164, 202
Litwak, Eugene, 156n
Lotrie, Dan C., 54
Lynn, Kenneth S., 46n

Maas, Henry S., 127n, 185n, 222n
Mann, John H., 211
Mauksch, Hans O., 154n
McCormick, Mary J., 47n, 124n
McDonald, Mary E., 222n

McEntrie, Davis, 32n
McGaugh, James L., 187n
McIsaac, Hugh, 128n
McRae, Robert H., 30n
Merton, Robert K., 32n, 46n, 58, 71, 120, 123n, 147, 190
Meyer, Henry J., 29n, 31n, 149, 222n
Meyerson, Emma Y., 130
Miller, Dorothy, 30n
Miller, Henry, 16-17
Miller, Irving, 70
Miller, Neal E., 186n
Miller, Walter B., 222n
Mills, Donald L., 46n
Mills, Theodore M., 217n
Mogulof, Melvin B., 30n
Moynihan, Daniel P., 30n
Mudd, Emily, 29n

Naegele, Kaspar D., 217n
Neubauer, Peter B., 184n
Northern, Helen, 222n

Ohlin, Lloyd E., 72, 93, 98, 156n, 218n

Parloff, M. B., 193
Parsons, Talcott, 32n, 50, 62n, 83n, 101, 103, 135, 171, 173, 175, 217n
Peabody, Robert L., 141, 143
Pearl, Arthur, 29n
Pearlin, Leonard J., 114
Perlman, Harris H., 30n, 94, 95, 183n
Piliavin, Irving, 16, 155n
Piven, Frances, 17-18, 156n
Polansky, Norman, 131, 202
Powers, Edwin, 29n, 222n
Preston, Malcolm G., 29n, 155n
Prins, Herschel A., 124n

Rachman, Stanley, 186n
Raven, Bertram, 125n, 127n
Ray, Florence, 183n
Redl, Fritz, 153n, 202
Reed, Ellery F., 222n
Reiff, Robert, 154n
Reiss, Albert Y., 153n
Reissman, Leonard, 82n
Richman, Williard C., 154n
Riessman, Frank, 29n, 154n
Riley, Donald P., 31n
Ripple, Lilian, 201

Ritti, R. R., 61n
Rogers, Carl R., 154n
Rose, Sheldon D., 77
Rosen, Sidney, 153n
Rosenberg, Morris, 114
Rosenfeld, Jona M., 219n
Rosow, Irving, 109

Sample, William C., 90
Schachter, Stanley, 196
Scheidlinger, Saul, 170
Schein, Edgar H., 185n
Scherz, Frances M., 69, 221n
Schiller, Jeffrey, 154n
Schorr, Alvin L., 47n, 222n
Schour, Esther, 84n
Schwartz, Edward E., 31n, 90, 162
Schwartz, William, 183n, 184n, 222n, 232n
Scott, W. Richard, 61n, 62n, 78, 146
Sherif, Muzafer, 126n
Sherman, Sanford N., 185n
Shils, Edward, 185n
Shyne, Anne W., 219n
Simmel, Georg, 62n, 191
Simpson, Ida, 55
Simpson, Richard, 55
Specht, Harry, 30n
Spellman, Eileen, 98
Stauffer, Robert E., 61n
Steiner, Gary A., 217n
Stetson, D., 31n
Strauss, Anselm, 31n
Strean, Herbert S., 183n
Strodtbeck, Fred L., 172
Studt, Elliott, 96
Suchman, Edward A., 222n
Sullivan, Dorothea, 165
Svarc, Irving, 125n

Taylor, A. L., 184n
Taylor, Robert K., 95, 97, 106
Terrell, Paul, 30n
Theobald, Robert, 31n
Thibaut, John W., 218n
Thomas, Edwin J., 156n, 232n
Thompson, Jane K., 31n
Tittle, Charles R., 32n
Tittle, Drollene P., 32n
Towey, Martin R., 218n
Towle, Charlotte, 31n, 68

Trecker, Harleigh B., 183n
Tropp, Emanuel, 208
Tuckman, Jacob, 219n
Tufts, Edith, 29n

Urban, Hugh B., 186n

Varley, Barbara K., 183n, 211
Vinter, Robert D., 82n, 151, 156n, 184n
Volkart, Edmund H., 126n
Vollmer, Howard M., 46n

Wax, John, 74
Weber, Max, 61n, 62n, 125n
Weisman, Irving, 125n
Wheeler, Stanton, 92, 156n
White, Clyde R., 130

White, Ralph, 155n
Wilensky, Harold L., 22, 46n, 50, 59, 73, 139, 155n
Wilkinson, Harold, 128n
Williamson, Margaret, 82n
Wilson, Gertrude, 166, 221n
Wilson, M. O., 126n
Witmer, Helen L., 29n, 222n
Wolins, Martin, 221n
Wolpe, Joseph, 186n
Woodruff, Cristine L., 126n
Wrong, Dennis H., 125n

Zander, Alvin F., 153n
Zetterberg, Hans L., 126n
Zlozower, Abraham, 31n

SUBJECT INDEX

Approach
    clinical-treatment: see Clinical-treatment approach
    individual-psychological: see Individual-psychological approach
    interpersonal-sociological: see Interpersonal-sociological approach
    learning: see Learning approach
    liberal: see Liberal approach
    social reform: see Social reform approach
    social science: see Social science approach
Adult education, 206
Agencies
    community, 203
    correctional, 97
    group work, 168, 171
    policy of, 139, 143
    private, 15, 139, 229
    public welfare, 15, 55, 97, 139, 142, 229
    study on family, 115-119
    and type of personnel, 15, 24
Authority, 114
    figure, 211
    formal and psychological, 96-97
    organizational, 141
    and personal relationship, 136-137
    professional, 41, 51-52, 193-194; see also Professional autonomy
    Weber's typology of, 100

Behaviorism, 176-178
Bureaucratic organization; see also Control, bureaucratic
    characteristics of, 50
    and professions, 50-51, 58-59
    rules and procedures of, 140, 141, 146
    and semi-professions, 53-55, 57
    and social work, 49

257

Casework; see also Groupwork, and its relation to casework
    criticism of, 13, 208, 225
    effectiveness of, 13, 93, 193-194, 205, 213-215, 225
    goals of, 13, 94-95, 107-108
    as medium of change and control, 91, 93-98, 152
    and normative power, 105-107; see also Power, of social workers
    relationship, 89-90, 93-94, 129, 136-137
    therapeutic, 35, 95, 122, 162
Change
    contagion of, 202-204
    environmental, 95
    induction in groups, 196-199, 211; see also Influence, in groups; Clients, attempts
        to change behavior of
    of opinion, 174-175
    personal, 91, 95, 108; see also Individual, growth
    of social institutions, 16, 18
Clients; see also Self-determination
    attempts to change, 19, 89-90, 95-96, 107-109, 119, 130, 150, 152, 178-182,
        214, 226
    and conformity, 13, 105-106
    direct problems of, 94-95, 201-202
    expectations of, 118-119, 151
    of group work, 169, 193
    interaction among, 199
    orientation of community to welfare, 148-149
    orientation of social workers to, 57, 145-147, 150
    power of, 100-101
    relationship between social workers and clients, 15, 25, 86, 94; see also Social
        workers, and relations with clients
    service to, 138-141, 225, 231
    social distance between professionals and, 133-134, 199
    welfare, 13, 18, 19, 148
Clinical-treatment approach, 93, 169, 171
Code of ethics, 39, 42, 226
    and organizational framework, 138-141
    of social work, 137-138, 179; see also Social work, basic values of
Compliance, 100-101, 104, 110-113, 117; see also Conformity
    and noncompliance, 114-115
Community
    action programs, 17-18
    centers, 171
    organization, 162, 166
    sanction, 39, 41
Conformity, 13, 96, 98, 104
    and group cohesion, 196-197
    to group norms, 92, 107, 123n, 204; see also Group, norms and standards;
        Power, and conformity
    needed resources for, 121, 126n, 175
    public and private, 109, 111
Continuance studies, 197-198; see also Motivation, Capacity and Opportunity
    studies

Control
    acceptance of, 117
    bureaucratic, 57, 226; see also Bureaucratic organization
    coercive and persuasive, 97
    community, 65
    different types of, 115-118, 120; see also Power, mechanisms of; Sources of
    in groups and in pairs, 191
    professional, 51-52, 66; see also Professional autonomy
    social, 96, 99
    and visibility, 54, 71-72, 89, 109-110; see also Supervision, and visibility
Credibility, 120, 195
    and attractiveness of group membership, 199, 200
    elements of, 200

Democratic
    action, 162, 167
    attitudes, 174, 179
    leadership, 203
    setting, 179
    society, 96, 165
Dependence, 99
    of client on social worker, 107, 151
    of patient on therapist, 173
Deprofessionalization, 43, 47n; see also Professionalization

Eligibility determination, 97, 135, 145, 225
Esprit de corps, 175, 191

Financial aid, 121, 142, 225; see also Income maintenance
    and casework, 23, 151
Functional prerequisites, 171-172
Functions
    adaptive and integrative, 172, 175; see also Functional prerequisites

Group
    cohesion, 191, 196
    definition of, 190-191
    dynamics, 90, 162, 164
    functions, 174
    membership and reference, 89, 93, 107, 115, 121, 123n
    natural and artificial, 208-211
    norms and standards, 92, 107, 191, 193, 196, 204; see also Conformity, to group
        norms
    personal change in the, 91, 190-194, 197
    solidarity, 172, 175
    structure and process, 15, 167, 171-172, 190-191, 199, 209-210
    task-oriented, 171-173, 211
    therapy, 169, 172, 181-182, 192-193, 206
    training, 170, 176, 207
    types of, 166-167
Group work, 18; see also Group workers

American Association for the Study of, 162
    clients of, 166, 227
    different approaches to, 170-171
    effectiveness of, 213-215
    goals of, 164-166, 169, 210-211, 227
    and group therapy, 206-208
    history of, 161-163
    methods, 166, 169-170
    and its relation to casework, 163-164
    as subfield of social work, 163
Group workers, 162
    American Association of, 163, 165
    position in groups of, 193-194
    social origins of, 167
    tasks of, 170
    training of, 168

Hatch Act, 230
Heteronomy; see Semi-professions and heteronomy

Identification, 104, 117, 120, 202
Income
    maintenance, 15, 18-19, 122, 151, 197, 226
    minimum, 225
Individual
    functioning, 13, 95
    growth, 165, 212-213
    responsibility, 148
    therapy, 162
    within the group, 165, 191-192; see also Group, personal change in the
Individual-psychological approach; 19-20, 163-166, 169, 170; see also Social work,
        basic dilemma in
Influence; see also Control; Power
    acceptance of, 110
    direct, 202
    in groups, 189-190, 192, 195-197, 199-202, 226
    mechanism of, 104
    range of, 134
    two-step flow of, 210
Intake, 198
Interpersonal-sociological approach, 164, 169, 170
Isolation
    of client-caseworker dyad, 14, 89, 107, 195, 205; see also Casework, relationship
    of different types of groups, 206-208
    of laboratory training, 179-180

Knowledge
    base, 14, 37, 39, 41, 135, 230, 261-262
    empirical, 96
    esoteric, 135
    expert, 200, 202

Laboratory training, 176, 178; see also Group, training; Learning process
    compared with group therapy, 180-182
    consequences of, 180, 182
    goals of, 179
Leaders
    types of, 203, 210
Learning
    deutero, 179
    process, 177-178
    theory, 176-177
Learning approach, 178; see also Learning
Liberal approach, 175

Manipulation, 177, 192; see also Rewards, manipulation of
Motivation, Capacity and Opportunity studies, 201-202
Movement studies, 212; see also Research, evaluation

Norms; see also Conformity; Group, norms and standards
    of client groups, 204
    commitment to, 103, 195
    deviation from, 92, 106, 148, 210
    of different subcultures, 105

Observability, 89, 109-110, 112, 204; see also Supervision, and visibility

Phase movement, 172-173
Poverty, 18, 94
    war on, 225
Power; see also Control; Influence
    and conformity, 105-106, 109, 111
    effects of, 109-113
    exercise, of, 111-114, 119-122
    field, 196
    in groups of clients, 194-195; see also Client, power of
    mechanisms of, 104, 115-118, 195
    of social workers, 25-26, 102, 113
    sources of, 110-112, 117-118
    types of, 25, 102, 114, 195, 197
Prestige
    of occupations, 130-132
    of professions, 129-130
    of semi-professions, 133
    of social workers, 130-132
Privileged communication, 54
Professional
    and bureaucratic orientations, 143-147
    identity, 167, 168
    orientation, 136-137
Professional autonomy, 14, 40, 49, 54, 226; see also Authority,
        professional
    in bureaucratic organizations, 79-80, 141; see also Control, bureaucratic

definition of, 65
differential zoning of, 53-54, 65, 66
and women, 55-56
Professionalization, 22-23, 37-38; see also Deprofessionalization
of group work, 163, 167-168
and social reform, 43-45
of social work, 39-42
and social work's values, 43-45
uneven, 40-42
Professions; see also Professional; Professionalization; Semi-professions
ambivalence toward, 147-148
characteristics of, 37, 39
established, 26, 38, 42, 53, 226
helping, 57, 146
human relations, 72
integration and differentiation of, 168
status symbols of, 136
types of, 38
Psychotherapy
effects of, 90-91, 177, 192
goals of, 176
and group work, 169-170
methods of, 169

Relationship; see also Casework relationship; Social workers and relations with clients
attractiveness of, 107, 110-111, 120, 197-198
dyadic, 189, 191, 192, 194, 226
one-to-one, 136, 199
personal, 93, 96, 116-117, 137, 195, 211
teacher-student, 179
therapeutic, 94, 173
treatment, 214
Research; see also Movement studies; Motivation, Capacity and Opportunity studies; Continuance studies
evaluation, 131, 180, 212
organizational, 90
on residential institutions, 93
small group, 163-164, 190
Resources, 18, 216
Rewards
manipulation of, 173
material, 102, 117
relational, 173, 195
symbolic, 106
Role
conflict, 15
differentiation, 172, 191, 204, 209
model, 105, 108
playing, 211-212
relationships, 209-210
set, 205
social, 171, 179, 183n, 227

Sanctions, 103-104
Self-determination
    the right of clients to, 96-98, 177
Semi-professions, 13-14, 26, 38
    and bureaucratic control, 53-55, 79-80; see also Bureaucratic organization, and
        social work; Social work, as semi-profession
    defined, 39
    and heteronomy, 52-53
Social; see also Role, social; Social reform approach
    approval, 106, 116
    class, 105
    distance, 133-134, 198-202
    functioning, 13, 108, 181, 205
    interaction, 92, 192
    milieu, 14, 180, 189, 206
    problems, 15, 193, 229
    skills, 165, 179, 189, 194, 227
    system, 172
Socialization
    adult, 90, 92; see also Adult education
    of children, 121
    objectives of, 109
    in residential institutions, 92-93
    and social control, 172; see also Casework, as medium of change and control
Social reform approach, 18-19, 22, 43, 167, 225
Social-science approach, 230
Social work
    basic dilemma in, 19-23, 26-27
    basic values of, 41, 57, 98, 164, 177
    and bureaucracy, 49, 140, 144, 226; see also Bureaucratic organization; Control,
        bureaucratic
    evaluation of effectiveness of, 212-213
    evaluation of performance in, 70, 72, 145
    goals of, 13-14, 34
    graduate schools of, 168
    intervention, 13, 203, 213
    as mechanism of control, 95-98, 152
    National Conference of, 162
    as semi-profession, 13-14, 39-42, 151-152, 226; see also Semi-professions
    specialization in, 21, 42
    suggestion to change practice of, 15-19, 229
    supervision in, 65-66; see also Supervisor, and social worker relationship;
        Supervision
    Working Definition of, 57, 139
Social workers
    attitude toward control function of, 97-98
    image of, 130-131
    National Association of, 41, 57, 78, 137, 146, 163
    orientation of clients toward, 150-151
    and relationship with clients, 25, 90, 106-107, 145
    role-conflict of, 23-24, 143

status of, 56; see also Prestige, of social workers
  teams of, 90
  training of, 22, 41, 132, 138
  in welfare agencies, 55, 142
Status
  consciousness, 133
  differentiation, 204
  symbols, 136
Stigma, 149-150
Supervision
  attitudes of social workers toward, 77-79, 146
  characteristics of, 75-77
  criticism of, 72-75
  of financial aid, 65-66
  purposes of, 67-69
  styles of, 53, 145-147
  techniques of, 70-72
  and visibility, 71-72; see also Observability
Supervisor; see also Supervision
  bureaucratic and professional orientations of, 144-146
  incompatible functions of, 68-71, 73-74
  role of, 78-79
  and social worker relationship, 67, 70, 75, 78-79, 141-142, 145
Symbolic-interaction, 137

Value; see also Social work, basic values of
  commitment, 105-106, 195
  internalization, 104, 111, 120-121

Welfare, 22-23; see also Social reform approach
  agencies, 55, 92, 225
  clients, 13, 18, 19, 148
  policy, 225; see also Income